THE MEANING OF SUNDAY

The Meaning of Sunday

The Practice of Belief in a Secular Age

JOEL THIESSEN

McGill-Queen's University Press
Montreal & Kingston • London • Chicago

© McGill-Queen's University Press 2015

ISBN 978-0-7735-4626-4 (cloth)
ISBN 978-0-7735-4627-1 (paper)
ISBN 978-0-7735-9802-7 (ePDF)
ISBN 978-0-7735-9803-4 (ePUB)

Legal deposit fourth quarter 2015
Bibliothèque nationale du Québec

Reprinted 2016, 2018

Printed in Canada on acid-free paper that is 100% ancient forest free (100% post-consumer recycled), processed chlorine free

This book has been published with the help of a grant from Ambrose University.

We acknowledge the support of the Canada Council for the Arts, which last year invested $153 million to bring the arts to Canadians throughout the country.

Nous remercions le Conseil des arts du Canada de son soutien. L'an dernier, le Conseil a investi 153 millions de dollars pour mettre de l'art dans la vie des Canadiennes et des Canadiens de tout le pays.

Library and Archives Canada Cataloguing in Publication

Thiessen, Joel, 1981–, author
    The meaning of Sunday: the practice of belief in a secular age / Joel Thiessen.

Includes bibliographical references and index.
Issued in print and electronic formats.
ISBN 978-0-7735-4626-4 (bound). – ISBN 978-0-7735-4627-1 (paperback). – ISBN 978-0-7735-9802-7 (ePDF). – ISBN 978-0-7735-9803-4 (ePUB)

1. Religion and sociology – Canada. 2. Secularization – Canada.
3. Rational choice theory. I. Title.

BL2530.C3T55 2015   306.6'0971   C2015-903988-6
                                         C2015-903989-4

This book was typeset by Marquis Interscript in 10.5/13 Sabon.

Contents

Acknowledgments   vii

1 In the Beginning   3
2 Active Affiliates: Religion Informed by God, Others, and Self   33
3 Marginal Affiliates: Cherry-Picking Religious Beliefs and Practices   65
4 Religious Nones: Freedom from Religion   94
5 Dwindling Demand: Stop Blaming Churches   126
6 Canada's Seat at the Secularization Table   160

APPENDICES

A Interview Schedule   193
B Interviewee Demographics   200

Bibliography   201

Index   223

Acknowledgments

This project could not exist without the ninety individuals who graciously set aside time to share their stories. I learned much from you, sociologically and personally – thank you. I hope that I adequately capture what you communicated and that you see a reflection of yourselves somewhere in this book. Thanks also to Reginald Bibby who, though we differ in how we interpret the Canadian religious landscape, generously contacted his survey participants to begin my sampling process. I appreciate our collegial yet rigorous dialogue about religion in Canada. An additional heartfelt thank you to five transcribers who faithfully completed this tedious task: Amy Hiebert, Chantelle Jipp, David Olson, Elizabeth Gripping, and Erin Baldwin. Amy Hiebert and Heather Ann Wicker also provided timely assistance with part of the literature review and data analysis. I am grateful for your attention to detail and your interest in this project – thank you.

The seeds for this project began in 2004 when I spoke with Lorne Dawson about studying under him as a graduate student at the University of Waterloo. Lorne's continued optimism, guidance, encouragement, and candid and constructive feedback since then are humbling and gratifying. Other mentors have also significantly shaped my scholarly development, including Michael Wilkinson during my undergraduate days, and my doctoral committee (Janice Aurini, Douglas E. Cowan, David Seljak, and Sam Reimer). Thank you.

Prior to starting this research in earnest, Ambrose University hired me in 2008. I value this environment to research and teach. Colleagues and students have shown great kindness and support, and many conversations inside and outside the classroom have animated my evolving thoughts about religion in Canada. Thank you for this academic space to come alive, to spur each other toward critical engagement with the world around.

Along the way several agencies have contributed funding to aspects of this project. These include the Social Sciences and Humanities Research Council of Canada, the Evangelical Fellowship of Canada Centre for Research on Canadian Evangelicalism, the Church of the Nazarene Canada, and Ambrose University. Thank you for investing in this research.

Kyla Madden and her team at McGill-Queen's University Press have been invaluable to work with. Thank you for patiently answering my many questions throughout and for helping to see this project through. Thanks also to the two anonymous reviewers who provided encouraging and constructive feedback to strengthen the book further.

Last, I acknowledge my family and friends who entertain my musings on religion, provide comic relief – often at my expense – and keep me grounded. My parents (Ken and Bev), sister and brother-in-law (Carissa and Scott), my wife's parents (John and Ann), and brother-in-law and sister-in-law (Ernie and Kathleen) have seen me through this project from the beginning, going back to the move from Calgary to Waterloo for graduate school. Thank you for your unending love and support. Few know me as well as my closest friends Stu and Ruthie and the kids (Lauren, Luke, and Alanna) and Jeremy and Bobbi and the kids (Gavin, Galen, Olivia, and Brooklyn). I am humbled by our collective friendship; I love the genuine joy and laughter in our gatherings; I value the honesty and transparency that we have. Thank you for this gift of community. My wife, Helen, has stood by my side in every phase of this research. Many times this meant you were left on your own as I hid away in a library, travelled evenings and weekends to conduct interviews, invested countless hours to write this book, and spent many days away to disseminate my findings with various groups. Thank you for being a sounding board, for your love, for your adventurous spirit, and for reminding me of what is important in life.

THE MEANING OF SUNDAY

I

In the Beginning

Larry Masters (all names used for interviewees are pseudonyms) is an Anglican in his late 50s who attends religious services for major religious holidays like Christmas and Easter. Trent Hooper is in his 70s and no longer identifies with any religion despite a strong religious upbringing in mainline Protestant and Roman Catholic settings. Larry and Trent are two of the first individuals who agreed to meet and discuss religion with me. Their reflections alerted me in the beginning of my research to two recurring themes that I would eventually hear more about with other interviewees – first, that religious affiliation, belief, and practice are ultimately about a person's individual faith, and, second, that people detest it when others push their religion on others.

In the beginning of my conversation with Larry I learned about the moral framework and "brainwashing" that he believes he received from his religious upbringing and attendance at a religious school. I heard about his questioning of "bloody religion" as a young adult, his wife being a "spiritual but not religious person," his uncertainty about "organized religion," and his current view that faith is a "crutch" in a time of need. At several points in the interview Larry describes what would become a central theme among many others in my study, that his faith is very personal and that "God helps those who help themselves." Similar to "Sheilaism," popularized by Bellah et al. (1985), Larry reflects on the religious beliefs and practices from his Anglican heritage: "Sometimes I don't agree with them. Sometimes I agree with them. Sometimes you cherry-pick, like everything in life … There's not a lot of black and white … You pick what you like: 'I like that. That one would be suitable. I'll keep that' … Whereas before, years ago, it used to be you couldn't cherry-pick. It was all inclusive. You got what you got."

Trent Hooper picks up on this individualist theme. He has his "own personal definition of a Supreme Being," and he rejects the idea that religious organizations should have much influence over people's attitudes and behaviours. Trent attributes his eventual departure from religious affiliation and involvement to religious exclusivity and pushing religious beliefs and practices on to others. Trent recalls that "priests tended to get involved very much in the ... lives of the individual parishioners ... even as far as dictating or suggesting at Mass who to vote for ... all kinds of things ... And I certainly never ever wanted that kind of involvement by anyone! So that was part of the reason I ... stayed away from all churches altogether because I didn't want ... to belong to a group where someone, a minister or whoever ... could lecture you on whatever on ... life; on behaviour." He goes on to single out his disdain for religious groups that "set down rules" regarding gender roles and norms that conflict with his personal views.

In this sociological study I draw on ninety interviews in Calgary, Alberta, and address three questions related to Christian beliefs and practices, with a particular focus on church attendance. First, what explains higher and lower levels of religiosity (e.g., belief in God, religious affiliation, church attendance, prayer, belief in the afterlife)? I tackle this simple yet surprisingly overlooked question by comparing the experiences, meanings, beliefs, and practices among and between three groups of people: active religious affiliates (those who identify with a religious group and attend religious services nearly every week), marginal religious affiliates (those who identify with a religious group and attend religious services primarily on Christmas and Easter, or for rites of passage such as weddings and funerals), and religious nones (those who do not identify with any religious group and never attend religious services). In what ways are these groups similar or dissimilar? Second, how might one assess scholarly debates about religiosity or secularity in light of the religious beliefs, practices, and involvements among active affiliates, marginal affiliates, and religious nones? For instance, should we expect active affiliates to decrease their level of religiosity in the future or marginal affiliates or religious nones to increase their levels of religiosity in the future? Third, depending on whether people are highly, moderately, or not at all religious, what impact does or could this have on a society's social and civic fabric? This "so what" or "who cares" question should interest the broader sociological community and the Canadian public as sociologists grapple with the relationship between religiosity levels and social and civic responsibilities in Canada and elsewhere (see, e.g., Putnam 2000; Bowen 2004; Stanczak 2006; Bibby 2007, 2011; Dillon and Wink 2007; Zuckerman 2008; Smith and Snell 2009; Putnam and Campbell 2010).

This study provides an in-depth window into "lived religion," defined by Meredith McGuire (2008, 12) as "how religion and spirituality are practiced, experienced, and expressed by ordinary people (rather than official spokespersons) in the context of their everyday lives." These experiences are culturally located in a Canadian urban centre, yet their approach to religion is informed by an overarching Canadian (and in some sense modern Western) cultural and religious narrative of choice and negotiation that transcends regional and religious variation. I do not aim to generalize the findings from this study to all of Canada or to resolve long-standing theoretical debates in the sociology of religion. The sample size, focus, and regional variations across Canada do not warrant such generalizations. However, I consider at times the wider points of intersection and "fit" between the results in this study and evidence from larger national and international studies. Namely, as repeatedly referred to in Peter Beyer and Rubina Ramji's (2013) edited volume on young Muslims, Hindus, and Buddhists growing up in Canada, thinking of faith in a highly individualistic fashion where religion is not forced on others is "quite typical in Canada" (Beyer 2013d, 56). In contrast to the United States, "In Canada, one notes a quite low level of what one might call religious aggressiveness, what some might want to call 'competitiveness' ... culturally, it seems, it is generally considered rather impolite and to that degree unacceptable to promote – 'push' – one's religion publicly or even to be too open about showing it publicly, to be 'in your face' about religion" (Beyer 2013c, 303). Regardless of one's religious or secular identification, Canadians generally believe that tolerance and accommodation ought to accompany religious and cultural diversity (see Beaman and Beyer 2008; Bibby 2011, 76–7). In practical terms this means that individuals can choose and construct a faith that works for them without forcing their religious beliefs and practices on to others, or fearing that others will impose their religion.

Without asserting generalizable findings, Calgary is an ideal location for data collection of this kind for several reasons. Levels of religiosity (e.g., religious affiliation, belief, and practice) in Calgary and Alberta are fairly close to the national average (see Bowen 2004, 54–5; Mata 2010; Bibby 2011, 51–3; Friesen and Clieff 2014, 10–18). Further, with high rates of migration into Calgary for employment opportunities, many interviewees had moved to Calgary from other parts of Canada. I listened to people frame their narratives based on urban or rural backgrounds across diverse locations from British Columbia to the East Coast. Additionally, unlike larger urban centres such as Toronto or Vancouver, where 40%–50% of residents are immigrants, only 26% of those in Calgary are immigrants, closer in line to the 20.6% national figure (Statistics Canada 2013). There could be value in gathering data similar to this study in places like Toronto or Vancouver, yet in some respects Calgary is a more modest representation of Canadian multiculturalism, including ethnic and religious diversity (12% of Calgarians identify with non-Christian faith traditions, which is higher than the 7.2% national figure but closer to the national picture than Toronto or Vancouver – see Mata 2010; Friesen and Clieff 2014).

Continuing with religious and ethnic diversity, my focus and scope is not on if or how my conceptualization, operationalization, and analysis of active affiliates, marginal affiliates, and religious nones applies among Jews, Muslims, Buddhists, Hindus, or Sikhs. Aside from the difficult task to make linkages between this study and the immense diversity within and between these other religions (see Beyer and Martin 2010), like any study I must begin somewhere to satisfactorily engage and extend the questions, theories, scholarship, and variables at the centre of this project. This means that I focus on religious identification, belief, and involvement among active affiliates, marginal affiliates, and religious nones. My approach reflects, in part, that scholarly definitions and measurements of religion are socially, contextually, and historically situated (see, e.g., Asad 1993; Greil and Bromley 2003). For better or worse this study follows a lineage of sociology of religion research that is heavily influenced by Protestant and European ideas about religion (Asad 1993). Church attendance is of particular interest given that social ties with other religious folk and regular religious gatherings with others are important to reinforce continued religious belief and practice, and for religion to have much personal and social significance in modern society (see, e.g., Durkheim 1915; Roof and McKinney 1987; Davie 1994; Beyer 1999; Bruce 2002; Jamieson 2002; Bowen 2004; Manning 2013, 151–2; Madge et al. 2014, 111). For instance, writing in the context of emerging adults Smith and Snell (2009, 252) claim, "The emerging adults who do sustain strong subjective religion in their lives, it turns out, are those who also maintain strong external expressions of faith, including religious service attendance. Most emerging adults, by contrast, who significantly reduce their external religious participation also substantially reduce their subjective, private, internal religious concerns." Steve Bruce (2002, 20) reinforces these claims when he proclaims that "the privatization of religion removes much of the social support that is vital to reinforcing beliefs, makes the maintenance of distinct lifestyles very difficult, weakens the impetus to evangelize and encourages a *de facto* relativism that is fatal to shared beliefs."

My emphasis on active affiliates, marginal affiliates, and religious nones does not entirely preclude attention to the variety of non-Christian religious traditions that importantly shape the Canadian religious landscape. As of 2011, 7.2% of the Canadian population identifies with a non-Christian religion and this figure, especially among Muslims, is on the rise as a result of immigration patterns and demographic trends over the past few decades (Beyer and Martin 2010; Mata 2010; Statistics Canada 2013). Excellent research has rightly given attention in this direction over the past decade in particular and countless projects are emerging nationally and internationally at the moment (see, e.g., Beyer 2005; Bramadat and Seljak 2005; Beyer and Martin 2010; Beyer and Ramji 2013). Where appropriate I address the impact that religious diversity (locally and globally) has on those I interviewed as well as on larger debates about secularization. Moreover I demonstrate how lived religion among active affiliates, marginal affiliates, and religious nones converges and diverges with experiences among those in non-Christian faith traditions. A central observation is that the guiding argument in this book, that faith is a private matter that should not be forced on to others, resonates strongly with young members of religious minority groups who are navigating their faith in Canada today (Beyer and Ramji 2013).

This said, a cautionary note that I return to in the concluding chapter regarding the larger Canadian religious picture: Canada is not as religiously diverse as the media, the state, and even some academics would have us believe. As Christian identification, belief, and practice slides, it is not to other religions mainly (even though religious diversity is on the rise). Christianity is losing ground as religious nones rapidly increase – the second largest "religious" category in all of Canada at 24% (Statistics Canada 2013). As such, I give some space to religious diversity, but my emphasis beyond Christianity is on the understudied and growing group of religious nones.

WHY THIS BOOK?

There are several reasons for this book. In terms of active religious affiliates, countless quantitative studies in the sociology of religion deal with people's Christian beliefs and practices. Lacking are in-depth qualitative understandings of the meanings and motivations behind individuals' religious beliefs and practices, to know, for example, what survey respondents mean when they say that religion is important to them or that they have spiritual needs. Qualitative research of this kind is increasingly common among religious minority groups in Canada, but Sam Reimer (2008) identifies this as a gap in our sociological study of Christianity in Canada.

With respect to marginal affiliates, it is stunning that few researchers anywhere in the world have explored the beliefs, practices, and circumstances that surround those who are committed to remain Roman Catholic, Anglican, or Baptist from birth until death and who faithfully attend religious services once or twice a year for religious holidays and rites of passage (passing references are made in the following sources: Walliss 2002; Lamoureux Scholes 2003; Inglis 2007; Zuckerman 2008; Day 2011) – a group that makes up between 40% and 50% of all Canadian adults (Bibby 2006, 192). How is this group similar to or different from the others in this study and what explains their steadfast commitment to a religious identity and group in spite of relatively low involvement in that group? What compels them to attend "religiously" once or twice a year and what are the chances, if any, of them attending more frequently in the future?

As for religious nones, growing research, particularly in the United States and the United Kingdom, is currently devoted to better understand the social, historic, and demographic realities of this rapidly growing group (see Bullivant and Lee 2012). Beyond contributing to this burgeoning set of empirical data, my research is the first of its kind to explore religious nones in detail in the Canadian context – an important contribution since 24% of Canadian adults claim to have no religion and 32% of Canadian teens say that they have no religion (Bibby 2011, 51; Statistics Canada 2013). In addition this study provides in-depth qualitative data on the "hard to find" religious none category, which Baker and Smith (2009, 730) identify as an important area needing research. For instance, I explore questions such as what religious beliefs or practices, if any, do religious nones adhere to, what past or present experiences and realities contribute to their current perspective on religion, and would they ever consider affiliating with or getting involved with a religious group?

In addition to better understanding these groups in their own right, this study intersects with the ongoing sociological conversation about the place of religion in contemporary society. Sociologists have long debated the relationship between modernity and religion, with some forecasting that religion will diminish or disappear altogether and others projecting that religion will remain a salient feature of modern society (see, e.g., Berger 1967; Martin 1978; Casanova 1994; Stark 1999b; Bruce 2002). In the Canadian context Reginald Bibby, one of Canada's influential sociologists of religion, has made important contributions to these discussions based on his survey data since 1975 on Canadian social and religious attitudes and behaviours. Bibby's conclusions during this time have ranged from secularization to revitalization to polarization.

Bibby initially suggested in *Fragmented Gods* (1987) and *Unknown Gods* (1993) that secularization was the appropriate lens for explaining religion in Canada based on declining religious authority and diminishing levels of individual religious belief and practice. Bibby stated in *Unknown Gods* (1993, 93) that secularization is evident in "not just the drop in the number of practicing [people but] also the impoverished faith of the participants." Until the 1960s religious leaders and organizations played a major role in providing education, health care, and social services, and frequently lobbying political leaders on issues of interest to religious groups (see O'Toole 1996; Grant 1998; Noll 2006). Religion's public presence became less influential as Canada modernized and institutions such as education, health care, or the family specialized and functioned apart from religious control (most notably in Quebec during the Quiet Revolution in the 1960s – see, e.g., Noll 1992; Baum 2000). At the same time Canadians became distrustful of religious leaders and organizations and many did not believe that religion should make much of a difference in one's life or Canadian society on the whole. Some religious organizations additionally modernized their beliefs and customs (e.g., the Roman Catholic Church after Vatican II or the United Church of Canada); religious groups struggled with aging congregations and rising costs associated with rapid building expansion during the 1950s; and individual religious affiliation, belief, and practice, which were higher in Canada compared to the United States until the 1950s, weakened between the 1950s and 1990s. When these were combined, it appeared as if modernization and religion did not mix well in Canada.

Bibby's interpretation changed in light of new data between 1995 and 2000, published in *Restless Gods* (2002, xii), in which he indicated that we might have reason to believe that a religious renaissance could occur in Canada: "organized religion is making something of a comeback, and that it is all to be expected." In part this conclusion was based on marginal increases in weekly attendance among 18- to 34-year-old and 55-years and older Protestants as well as conservative Protestant adults and teens, and monthly attendance increases among mainline Protestants and Roman Catholics. Religious identification and involvement among non-Christian religious groups such as Muslims and Buddhists also showed modest increases, particularly among teenagers. Additionally, several indicators of spiritual interest remained consistently high among Canadians in areas such as asking ultimate questions about meaning and purpose in life or happiness and suffering, believing in a supernatural being or in the afterlife, claiming to have experienced God or a supernatural being, or praying. Still, the most significant finding to emerge, one that was the basis of *Restless Churches* (2004), was that marginal religious affiliates reportedly desired greater involvement in their religious group if they found it to be worthwhile for them and their family. For instance, if various ministry, organizational, and personal factors were accounted for, such as more relevant preaching, better programming, livelier music, or a congregation that cared for them, or they were at a different stage of life like getting married or having children, then they would consider more involvement in their religious group.

Bibby's most recent interpretation in *Beyond the Gods and Back* (2011, 51–2) is a hybrid of his secularization and revitalization theses, a conclusion that supports a polarization narrative: "Solid cores of people are either involved or not involved in religious groups, either identify with traditions or do not identify with any, and are either theists or atheists … as some Canadians in the 'ambivalent middle' have moved toward religion, observers – including myself – have suggested that a measure of 'renaissance' and 'revitalization' might be taking place. As others in the 'ambivalent middle' have moved away from religion, we have suggested that we are witnessing the latest manifestations of secularization. More accurately, what has been emerging is polarization – two dominant postures toward religion." Among Canadian adults 31% attended religious services weekly in 1975 compared with 25% in 2005 (18% never attended in 1975 versus 23% in 2005); 91% identified with a religion in 1975 while 85% did so in 2005 (9% did not so identify in 1975, up to 15% in 2005); 61% claimed to believe in God in 1975, down to 49% in 2005. In terms of Canadian teens 23% attended religious services weekly in 1984 versus 21% in 2008 (28% never attended in 1984 and 47% never attend as of 2008); 88% identified with a religion in 1984 whereas 68% identified with one in 2008 (12% did not identify in 1984 versus 32% in 2008); 54% claimed to believe in God in 1984, dropping to 37% in 2008. In short, there is a notable division between those who attend religious services weekly versus never attending at all, those who identify with a religious group versus not identifying with one, and those who believe in God versus not believing. These statistics are especially pronounced among teenagers.

As useful as Bibby's quantitative data and conclusions are, qualitative data uniquely provide us depth and context to appropriately interpret, extend, and challenge quantitative findings. I have written elsewhere about my suspicions, on methodological grounds, over the revitalization thesis (Thiessen and Dawson 2008; Thiessen 2012) and more recently the polarization thesis (Thiessen 2011) in favour of Bibby's original secularization interpretation. Interviews enable researchers to tackle "why" and "how" questions (in contrast to "what" questions), examine the meanings, motivations, and processes behind religious decisions, and create space for new and unanticipated theoretical categories to emerge from the data (see Ragin 1987; Strauss and Corbin 1998; Goodwin and Horowitz 2002, 36–7; Johnson 2002, 112–13; Espeland 2005, 3; Lamont 2005, 2; Duneier 2006, 686; Day 2011; Wuthnow 2011). The narratives and experiences that arise from the interview data in this study advance our ability to evaluate which if any of Bibby's interpretations are accurate based in large part on the meanings and motivations behind people's religious activities.

Some might question whether individuals can reliably call forth conscious and intentional motivations for their behaviours because of faulty memory or social desirability bias, or if researchers or participants can tap into people's unconscious motivations, and therefore whether researchers should have the freedom to challenge or override the motivations that actors give for their own behaviour (see, e.g.,

Mills 1940; Martin 2011). Qualitative data are not perfect (neither are quantitative data), yet I agree with Wuthnow (2011, 6) that researchers can obtain valuable information when participants speak, especially during post-behaviour deliberations on motivations for past actions. I take a pragmatic approach to the aforementioned limitations. For example, I asked people to reflect on why they made certain religious decisions in the past and to reflect on motivations for current as well as possible future religious beliefs and behaviours. These latter questions helped to jog people's memories if they struggled to recall things from the past and, when these questions and responses were taken as a body of information and then compared within and between interviews as well as with the current literature, helped to discern people's true motivations for religious attitudes and practices. Social desirability bias did play a part in some interviews, but I detected this when shared information did not align, at which point I gently pressed interviewees to reconcile the discrepancies. For instance, some religious nones stated they believed in God and at other points in the same interview were far less confident. As I explored these inconsistencies further they expressed that they "should" believe in God because it seemed like the right belief to adopt, but when push came to shove they really did not believe in God. Social desirability also emerged among marginal affiliates who indicated that they would consider greater involvement in their religious organization if they felt it was worthwhile to them or their family, yet when prompted on this further they conceded that they were unlikely to pursue greater involvement and any initial response to my question about a desire for greater involvement was likely due to perceived pressure from their family, friends, religious group, or society – attending church more regularly was a "good" thing to do. By probing interviewees further on these and other topics I attempted to keep their perspectives, understandings, and narratives at the centre of my research as opposed to dismissing their perceptions with an outsider's authoritative or expert view (see Hesse-Biber and Leavy 2004; Martin 2011).

One final point about the quantitative-qualitative debate. In his recent article "Taking Talk Seriously: Religious Discourse as Social Practice," Robert Wuthnow (2011) argues for the merits of qualitative research in its own right rather than trying to legitimate qualitative findings by using quantitative language (e.g., "participants frequently spoke of …"). He makes several good points concerning how qualitative researchers minimize "talk" by quantifying their results rather than focusing on process, meaning, and identity in people's lives. I think there remains a place for quantification within qualitative studies without generalizing qualitative findings to the larger population or disregarding the core emphasis of qualitative research on meaning, process, and identity. The latter objective should remain at the heart of qualitative studies, but quantifying qualitative data provides transparency and precision when reporting it and helps with issues of reliability and validity that qualitative researchers are often criticized for. For instance, revealing how many interviewees say they are too busy to attend church shows how strongly this theme was evident and alleviates ambiguity surrounding phrases such as "many" or "most" participants believe or behave in certain ways. For this reason I include many quantitative references when presenting my data, but my main interest remains on how "talk plays an active role in subjects' lives" (Wuthnow 2011, 6); this study is not about overextending ninety interviews to explain all Canadians or to lose people's stories and experiences in numbers. My goal is that the following research findings and analysis will advance a carefully nuanced understanding of active affiliates, marginal affiliates, and religious nones in the early twenty-first century.

THEORETICAL FRAMEWORK

Two theories are particularly influential in the current sociology of religion literature and the sociological understanding of religion in Canada: secularization theory and rational choice theory. Many reading this book will be quite familiar with them. My purpose is not to present every aspect of these theories, to support or critique each theory, or to give detailed empirical data – much of which emerges as I progress in the book – but simply to outline the aspects of these theories that help lay the groundwork for interpreting my interview data moving forward. Along the way I highlight prevailing Canadian values and realities that aid to set the context for assessing the past, present, and possible future religious beliefs and practices among active affiliates, marginal affiliates, and religious nones.

Building a Case for Secularization Theory

There is a vast literature on secularization, one too large to cover in detail for my purposes here (see, e.g., Cox 1966; Luckmann 1967; Martin 1969, 1978, 1991, 2005; Lyon 1985; Lechner 1991; Tschannen 1991; Chaves 1994; Yamane 1997; Beyer 1999; Swatos Jr and

Christiano 1999; Gorski 2000; Heelas et al. 2005; Casanova 2007, 2008; Berger et al. 2008; Neuhaus 2009; Norris and Inglehart 2011). As such I limit my overview only to those scholars and ideas that apply directly to my argument in this book.

The premise of secularization theory, largely supported among European scholars, is that societies and individuals are less religious today than in the past because of social structural shifts associated with modern society, including structural and societal differentiation, rationalization, pluralism, and individualism (e.g., Berger 1967; Wilson 1982, 1985, 2001; Davie 1994; Bruce 2002, 2011; Voas and Crockett 2005; Crockett and Voas 2006; Voas 2009). Secularization proponents (Martin 1978; Wilson 1985; Yamane 1997; Berger et al. 2008; Bruce 2011; Norris and Inglehart 2011) are careful to point out that secularization unfolds differently across time and space, depending on a range of historical, social, and cultural factors in local societies. Further, secularization is not inevitable, straightforward, or irreversible in modern society.

Opponents of secularization theory, mainly from the United States, incorrectly attack secularization theorists for supposedly predicting the end of religion. They point instead to strong signs of religious vitality in the twenty-first century, including new religious movements, the public presence of religion, and ongoing signs of "spirituality" in many regions of the world (e.g., Hadden 1987; Casanova 1994, 2007; Stark and Finke 2000; Finke and Stark 2005). Incidentally, recent findings in the United States challenge these claims by foes of secularization theory, showing secularizing trends in the United States (see, e.g., Kosmin and Keysar 2008; Pew Forum on Religion and Public Life 2008, 2010; Putnam and Campbell 2010; Chaves 2011; Sherkat 2014).

Part of the challenge in debates over secularization is that many scholars clumsily make unstated assumptions about what they mean by secularization, they measure it differently, and as a result they often talk past each other. My conception of secularization is informed by the Belgian sociologist Karel Dobbelaere (1981, 2002), whose multi-pronged understanding of societal, organizational, and individual secularization is instructive for defining, measuring, and analyzing secularization. He defines societal secularization as "the shrinking relevance of the values institutionalized in church religion, for the integration and legitimation of everyday life in modern society" (Dobbelaere 2002, 19). In short, religion's place in the public sphere diminishes. The Quiet Revolution and the separation of religion from other secular institutions across Canada (and many liberal democracies in industrial settings) in the mid-twentieth century exemplify this type of secularization. Organizational secularization is the liberalization or modernization of religious belief and practice that occurs within a religious group (Dobbelaere 2002, 21). Depending on a group's social context this could include relaxing religious beliefs to allow women in religious leadership, accept gay marriage, permit alcohol consumption, include drums and guitars in church music, or allow adherents to wear jeans to church. Individual secularization refers to any "decline in involvement in churches and denominations" (Dobbelaere 2002, 18), or personal belief and practice such as belief in God, belief in life after death, prayer, or reading a sacred text. This final category is particularly problematic in secularization discourse because many individuals in Canada and elsewhere continue to identify with a religious group, pray in private, and believe in God all the while rarely if ever attending religious services. The question becomes, how should we interpret such individuals at the level of individual secularization? Should we privilege some types of religious belief and behaviour beyond one's religious group over active involvement in that religious group? However one approaches the secularization debate, clarity about which level of secularization one is referring to, and clear evidence along the way, is imperative.

Peter Berger (1967) and Steve Bruce (2002, 2011) are two of the most influential secularization proponents (Berger later renounced his theory in 1999). Like Dobbelaere, with his concept of societal secularization, Berger and Bruce believe that religion progressively plays a less dominant role in modern society, a result of rationalization processes such as structural and social differentiation in industrial societies. As societies become more complex and social institutional efficiencies are sought in turn, single institutions such as religion no longer fulfil the functions associated with other social institutions like education or health care. The result of growing societal complexity is individual and institutional division of labour and specialization to the point that religion is pushed to the margins of society as politics, the economy, education, and the legal system emerge as dominant social institutions. Drawing on historical and empirical examples from around the globe, Berger and Bruce argue that if religion plays a diminishing role in key social institutions it is only a matter of time before individuals look on the world through a lens that does not include much religion.

There are internal and external causes of secularization. Internal to religious organizations, Berger singles out ancient Israelite religion in the Old Testament as well as the Protestant Reformation as unintentional catalysts for individuals to view their faith in an individualist manner. For my purposes I briefly touch on the shifts caused by the Protestant Reformation. In an attempt to aid religious adherents toward what some believed was a more authentic and personal faith, the Protestant Reformation contributed to a faith devoid of many religious social reinforcements associated with church sacraments, priestly authority, and miracles. Because these elements to a community's religious life were diminished, the gap between God and humanity was enlarged, leaving many people subsequently to view their day-to-day lives with little reference to religion. Without a dominant religious narrative constantly reinforced in most aspects of one's life, people were freed to explore non-religious perspectives and world views.

Steve Bruce also deals with internal secularization. He argues that many religious beliefs and practices that people are currently drawn to epitomize secularized religious forms. In response to signs of religious life that some cite to refute secularization arguments such as the New Age Movement, growing interest in Eastern religions in the West, and rapid growth among Pentecostal and Charismatic groups worldwide, Bruce suggests that such movements are primarily individualist and subjectivist in orientation, raising doubts about how unifying or sustainable these belief and practice systems are in modern society. For instance, the New Age emphasis on elevating personal experience over external authority figures, the prominence given to personal experience over shared doctrine, or focusing on a personal relationship with Jesus Christ in some Pentecostal or Charismatic settings leads Bruce to align with Dobbelaere's concept of "organizational secularization." For Bruce these religious beliefs and practices forsake traditional religious emphases on otherworldly concerns that entail more demanding and sacrificial components and they lack the rigour and group accountability around a shared collection of beliefs and practices typically found in religious contexts. Furthermore, people gravitate toward groups that endorse individualism, autonomy, and diversity, making it even more problematic for a religious group to compel people to embrace a shared set of religious attitudes and behaviours.

External contributors to secularization include pluralism and privatization. As religion loses its grip on other social institutions religious and social pluralism emerge. With religious pluralism no single religious group benefits from the state as its official ally (e.g., as did the Lutheran church in some parts of Germany) and religions must compete on "neutral ground" with other religious and secular influences for people's devotion. Once taken-for-granted, the status for religion in a plural society is marginalized at best. This relegated position means that families and religious organizations are the main (or sole) source of religious instruction and reinforcement. Additionally, awareness that many religious options exist sets the stage for religion to be perceived as a subjective and relativized world view in contrast to a set of objective and absolute beliefs and practices. Countless examples of Berger's projection emerged in my research as interviewees found religion to be less believable and firm in an era dominated by many religious and non-religious belief systems. I heard phrases such as "there's so many of them ... they can all be right, they can all be wrong"; "the more open minded we become ... people see that there are aspects of each religion that people kind of skew"; "then maybe more people think nobody really has the answer"; or "I'm so fed up with every church thinking that they have the only Christian faith." These sentiments are embedded in a Canadian social climate that celebrates multiculturalism and immigration from non-Western countries where many identify with non-Christian religious traditions such as Islam, Buddhism, or Hinduism. These reflections are exacerbated in a globalized era where people are exposed to and can learn about anything in the world at the click of a finger, quickly realizing just how many perspectives about the world and religion exist beyond their own.

Social pluralism is another certainty in modern society, a point that Bruce picks up on when discussing social differentiation, and an idea stressed earlier by Karl Marx and Emile Durkheim. With geographic mobility the norm in modern societies, particularly from rural to urban settings, individuals increasingly find themselves in social settings with people who have different backgrounds and views than themselves. No longer are individuals surrounded by their families and traditional beliefs and practices at home that bind them and entire communities together. Instead, individuals, often working in highly specialized roles, now rub shoulders with doctors, cash clerks, mechanics, and business executives who have very little in common with them, least of all religion to hold them together around a common world view.

One extension of religious and social pluralism and the separation between church and state is the privatization of religion. Here religion is relegated to the private realm of families and individuals, apart from work or politics or education. In this social setting people want religion kept out of public life because no one religion should have a privileged status over another religion. Since no religion can be authoritatively true in a pluralist context, people limit religion to the private realm so as to avoid public controversy over competing world views. Here too, this acceptance of privatized religion is well documented among those that I interviewed. James Setton, a religious none in his 30s, says "I do have a kind of problem with religion ... you can't hardly ... open up the newspaper, turn on the television without learning about yet another religious group trying to involve themselves in public policy." Connie Firth, a Roman Catholic marginal affiliate agrees: "I don't think that [religion] should be enforced or regulated at all." Peter Reagle, a conservative Protestant marginal affiliate reinforces these views when he thinks religious groups are already too "influential ... [they] shouldn't be ... let the person shape their own religious beliefs."

Beyond keeping religion out of the public sphere, those I interviewed are adamant that others do not push their religion on them. Carol Ward, a religious none in her mid-30s, expresses that religion "should be more individual ... I really don't like when people push religion onto others. I have a really big issue with that." Similarly, Jennifer Redden, in her mid-40s, and a marginal affiliate, says, "I don't believe pushing anything onto anybody ... I can talk about how I feel. I can talk about ... what I believe and what I do, but I don't think that I would have a right to push it onto somebody else." Even from the active affiliate perspective, Kelvin Nill, a regular attender in the United Church of Canada, declares "I don't need somebody in the pulpit telling me what's right and what's wrong ... I don't think religious groups should be thumping away at their own beliefs."

Building on a Durkheimian and functionalist approach to sociology, Berger concludes that in a religiously and socially plural climate religion ceases to fulfill one of its main functions in society, to provide a common base for ultimate meaning that binds society together. There is merit to this taken-for-granted line of reasoning as historically religion has functioned as a common base for some societies. Still, based on my interviews with active affiliates, marginal affiliates, and religious nones several questions arise that deserve careful consideration. Was social solidarity one of the main functions of religion in traditional society (i.e., mechanical solidarity, to use Durkheim's terms), but no longer in modern society (i.e., organic solidarity, to borrow from Durkheim)? Does the function of religion, particularly to draw a society together around a common "ultimate" world view, depend on social and cultural context, and if so in what ways and how so? In other words, does the function of religion vary across time and space? Are there other primary functions for religion in society, ones that replace or supersede what Berger thought? Is it possible that as secularization takes hold of a religiously and socially diverse society, other grand narratives come to the surface to bind people together? For example, could one plausibly argue that rather than religious belief and practice unifying active affiliates, marginal affiliates, and religious nones, it is a shared world view around individualism, inclusivity, and tolerance that binds them together (see Bibby 2006)? Relative to religion, do most interviewees share the perspective that religion should stay out of the public domain and that individuals or groups should not push their religion on to others? Going one step further, does religion function more as a divisive rather than unifying force in plural modern societies? I address many of these questions at different points throughout the book.

Berger continues in his theory of secularization to suggest that like any product that is marketed in a competitive context, religion is also marketed in a pluralist and privatized social setting, with different religious groups emphasizing and de-emphasizing beliefs or practices to set themselves apart from other religions. For instance, some groups stress the relevance of their preaching or music while others emphasize theological distinctives such as joy and happiness in this life, escaping to a better next life, or helping the less fortunate. Religious groups appeal to different niche markets, but the plausibility of any single religious group is generally tarnished as people believe religious groups are less credible when they modify their product in hopes of drawing in new adherents.

The cumulative effect of pluralism, privatization, and marketing religion is the subjectivization of religion where individuals legitimate what is "true" based on their individual emotions and experiences rather than objective dogma. Thomas Luckmann (1967, 1990) famously projected that "invisible religion" would characterize people's appropriation of religion in socially differentiated societies. He contends that the shrinking span of great, intermediate, and little transcendence in modern society, transcendences historically tied to traditional institutional expressions of religious life, yields religious expressions that change but do not secularize. Akin in some ways to rational choice rejections of secularization theory, "invisible religion" entails that people turn to emerging and alternative New Age, cult, or do-it-yourself religiosity in a religious marketplace that sacralizes individual autonomy.

However one interprets this shift, it is clear that individuals' beliefs and practices are relativized to other people's beliefs and practices in modern society. As many interviewed in this study indicate, "What is true for you is true for you and what is true for me is true for me." This reality creates a crisis of legitimacy for religious organizations and those who belong to them. According to Berger (1979) this crisis results either in groups that reaffirm their traditional religious beliefs and practices in strong religious subcultures (e.g., evangelical and Roman Catholic traditions), groups that modernize and change their beliefs and practices to align with modern sensibilities (e.g., the United Church of Canada), or individuals who choose their own feelings and experiences over and against traditional religious authorities as the ultimate authority over their world view. This final response is the prevalent one among religious nones, marginal affiliates, and even active affiliates as they embrace the idea that individuals ultimately hold authority over their religious beliefs and practices – a posture amplified in a religiously plural context where individuals are keenly aware of the many religious options available, even within their own religious tradition (e.g., between Catholics and Protestants, Baptists and Lutherans, and within the Anglican tradition).

To bring this theory full circle, if religion is set to the margins of society, it is restricted to the private realm, and individuals adopt a subjectivist and relativist approach to their faith, then religion will have little significance for individuals or entire societies. This outcome is because the "common" social infrastructure to support continued and meaningful religious belief and practice is basically absent. Steve Bruce (2011, 2–3) echoes this conclusion in the following way:

> The declining power of religion causes a decline in the number of religious people and the extent to which people are religious. As religious faith loses social power, it becomes harder for each generation to socialize its children in the faith. It also becomes progressively harder for those who remain religious to preserve the cohesion and integrity of their particular belief system. As religion becomes increasingly a matter of free choice, it becomes

harder to maintain boundaries. Alternative reworkings of once-dominant ideologies proliferate, and increasing variation encourages first relativism – all roads lead to God – and then indifference as it becomes harder to persuade people that there is special merit in any particular road.

To reinforce his position, Bruce draws on figures in Britain to show that religious belief and practice is on the decline and even modest signs of growth in New Age expressions of spirituality or new religious movements pale in comparison to declines in traditional religious sectors. He also documents that in places like the United States where levels of religiosity are higher than most other Western countries, American churchgoers do not look much different from their non-religious counterparts in terms of smoking, dancing, divorce, or how they dress (i.e., evidence of organizational secularization, to use Dobbelaere's language).

Building a Case against Secularization Theory

Secularization theory is not as widely endorsed in the United States. Jeffrey Hadden's seminal article in 1987, "Toward Desacralizing Secularization Theory," laid the base for growing concern toward secularization theory. He suggests that sociology, given its roots in the Enlightenment, has long held a bias in favour of secularization to the point that scholars fail to adequately or fairly evaluate the assumptions behind secularization theory. If sociologists impartially examined the secularization thesis in light of empirical data, Hadden suggests that they would find, in the United States, stable levels of religious belief and practice – a finding reinforced by other American sociologists (see Greeley 1989; Presser and Chaves 2007). Others, in response to assertions that features of modernization such as economic, educational, and scientific advances inevitably lead to secularization, go further than Hadden to suggest that Americans have grown more religious over the course of history (Finke and Stark 2005), often measured by institutional expressions of religiosity (e.g., church attendance). In the European context people are not as secular relative to the past because Europeans were not as religious previously as many indicate. There are also many scholars who conclude that expressions of religious life have changed but not diminished, with many people maintaining nominal religious affiliation, belief, and involvement, reflecting the continued need and desire for religion in the modern era (see also Davie 1994; Miller 1997; Stark and Finke 2000; Bibby 2002, 2011; Stark et al. 2004; Heelas et al. 2005; Houtman and Aupers 2007; Lynch 2007; Wuthnow 2007).

Rodney Stark and William Bainbridge (1985), Jeffrey Hadden (1987), and Jose Casanova (1994) also refute secularization theory by highlighting the growth of new religious movements since the 1960s, which tend to arise in areas where adherence to conventional religious groups is low. Stark and Bainbridge (1985) frame their discussion of cults and new religious movements in response to those who suggest that secularization is irreversible. Acknowledging that religious groups are not always effective to attract or keep adherents and that organizations have the propensity to diminish strict beliefs and practices in response, they document that sometimes stricter religious groups (i.e., sects or cults) arise to fill a gap in the religious marketplace. Over time these religions tend to relax their positions to appeal to the masses to the point that new sects and cults arise in response. Stark and Bainbridge contend that this is a cyclical secularization process; do not mistake the absence of conventional religion for secularization when new religious expressions appear to fill the void. In turn, sociological interest surrounding new religious movements has gained enormous ground (e.g., Bromley and Hadden 1993; Lewis 2004; Dawson 2006), resisting the pro-secularization narrative that long dominated sociological research on religion.

Perhaps the most cited rebuttal of secularization is the strong public and political presence that religion has in many regions of the world (see Hadden and Shupe 1989; Casanova 1994; Berger 1999; Bramadat and Seljak 2005; Martin 2005; Berger et al. 2008). Jose Casanova refers to this phenomenon as the "deprivatization" of religion whereby religious groups refuse to accept their marginalized status in modern society. From the Christian Right in the United States to the continued struggle between Jews, Muslims, and Christians in the Middle East to tensions between Hindus, Muslims, and Sikhs in India, religion continues to play a prolific role in public life around the world. Even in Canada where many presume that religion is left dormant in the private sphere, religion is a hot topic in the political realm, especially as it relates to religious diversity. For instance, recent contentious debates include whether Sikhs should be allowed to carry their kirpans at school, Muslim women should be allowed to wear a niqab when boarding a plane or testifying in court, religious schools should receive public funding, or Canada should legalize homosexuality, abortion, or euthanasia. According to Casanova, deprivatization occurs for several reasons, including groups that hold a theological belief that God requires them to have a public presence, religions that fear their public influence is giving way to secular pressures, organizations that have global ties that fuel a group's propensity and confidence to assert themselves, or in fairly secular societies where the relationship between immigration and religious diversity fosters public discussion.

I could summarize far more about the secularization debate, but the major points covered here reveal some of the core ways that scholars define, measure, and analyze secularization. Based on the "fit" between the interview data in this study and countless national and international studies that I refer to throughout, I advance a case that supports Berger and Bruce's assessment that the conditions of modernity provide an environment for societal, organizational, and eventually individual secularization to flourish and that pluralism sets the stage for individualism and relativism to set in (see Hay 2014 for a quantitative defence of this position in Canada). I agree with Steve Bruce that it is more difficult (though not impossible) to remain highly religious *at the individual level* in the face of modernity, and once secularization sets in, it is incredibly difficult to reverse the trend.

Rational Choice Theory

A second theory garnering attention in the sociology of religion and one at the heart of Reginald Bibby's sociological examination of religion in Canada is rational choice theory. I am not as interested here in rational choice theory as a whole (see, e.g., Homans 1961; Blau 1964; Becker 1976; Stark and Bainbridge 1985, 1996 [1987]; Iannaccone 1988, 1990, 1992, 1994, 1995a, 1995b, 1997a, 1997b; Stark and Iannaccone 1994; Iannaccone et al. 1995; Stark and Finke 2000; Iannaccone and Everton 2004; Finke and Stark 2005) as I am in Rodney Stark and Roger Finke's (2000) exploration of the micro-aspects of individual religious decision-making processes as well as some of the structural variables associated with religious supply and demand.

This theoretical area is sociologically and empirically significant to this study for two reasons. First, the sociological study of religion in Canada has been importantly shaped by Reginald Bibby, who draws heavily on elements of rational choice theory in his nationally representative survey research. For instance, Bibby once argued (2002), and to some degree still does (2011, 186–206), that we should expect a renaissance of religion in Canada, particularly among marginal affiliates who are already tied to a religious group and have an ongoing need and desire for the things that religion provides. He draws directly on the supply and demand argument in Stark and Finke's work to support this conclusion: if religious demand is constant – and he believes it is – then changes to religious supply should yield greater levels of religious involvement. Understanding and testing the theoretical underpinnings to Bibby's work is imperative in order to evaluate fairly the legitimacy of his analysis and conclusions. Findings from the ninety interviews differ from the kind of data that Bibby draws on, yet interview data on people's past, present, and possible future levels of religiosity can help to account for individual's religious decision-making process in ways that survey data do not (see Day 2011). In turn these data will help us to appropriately address the second key issue in this book regarding debates about religiosity or secularity in light of the religious beliefs, practices, and involvements among active affiliates, marginal affiliates, and religious nones.

A second reason for examining these rational choice assumptions is because some of the core axioms and propositions in Stark and Finke's (2000) work, surprisingly, lack concrete empirical data or are logically suspect. Laurence Iannaccone (1997a, 41), a proponent of rational choice, acknowledges this weaknesses when he admits that he does not *know* whether or not people are rational, but that rational choice assumptions have been useful in the social sciences for building and testing models of human behaviour. He goes on to encourage empirical research that addresses micro-level questions relative to rational choice theory and religion. Mark Chaves (1995, 99), N. Jay Demerath III (1995, 105–6), Mary Jo Neitz and Peter Mueser (1997, 111–17), and Steve Bruce (1999, 43–4, 121) all echo Iannaccone's endorsement of micro-level research, calling for qualitative studies that examine individuals' stories, cultural context, the variation between cases, and religious production processes. Here too, though findings from ninety interviews will not lead the social scientific community to categorically support or reject the axioms and propositions within Stark and Finke's work, interview data can help to move this discussion forward from the theoretical to the empirical and to get at what explains higher and lower levels of religiosity between active affiliates, marginal affiliates, and religious nones.

Three propositions from Stark and Finke's *Acts of Faith* (2000) are helpful for examining how and why people make religious decisions in the ways that they do. The first proposition: "people make religious choices in the same way that they make other choices, by weighing the costs against the benefits ... within the limits of their information and understanding, restricted by available options, guided by their preferences and tastes, humans attempt to make rational choices" (Stark and Finke 2000, 85). Rewards are "anything humans will incur costs to obtain," while costs are "whatever humans attempt to avoid" (Stark and Bainbridge 1996 [1987], 27). Stark and Finke (2000, 85) carefully declare that "intention is everything"; people consciously and strategically intend to act rationally based on the available information at hand. Implicit in this argument are individuals who possess high levels of agency in their decision-making processes, a point that has received significant criticism over the years (see Heath 1976, 46; Ellison 1995, 95; Sherkat 1997, 68; Bruce 1999, 36, 78, 126–7). For instance, social ties, the way one is socialized, and lack of available options restrict the degree of agency one has over their religious decision-making processes.

In their discussion of religious costs and rewards, Stark and Finke extend social exchange theory (see Homans 1961; Blau 1964; Becker 1976) to account for exchanges between humans and the gods (Stark and Bainbridge 1996 [1987], 81–6; Stark and Finke 2000, 83–113). Stark and Finke (2000, 97–8) suggest that humans will pay higher costs to the extent that the gods are believed to be dependable, responsive, and of great scope. A dependable god can be relied on to keep their word with humans, a responsive god is concerned about and acts on behalf of humans, while a god of great scope has a diverse array of powers and range of influence with which to meet human needs. To the degree that individuals believe their god or gods score high in these areas, they are more likely to engage in extended and exclusive exchanges with them (Stark and Finke 2000, 99–100). This means that people will make periodic payments over an extended period of time and they will make exchanges with one god only.

Stark and Finke (2000, 96–113) note that when individuals make exchanges with people or gods, some exchanges are riskier than others (also see Heath 1976, 7–18, 46; Iannaccone 1997a, 33–5). Riskless exchanges occur after comparing all of the available options, and then proceeding with the one that gives the actor a high level of certainty that the desired outcome will occur. Riskless exchanges tend to be informed by past experiences, when individuals or groups experienced their god as dependable and responsive and in turn responded with extended and exclusive exchanges. A person's level of risk is also decreased when others share the same religious explanations and when they jointly participate in or witness an array of religious phenomena (e.g., religious rituals, prayers, miracles, or mystical experiences).

High-risk exchanges involve people's attempts to minimize their losses rather than maximize their gains. This is why people have house insurance. The thought of losing all of one's possessions is a greater burden than spending ninety dollars a month to insure everything, even if one never uses the insurance. This is akin to Pascal's Wager, where people assume a 50/50 chance that God exists. Rather than assuming that God does not exist and running the risk of going to hell, people choose to believe that God does exist. If they are correct, great, but if not, the costs are minimal, relative to the risks (i.e., cost) of eternal damnation. Some marginal affiliates that I interviewed adopt this position. Lance Couth, in his early 40s, admits that "if I don't attend then, I'm going to hell." Tracie Pearson, a Roman Catholic marginal affiliate in her late 40s, comments about people in general and says that "we were taught that if you don't go any other time of the year, you have to go then [Christmas and Easter]. Maybe they're afraid they won't go to heaven if they don't go." I ask her if this is a personal fear, and she says, "I guess I would feel that way." I then ask if she shares the same fear for her children, if they do not attend for religious holidays, and she again responded affirmatively. In total, people's assessment of costs, rewards, and risks informs how and why they make exchanges with the gods.

It may be true that individuals make religious decisions by weighing costs and rewards. However, aside from the standard costs of time and money (see, e.g., Iannaccone 1997a; Iannaccone and Everton 2004), we know very little about what those costs and rewards are, particularly in relation to church attendance, as framed by the very individuals who make religious decisions. Part of my objective in this study is to measure interviewee's subjective understanding of the costs and rewards that they associate with their religious beliefs and practices. I also explore the degree to which interviewees believe that their god (if they believe) is dependable, responsive, and of great scope, and in turn their willingness to enter into or remain in extended and exclusive exchanges with that god. Going one step further, I explore Stark and Finke's theory in the context of people's relationship with religious organizations. If individuals believe that those in their congregation are dependable and responsive, then the theory reasons that people would be more likely to participate in extended and exclusive exchanges with their congregations.

Stark and Finke (2000, 145, 147) say that "among religious organizations, there is a reciprocal relationship between expense and the value of the rewards of membership ... to the extent that one is motivated by religious value, one must prefer a higher priced supplier. Not only do more expensive religious groups offer a far more valuable product, but in doing so, they generate levels of commitment needed to maximize individual levels of confidence in the religion." This set of ideas builds on "strict thesis" assumptions where stricter religious groups supposedly generate deeper levels of religious commitment among adherents (Kelley 1972; Iannaccone 1994). The rationale is that strict religious groups offer definitive answers to questions of ultimate meaning, giving members a sense that God is on their side if they subscribe to the group's beliefs and practices. These groups provide clear boundaries between "insiders" and "outsiders" so that those on the inside are required to commit to ongoing belief in and loyalty to a unique way of life (e.g., to abstain from premarital sex, drinking alcohol, or wearing certain attire). These commitments facilitate a mutually supportive environment, rooted in common beliefs, which tend to motivate individuals to subordinate personal desires to the group and solidify their confidence in the religious beliefs and practices that frame their exchanges with the gods. As a result, "free riders," or those who are not fully committed to the group, are left on the outside. Iannaccone (1994, 1197) reasons that "increased strictness (or distinctiveness, or costliness) leads to higher levels of church attendance and church contributions, closer ties to the group, and reduced involvement in competing groups." As I explore rewards, costs, and exchanges among active affiliates, marginal affiliates, and religious nones I pay attention to the strictness thesis. Is strictness a magnet or deterrent for religiosity, particularly in its institutional forms?

The second proposition is that individuals have an inexhaustible demand for rewards that only religion provides, such as life after death, and religious supply is critical to meeting this constant demand. Stark and Bainbridge (1985, 6) insist that "the single most urgent human desire" is eternal life. In *A Theory of Religion*, Stark and Bainbridge (1996 [1987], 315) comment that "all humans share the desire for very general rewards, such as everlasting life, which seem unavailable to anyone this side of paradise." Stark and Finke (2000, 85) assert that "religion is the only plausible source of certain rewards for which there is a general and inexhaustible demand." Arguments to this effect are repeated in several other contexts too (see, e.g., Stark and Bainbridge 1985, 6–8, 431; Stark and Bainbridge 1996 [1987], 101, 315; Iannaccone 1997a, 28–9; Stark 1997, 46–8; Stark and Finke 2000, 85, 89), including by Bibby (2002; 2004) in the Canadian milieu. In a related way, Stark and Finke (2000, 103) contend that religious organizations' "primary purpose is to create, maintain, and supply religion to some set of individuals and to support and supervise their exchanges with a god or gods." In other words, religious organizations have an important role to help individuals make exchanges with a god or gods as they pursue their desire of life after death. But if religious demand is constant, then how does one explain varying levels of religious belief and practice?

The rational choice response is that religious supply shapes individuals' preferences and tastes, thus if levels of religiosity decline it is because of faulty religious supply (see Iannaccone 1994; Stark and Iannaccone 1994; Stark and Bainbridge 1996 [1987]; Finke 1997; Stark and Finke 2000; Finke and Stark 2005). Rational choice theorists arrived at this conclusion when considering why America was more religious than Europe. They highlighted America's official separation of church and state, which created a setting for religious groups to openly compete for people's allegiances by sharpening their supply of religion (e.g., livelier music, better preaching, or more parking). In return, people are more willing to incur greater costs to obtain what they believe is a better product and thus a better reward.

In contrast, many European nations such as France, Germany, Italy, or Belgium closely align church and state so there is less need for churches to compete for people's time, money, or devotion. According to Stark and Finke (2000, 228–39) many European religious organizations are weaker because they lack the impetus to sharpen their supply as clergy and lay members grow lazy, their beliefs and practices liberalize over time, and they screen out competition from other religious groups through legal sanctions, all with little fear of losing social or financial support to other religious groups. Stark and Finke (2000, 201) summarize the above conjectures this way: "Religious pluralism (the presence of multiple suppliers) is important only insofar as it increases choices and competition, offering consumers a wider range of religious rewards and forcing suppliers to be more responsive and efficient."

The questions that arise from their theory are whether active affiliates, marginal affiliates, and religious nones do, in fact, have an inexhaustible demand for life after death or meaning and purpose in life, and whether religious supply is the key variable to understanding the religious marketplace? I am particularly drawn to these questions given Reginald Bibby's continued preoccupation with the "ongoing reluctance of people to rule out the possibility of life after death ... the market for answers to the ongoing, universal question of what happens after we die remains extremely vast ... the desire for increasing clarity on this critical issue is something most of us want. That widespread desire guarantees a permanent place for religion" (2011, 170, 184–5).

The third aspect to Stark and Finke's work concerns the social side of religion: "in making religious choices, people will attempt to conserve their social capital [interpersonal attachments]" (Stark and Finke 2000, 119). For instance, social ties are critical for those who convert and join a religious group (Stark and Bainbridge 1985, 308–9) and for people already in a religious group to promote and sustain religious commitments via shared religious explanations. As Stark and Bainbridge (1985, 343–4) put it: "Living religion is a social enterprise, and religious beliefs take on significance for human affairs only as they are tied to social exchanges. Lone individuals, and even pairs of exchange partners, are seldom able to sustain strong supernatural orientations without powerful outside assistance ... therefore, vigorous, formal religious organizations and social movements can give beliefs and attitudes considerable salience for personal relationships; in the absence of such mass social support, beliefs and attitudes are not generally salient." This is why Stark and Finke (2000, 160–2) contend that when there are less dense social networks within a congregation there will also be low levels of reinforcement for commitment and less efficient means of monitoring member behaviour. Therefore, Stark and Finke (2000, 106–38) conclude that an individual's confidence in religious explanations is strengthened to the degree that others express confidence in the same explanations, that individuals participate in collective religious ceremonies, and that people conserve their religious and social capital (also see Iannaccone 1994; Ellison 1995; Sherkat 1997). Sociologically, their line of reasoning makes sense. My purpose is to explore active affiliates, marginal affiliates, and religious nones and the relationship between the social side of one's faith and their level of confidence in religious explanations.

THE PRESENT STUDY

I originally interviewed 42 individuals between May 2008 and July 2009 as part of my doctoral research on active and marginal religious affiliates. Upon completing that project I extended the research to include religious nones as well as a larger sample of active and marginal religious affiliates. Between May 2012 and August 2013 I conducted an additional 48 interviews. With the exception of two interviews that occurred over the telephone (to accommodate their schedules), all interviews were face-to-face and took place in coffee shops, people's homes, or places of employment. The interviews lasted around one hour on average, and ranged from 24 to 108 minutes long (see Appendix A for the Interview Schedule). All interviews were digitally recorded and then transcribed, and detailed field notes were taken during the interviews. Throughout the interview process I used NVivo, a qualitative data software package, to sort, organize, code, and analyze the data.

My sampling began with Reginald Bibby agreeing to contact 160 active and marginal affiliates in Calgary, Alberta, who had filled out his 2005 national survey, requesting their participation in my project. Nine individuals came forward and were interviewed for this study. I then relied on a snowball sample from those I interviewed throughout the project, along with referrals from personal friends, family members, colleagues, and students. In total I interviewed 30 active affiliates, 30 marginal affiliates, and 30 religious nones. Of the 90 people interviewed, there are 43 males and 47 females. Thirty-two are between 18 and 34 years old, 35 are between 35 and 54, and 23 are 55 or older. Twenty-three individuals are single, three are cohabitating with their partners, 3 are engaged to be married, 43 are in their first marriage, 9 are in their second marriage, 5 are divorced or separated, and 5 are widowed. With respect to highest level of completed education, 2 people did not finish high school, 7 did not pursue education beyond their high school graduation, 17 have a diploma or certificate, 13 have some college or university training, 39 possess a Bachelor's degree, 10 hold a Master's degree, and 2 have Doctorates. Within active and marginal affiliate groups, 20 identify themselves as Roman Catholic, 18 are part of mainline Protestant groups (e.g., Anglican, Lutheran,

United Church of Canada), 14 associate with a conservative Protestant tradition (e.g., Baptist, Christian and Missionary Alliance, Evangelical Missionary Church, Nazarene, Pentecostal, Salvation Army), and 8 are part of a non-denominational tradition or do not align to any single stream of Christianity. For religious nones, 7 previously had Roman Catholic ties, 10 had links in mainline Protestant traditions, 6 left conservative Protestant denominations, one left the Mormon Church, and 6 were not raised with any religion (for a comprehensive demographic overview, see Appendix B).

OUTLINE OF THE BOOK

In chapters 2, 3, and 4 I deal with active affiliates, marginal affiliates, and religious nones, respectively. I begin each chapter with three vignettes from those that I interviewed. These stories provide a window into several beliefs, practices, and experiences that resonate with many others whom I met as well as points of departure between interviewees, advancing my chief interest to explore what explains higher and lower levels of religiosity. In line with a modified grounded theory methodology, I focus my data analysis around secularization and rational choice theory and give attention to emerging themes from the data not currently found in the literature. As I present the many vignettes I am reminded of the privileged position that I was in to hear individuals express their thoughts and experiences regarding religion, life, and society, and in turn to communicate these sentiments to others. My hope is that I honestly and accurately represent those I interviewed (see Fine 1993).

In chapter 5 I explore the variables that surround the transition for once active affiliates who now identify as marginal affiliates and religious nones (48 in total). Following Bibby's research I also deal with any possible interest in greater involvement in a religious group and if so, what catalysts may be necessary for this to potentially occur. Additionally I examine how marginal affiliates and religious nones approach religious socialization with their own children. I centre my discussion and analysis of this data on the supply and demand debate within rational choice theory as well as secularization discourse. Specifically, should we expect a reversal of secularizing trends based on any possible future religious involvement among marginal affiliates and religious nones? Incidentally this research study will lay the tracks to a longitudinal study with many of those I interviewed, to see how their religious beliefs and practices evolve in the next ten to fifteen years and beyond – a rare opportunity in qualitative research (see Dillon and Wink 2007; Bengtson et al. 2013).

In the final chapter I do four things. First, I directly answer the main research question of the book (what explains higher and lower levels of religiosity?) by summarizing the major similarities and differences between active affiliates, marginal affiliates, and religious nones in my study. Second, I utilize Karel Dobbelaere's secularization framework to address scholarly debates about religiosity and secularity in light of the empirical findings from this study and elsewhere. Third, I explore the potential social and civic implications of a secularized society, drawing on theoretical and empirical discussions from both those who argue that religion is "good" and "bad" for society. Finally, I identify areas of research that ought to be conducted in the future to build on the findings of this study and our sociological understanding of religion in general and in Canada more specifically.

2

Active Affiliates: Religion Informed by God, Others, and Self

Stephen Nettle, Elizabeth Hickory, and Brooklyn Strait span the age spectrum from 18 years old through to 75. Each finds a home in one of the three dominant streams of Christianity in Canada, Roman Catholicism, mainline Protestantism, or conservative Protestantism. Similar to many active affiliates that I interviewed Stephen, Elizabeth, and Brooklyn attend religious services nearly every week and previously or currently volunteer time in their local congregations in the areas of music, children or youth, church governance, Sunday school or small groups, or serving the homeless. They also pray daily, some read the Bible several times a week, and all strive to live moral lives. All acknowledge in diverse ways how and why their religious attitudes and behaviours are informed by God, others, and themselves. They believe that God speaks through prayer, Scripture, and song, that others (friends, family, church leaders) affirm or challenge certain orientations to the world, and that individuals ultimately settle on what they believe to be true. Amidst these similar approaches to their religion Stephen, Elizabeth, Brooklyn, and the remaining 27 active affiliates embody a personal and unique religious narrative. They come from different backgrounds, have varying religious experiences, grapple with several aspects to faith and personal and public life, and subjectively appropriate religious belief and practice in their own way. In-depth insights into the attitudes, behaviours, and experiences of active affiliates open a window into religious decision-making processes and outcomes that assist a well-rounded exploration into the similarities and differences among and between groups ranging from the very religious to the relatively irreligious.

STEPHEN NETTLE

Stephen Nettle is 75 years old. He invited me into his home on a sunny June afternoon, led me to his kitchen with a view out to his back garden, and offered me a drink. Stephen is married and has three children and currently enjoys life as a retired schoolteacher. One of five children, he grew up in England where his father was in the British Army before becoming an engineer in an aeronautical factory. While growing up Stephen and his family regularly attended a Salvation Army church and he describes his family as "*very* religious."

Following high school, Stephen joined the British Army as a musician. There he was exposed to a book that would forever change him, written by the Roman Catholic monk Thomas Merton. Stephen appreciated the emphasis in his evangelical upbringing on a personal relationship with Jesus but Merton's book opened his eyes to the sacramental and monastic aspects to the Christian life that he was less familiar with. This spiritual awakening of sorts led Stephen to eventually join the Roman Catholic Church and to become a monk. Through this experience he developed an all-encompassing life commitment to God and he incorporated liturgical and structured elements into his spirituality, behaviours that remain with him to this day. Following many years in a monastery, Stephen sensed God drawing him in a different direction, to that of husband and teacher.

Stephen still identifies himself as a Catholic, though he regularly attends an Anglican church. His passion for music initially contributed to him joining a choir at an Anglican church in his neighbourhood, where he currently attends. In terms of his religious affiliation, Stephen states, "I don't think there's any reason why I should become an Anglican. I see myself ... as a Catholic Christian." When I ask Stephen how important his religious affiliation is, he promptly interrupts that I "have to define the word *religion*." This is a repeated reaction among many interviewees. The term "religion" is troubling, calling forth negative images of authoritarianism, dogmatism, legalism, and sexism. Interviewees favour terms like "faith," "spirituality," or "personal relationship with God," words that are socially acceptable, inclusive, and less threatening. This finding validates much of what scholars have documented over the last decade too (see, e.g., Wuthnow 1998, 2001; Zinnbauer et al. 1999, 901; Fuller 2001; Bibby 2002, 194–202; Marler and Hadaway 2002, 294; Hood Jr 2003, 249; Dillon and Wink 2007). What might surprise some is that active affiliates are just as troubled with the word "religion" as those not actively involved in a religious group (see, e.g., Levan 1995; Cavey 2005). Rebecca Anderson is part of a conservative Protestant congregation and is about to begin university. She says, "I don't try to get caught up in religion ... I think, just having a relationship with God."

After Stephen expresses his disdain with the term "religion," he highlights that his Christian identification is far more important than being Roman Catholic or Anglican: "My Christian faith isn't something which is ... laid on top ... it's not *part of* my life. My religious faith is an expression of what is ultimately true in my life ... Being a committed Christian doesn't mean that you say goodbye to all the other parts of life. It is something which is part *of* life ... the Christian faith is a way of looking *at* life as a whole ... There is no conflict between the ordinary and the spiritual. There is no conflict. It is the same thing as two things." Stephen's reflection resonates with one third of active affiliates: denominational affiliation matters little to them (see Miller 1997), to the point that many Protestants would consider changing religious affiliation, albeit only within their stream of mainline or conservative Protestantism. More important than denominational tie is defining themselves as Christian first (see Clarke and Macdonald 2007), an identifier that they believe is central to their life.

Stephen continues to believe many of the things that he learned in his Salvation Army upbringing, such as a belief in a personal God who is actively involved in the world. He believes that the Holy Spirit provides guidance and direction for "believers" to live a moral life. These values are clear in Stephen's reflection on the unspeakable and intense restlessness of the human soul that lured him to faith in God and to regular church adherence. Referencing St Augustine's *Confessions*, he declares, "Lord, you have made us for yourself, and our hearts are restless until they rest in you."

I then ask Stephen, "Do you find that you gain anything specifically from your personal faith commitments?" In contrast to many others that I interviewed who frequently responded with a list of rewards tied to their religious beliefs and practices, Stephen shares the following statement: "At least for the Christian, there's only one road to God, and that is by way of the cross. And the cross is not peace or tranquility ... The cross is painful ... If you're going to follow Christ ... who is ... the *crucified* Lord, then there is no way to avoid the cross ... That means ... that you cannot expect total peace. You can't expect an escape from conflict ... the Christian life is not a departure

... an escape from the ... problems and the pains ... of everyday life ... it's ... a more intense way of living everyday life. It's an intensity of living, and it's an intensity of joy, and it's an intensity of pain."

When I ask Stephen if religion is mainly an individual journey or one that should be shared in community, he responds that religion is essentially individual, but that our surroundings influence our approach to religion. Individuals intentionally choose to believe in God or not and they make decisions about how to live their life according to religious convictions. Still, they gather their religious beliefs and practices from other people, and community gatherings are an important setting to either test or validate their religious attitudes and behaviours. I probe Stephen, "How influential is your own congregation in shaping your beliefs and practices?" He replies, "Indirectly only ... when I was younger ... I'm not so impressionable now as I was." Stephen's exposure to Thomas Merton and the Roman Catholic Church were influential catalysts as a young adult to change his views toward religion, but since then his religious attitudes and behaviours have essentially stabilized.

To summarize, Stephen's narrative sheds light on the realities of several other active affiliates that I interviewed. They insist that their religious world view informs the decisions that they make in all aspects of life, particularly evident among those who grew up in strong Christian families. This is magnified in Stephen's acknowledgement that submitting one's life to God is the requirement for total commitment to Christianity. He and others in my study do not see their life as their own and God can do with them as He wants; marginal affiliates do not share the same belief. Furthermore, regardless of age, denominational ties pale in importance to active affiliate's Christian identification, especially for those with strong religious roots and who have maintained high levels of religiosity throughout their life. This is demonstrated in Stephen's contact with different denominations and the subsequent low priority that he associates with each denominational identity marker. This is also reflected in Elizabeth Hickory's story.

ELIZABETH HICKORY

Elizabeth Hickory, 18 years old, met me in late July at one of several Tim Horton's coffee and doughnut shops that I frequented during this study. The youngest of three siblings, she currently works a few part-time summer jobs in anticipation of attending university in the fall to become a nurse. Her mom and dad raised her in the Pentecostal denomination where she participated in church, Sunday school, and eventually youth group on a weekly basis, and she attended a Roman Catholic school growing up. I ask Elizabeth if religion was important to her family when she was younger and she states, "It's always been a part of my family, and even ... my grandparents ... it was a very important part of ... our whole family." When she reflects on the importance of religion to her personally growing up, she speaks about meaningful relationships as well as the guidance that comes from her faith: "It was important. It was ... how I connected with a lot of my closest friends, and ... it's always been something instilled in my life, and it kind of helps bring purpose and meaning to your life." For many of the 90 people I interviewed who attended a church youth group, friendships were a drawing card for involvement in their local church, sometimes even more important than any religious component to youth group gatherings – especially for those who now consider themselves marginal affiliates or religious nones. For those who remain active affiliates relationships were valuable, but the meaning and purpose that they gleaned from their religious experiences were equally if not more valuable, enough to sustain their continued involvement to this day.

At present Elizabeth is actively involved in her local congregation. In addition to Sunday morning services, she attends a weekly young adult service, she volunteers with the youth group, and she helps out with the coffee shop at the church where all proceeds go toward youth mission trips. I ask how important her Pentecostal identification is and similar to Stephen, her denominational ties are less important than being Christian: "Growing up in the Catholic school and then Pentecostal church, I didn't even really know that I was going to a Pentecostal church until I was ... probably twelve or something, and I asked my dad, and I didn't understand ... there's so many different denominations ... There's Baptists. There's Pentecostals. Anglicans ... for me, it's just about being a Christian. I'm affiliated with the Pentecostal church, and that's what I've grown up in, but ... it's more just about having a relationship with God and being somewhere where I feel like I'm being, I guess, spiritually fed." She carries on to indicate that Christianity is the most important thing in her life: "Christianity – like, my faith, my relationship with God – is ... well, I try to ... hold it as the most important thing in my life ... My life is just ... given meaning through Christ."

I inquire about Elizabeth's reasons for being actively religious as well as some of the possible trade-offs that she has incurred along the way. Religious community is a notable benefit of her religious involvement. From her close friends, most of whom attend church regularly, to those who have mentored her to those she mentors, she values the support and prayer for each other through difficult times in life. She says, "I attend because I have friends in the church … I gain moral support through the church … I can relate most with [the] friends I have made through the church or mentors that I have made through the church … just to have someone who … is there for you and will pray for you if you're going through a tough time." She goes on to provide many instances where fellow church members rallied around her in a time of need or where she participated with friends to help others in her congregation. For Elizabeth the church is a place where she can depend on others and she believes that they care about each other.

Church is also a place where Elizabeth learns about God, which draw her closer to God, and she benefits from the conversations and discussions with others who help her to understand the Bible and God more clearly. It is not surprising then that she says her church is "very influential" in shaping her beliefs and practices including belief in God, belief in the afterlife, consistent "quiet times" with God each day, attempts to positively influence those around her, and involvement on mission trips.

She references different experiences in high school as trade-offs for being fairly religious. For example, most people were out partying on weekends but for religious reasons her and some of her friends did not. Some made fun of her for being open about her Christian faith. She concludes that "you just have to accept it and move on and try to … still be friends with those people who maybe don't want to associate with you because of your faith, and … you can show them … try to be a … positive guidance to them." Implicit in this response is her view toward the afterlife, which she spoke about later in the interview. She believes that only those who believe and behave according to biblical precepts will be allowed into heaven, and it is her job as a Christian to encourage those around her to "become Christian."

Near the end of our interview I asked Elizabeth, as I did with the other 89 interviewees, whether she thought religion was a positive or negative social force in society. Similar to most other active affiliates that I interviewed (unlike marginal affiliates or religious nones), she believes that religion plays a positive role in society, though her response signals elements of exclusivity that partially fuel an emerging polarization between the two extremes of the religious continuum all around the world, including Canada (see, e.g., Putnam and Campbell 2010; Bibby 2011; Wilkins-Laflamme 2014): "I believe that it's positive ... in society ... it's a needed force ... Because, if not ... the world's getting run by ... secularism, and that's ... scary ... it's sad, but sometimes ... religion doesn't have enough of a ... force as it should ... Because you see ... in politics ... gay marriage being approved and stuff, which, as a Christian ... it's hard because it shows that the world's going that way ... and it easily pitfalls ... one thing ... that changes in politics, and then it's, like, okay, well, if this ... is now being allowed ... what's going to happen next? ... Christianity and religion needs to be almost ... I wish it could be more of a force because there's a lot of things going on in the world." Elizabeth says all of these things with a sincere belief that religion is good for society and that even more religious influence in society would be better, all without a deep-seated desire to bring harm or destruction to others. She is not alone. Other active affiliates that I met share these views, some more stridently than Elizabeth, and it is views such as these, even if presented in an innocent and non-vindictive manner, that contribute to a strong aversion among many marginal affiliates and religious nones toward organized religion.

I follow up with Elizabeth and ask whether she thinks people need religion in order to be moral or ethical beings: "No, not necessarily. Religion certainly helps, but ... you'll meet people who are ... just amazing human beings ... but they don't actually fully follow religion or follow a belief. And it's hard ... when you find that out, you're like, 'Are you serious? You're not ... involved in a church?' And they're like, 'No, I'm not' ... it's hard to believe because ... they're living their life very morally. I don't know. Some people are, I guess, just good human beings ... The world needs good human beings ... So people can live morally and ethically without religion. I think religion obviously, helps, but people do without it." Only a handful of the ninety people that I interviewed believe that religion is necessary for individuals or entire societies to be moral or ethical, but active affiliates more than anyone else believe that religion is not necessary, but it certainly helps.

We conclude our interview by talking about many volunteer involvements, clubs and social groups that she is part of, as well as how she spends her leisure time. I leave the interview thinking about the profound impact that Elizabeth's religious upbringing has on her religious world view, the central place that Christianity has in her life, the strong social ties that shape her experiences with God and her local congregation, and the possible negative reactions that marginal affiliates and religious nones might have toward her views on what is required to obtain the afterlife or the role that religion ought to possibly play in society.

BROOKLYN STRAIT

On my way to meet Brooklyn Strait, seven years to the day after the terrorist events in the United States on 11 September 2001, my sociological imagination was racing. I was thinking about the profound worldwide impact that 9/11 had on people's perceptions toward religion and how my conversation with Brooklyn might intersect with this emerging global discussion.

Brooklyn is a Roman Catholic in her 40s. She is divorced with one teenage child who lives with her, and she has taught English as a Second Language for over two decades in several Canadian and international locations. Both her parents were teachers in the Catholic school system, which partially contributed to her career path.

On the topic of religion all of Brooklyn's education, including college, took place in Catholic settings. She joked that she never met a Jewish person until she moved to Montreal for a period of her adult life. Brooklyn was confirmed and took her first communion as a child, and attended mass weekly with her family until her teen years. She reflects, "[We had a] real strong Catholic upbringing. But ... not traditional. My parents are very ... liberal thinkers ... they both are quite educated ... they're not super stuck as conservatives." This final statement later rubbed off on Brooklyn's approach to religion. During her teen years Brooklyn's parents gave her the option to continue attending mass. She reduced her involvement to monthly at that point because attending church each week was "not cool." Brooklyn claims that religion was not that important to her personally growing up, thinking of it simply as a tradition.

Brooklyn's approach to religion changed in her 20s when she moved overseas:

> When I got into university ... then it became more important ... I needed something ... I needed that sense of security and that sense

of home that you ... lose when you start getting more out in the world ... I was away from home, and I didn't have any friends ... So I started going to church at that point because it was ... first of all, I didn't have anything to do on Sunday except wander around and study ... I thought, "Gee, you know, this is really interesting, because, no matter where I am in the world, they still do the same thing in this church." So you feel comfortable. It's sort of like going to McDonalds except it's not McDonalds.

She expands on the ritualistic elements of the Catholic Church, which comfort her: "Everyone does the same thing in whatever language or whatever culture, so that's a real common point ... I know when to stand up, when to sit down, when to kneel, what he's going to do now, when it's communion ... So that's kind of ... nice, especially when you feel like you're a stranger." Upon her return to Canada regular church involvement continued because unlike her friends and parents, Brooklyn believed that God could provide direction on what to do with her life.

Brooklyn currently attends mass weekly along with her daughter. Over the years she has provided leadership with Rites of Christian Initiation of Adults for adult converts to Catholicism, reading Scripture during church services, plus her daughter is an altar server. Some of her closest friends are also actively involved in a Catholic church. Asked if her Catholic identification is important, Brooklyn responds, "Very important ... It's kind of a defining thing for me ... But I'd have to say it's not only Catholicism but just the way I live my life." Her faith is regularly informed by starting and ending each day in prayer, sometimes a joint activity with her daughter. She rejects media or politics influencing people's thinking, favouring how religion can instead help people to avoid taking everything at face value.

Mindful of traditional Roman Catholic opposition to divorce, I ask Brooklyn about how she and her ex-husband approached religion, and whether religion was a source of tension that contributed to their divorce. Her husband was not that religious. He attended mass on some occasions when Brooklyn asked him to, but religion was not the reason for the divorce. She then qualifies her initial comments: "If he would have had religious beliefs, he might have thought differently. It might have affected the way he looked at things. Like, for instance, money was a big point of contention, so if he had more religious background, maybe he wouldn't have put money number one in his life." When speaking about the impact of this mixed-faith union on her daughter, Brooklyn points out that her husband supported her raising their daughter however she wanted. On this point she stresses the importance of baptizing her daughter, reinforcing a theology of baptism to arise from several active and marginal affiliate Roman Catholics: "I just think that because then she's accepted into the church ... that was very important ... there's a certain protection in belonging to the church. I feel that you're in the ... group of ... the circle of prayer ... you're being held by people."

Commenting on the reasons for her weekly mass attendance, Brooklyn highlights the "spiritual nourishment" that she receives — like food for the body — and the quiet and solitude away from the hectic pace of "normal" life. She likens her church to a "home" and safe refuge where she receives "messages from God" through prayer, the priest, and the sermon. She also values her religious bonds with other people: "Being with people who are of the same mind is very important ... I think there's a lot of power in a ... group of people in prayer together. There's more power than just being by yourself." At the same time she values time on her own when she prays, which gives her "peace of mind" and helps to "put things into perspective."

Does Brooklyn believe she sacrifices anything while experiencing these benefits of her faith? She replies, "You can't ... just go living ... a completely different life ... You can't just ... receive things and say ... 'I'm not going to do anything with that' because then you'll stop receiving ... Sometimes it's hard to listen. Sometimes the message is not really what you want to hear. Or sometimes you have to persevere. Sometimes you have to keep going in that direction, even though it seems very difficult and like you're not gaining anything ... in that way, you do have to sacrifice ... It's always a mystery. So you have to live with that mystery. If you can't live with it ... it's a bit of a sacrifice to live with that. We can't just get answers for everything."

On the afterlife, Brooklyn definitely believes in life after death though she is not "black and white" on what the afterlife entails. She describes purgatory as a place of love that prepares all individuals for a more permanent place. Brooklyn is less clear if it is as simple as good people go to one place and those who are not good go to another. She summarizes her evolving understanding this way: "I can't say where I'm going exactly, but I know what I strive to do and what I like to do ... I just rely on God's grace ... I do believe that there is an afterlife. And I believe that the people who have gone before me

... there's some connection with them ... I believe ... in prayer for ... people who have died and prayer for people who ... we're all one big community." She rejects the evangelical belief that only those who accept Jesus as their saviour will go to heaven. She believes God is inclusive and gracious to allow others into the next life, but she is unclear about what those other variables might entail. In the end she summarizes, "Jesus is love, and God is love."

We change topics slightly. I ask Brooklyn if she believes that she can depend on God. She does, but brackets her response around how slow God is to respond to prayers and the subsequent challenge to fully trust and hand over control to God. Brooklyn maintains that God cares about and acts in the best interests of humans, though humans sometimes get in the way by doing things their own way rather than what in her mind is the ideal, to fully depend on God.

Brooklyn proceeds to offer her thoughts about trusting others in her congregation. She could if she were to ask them, however her perception is that this is not a "Catholic" thing to do – Catholics are very private people. This stood out to her when attending an American evangelical church when she was in her 30s. She had a fall out with her family that contributed to her moving locations and trying to do everything opposite to what her family wanted, which included going to an evangelical church. There she experienced people who, unsolicited, got to know and help other people. She also learned to value scripture, which she repeatedly referenced in our interview as a deficiency in Catholic settings: "You know, it's like going to the lecture all your life and then finally reading the text that goes with the lecture."

The drawback with evangelicals, however, was that "they thought their church was the only church that was right ... I can't deal with that ... that's against my liberal thought ... I can't tell anyone my church that, and I can't have someone telling me that." This is why she accepts most of what Catholicism teaches, but not everything (she does not elaborate), and she rejects religious groups that are too exclusive in their faith. On this latter point she singles out Muslims for "walking around with a hood over [their] head looking like a fool." She carries on to speak of all exclusive religions: "Religions ... that are too ... narrow ... They restrict people too much ... If you're always told what to do and you're always trying to do what someone expects you to do, then ... That's why the personal aspect is so important ... And if you have too many rigid rules and structures and hierarchies in there, you're not going to do that. So that's why I think people do see religions negatively. I think they can't get past that. There are these rules. That's nice. But, within that, I have to live my own ... I have to be who I am."

Based on my other interviews with active affiliates I was surprised to hear that Brooklyn does not believe that her church, located downtown where many marginalized populations reside (e.g., homeless, addicts), cares for and acts in the best interests of people. She acknowledges that some individuals do good things, but her church culture discourages the rowdy "bums" (her word) from hanging around church services or giving money to those who ask because they will likely use it for drugs or alcohol. I could not discern if this culture was formally encouraged and legitimated by local church leaders or whether this was a culture that somehow emerged from within the congregation. Either way, Brooklyn does not believe that her church is as caring and loving toward people as they could or should be.

Near the end of our interview we converse about those who attend Catholic mass mainly for Christmas and Easter. Some Catholics that I interviewed have a problem with "free riders" showing up for these services, but Brooklyn is not among the critics: "Whether or not you think you believe, they're still there ... if you go on Easter and Christmas ... that's just fine. What's wrong with that? ... I think that, as Christians, we should always be welcoming ... that's what our purpose is ... to try to tell people the good news ... it's free admission ... if we don't model that, who's going to?" Brooklyn's sentiments reinforce her earlier stance of opposition against religious groups that are too exclusive and inaccessible.

As I leave the coffee shop I am not sure if there is any direct connection between the 9/11 terrorist acts seven years prior and Brooklyn's aversion to strict expressions of religious life. I imagine these events did not help. Nevertheless Brooklyn, Elizabeth, and Stephen's stories provide a helpful lens for making sense of active affiliates in this study as well as to compare with marginal affiliates and religious nones.

GROUNDED IN LIFE

How do active affiliates think about their religious decisions? What rewards do they attach to their beliefs and practices and what trade-offs do they incur along the way? Stephen, Elizabeth, and Brooklyn's vignettes introduce us to some of the rewards and costs that active affiliates associate with their religious faith. The rewards that emerged in my interviews range from individual gains, such as feeling good about themselves, knowing that they are loved by God and others, and experiencing a break from the strains and busyness of life when they pray, read the Bible, or attend church, to social things, like participating in social justice initiatives (e.g., helping the poor in society) and carrying on their family or religious group's tradition. Three rewards or functions stand above the rest: participating in a likeminded community; receiving meaning, purpose, direction, and morals for daily living; and developing and affirming their faith by learning more about the Bible from a trained specialist and singing worship songs, and praying in a larger social setting (see Bibby 2012, 96).

Similar to Elizabeth Hickory and Brooklyn Strait, for seventeen of the thirty active affiliates the greatest benefit of their faith is the community that they experience with fellow believers. This includes surrounding themselves with people who share similar beliefs and practices and seeking social and spiritual supports with others in their church. Zach Tuttle, in his late 30s, states that the "regular Sunday morning community is regular enough that it does kind of keep me grounded, reminds me of who I am, what I believe, and it surrounds me with others that hold those similar beliefs, so it does kind of give me that weekly grounding." Jennifer Reed, a mother-to-be in her 20s and part of a conservative Protestant church, shares the benefits to participating in a small group: "Accountability in our small group because we're really honest with each other. Gain friendship. People who will support you when you need it ... you get just a sense of peace about things ... when you pray and do your Bible study and you're being consistent and you're being faithful ... you can handle life's problems." From this quotation (and others like it) active affiliates see their involvement in the religious community as an insurance of sorts that someone will be there to help in times of need, and vice versa. This mutual aid is reassuring for many, especially in a world where now it is even hard to count on family support (who may not be emotionally or physically present), let alone neighbours.

Stephen Nettle, Elizabeth Hickory, and Brooklyn Strait all spoke clearly about the meaning, direction, and purpose that they receive from their faith and their regular involvement in their religious group, and fifteen active affiliates echo this perspective. They believe that the combination of regular church attendance, belief in God, along with a host of private practices (e.g., prayer, Bible reading, and meditation and reflection) provides a source of meaning in life. It gives them a framework to interpret their social roles in the home, at the workplace, and as a citizen of the world. They articulated that God "helps bring purpose and meaning to your life," God "puts things into perspective for me," or God reminds them "of the way you should be living your life." Zach Tuttle says that prayer "keeps me continually grounded in God. Therefore, it just helps me be a better husband and father and neighbour and worker. I mean, everything I do, I try to filter through my belief system, so it definitely benefits. I think it makes my life better because I try to do things that are wise and good ... I believe that my marriage is better off for it. My family is better off for it. My finances are better off for it. My relationships, in general. My personal health, even, physically and emotionally." Other active affiliates similarly maintain that their lives are improved because they believe in God and they share in that faith with fellow believers on a regular basis. What differentiates active affiliates from marginal affiliates is that active affiliates believe that they need weekly church attendance to remind them that God ought to strongly influence their morals and structure their daily activities in religiously meaningful ways. Marginal affiliates maintain that only a few church appearances a year will "do the trick" though most admit they do not consciously seek to align their daily activities in accordance with God's will.

Another reward that twelve active affiliates discuss is the development and affirmation of their faith by learning more about the Bible from the religious leader, singing worship songs, and lifting prayers to God in a larger social setting. Active affiliates are drawn to their religious leaders who offer insights into the Bible that they would not have discerned on their own. As Adam Major, an elderly gentleman in the United Church of Canada, states, "The points in Scripture have often been difficult to understand, and the guys at [Alpha Church] have been just tremendous in giving different insights into the meaning of Scripture." This is perceived as a reward because it helps people to learn about God, so that they can uphold the beliefs and practices common to their religious tradition and experience a good life here on earth and in the afterlife. Deferring to an expert authority is characteristic of this day-and-age when individuals turn to experts on subjects that they are not as knowledgeable about and when people are unable or unwilling to invest the time to become experts themselves (Giddens 1990).

These gains are enhanced when individuals see people around them also learning and striving for the religious ideals that the religious leader preaches about. The same can be said about singing songs and lifting prayers with others. As Zach Tuttle put it, "Even though I can just stick a praise tape on at home if I want to or a praise CD in the car by myself, there's something more powerful about larger corporate worship times." The strength, energy, and development and affirmation of personal faith that people experience at church epitomizes the "collective effervescence" that Emile Durkheim (1915, 209–10) discusses: "In the midst of an assembly animated by a common passion, we become susceptible of acts and sentiments of which we are incapable when reduced to our own forces." He goes on to say that religious ceremonies function "to bring men together, to put the masses into movement and thus to excite a state of effervescence, and sometimes even of delirium ... a man is carried outside himself and diverted from his ordinary occupation and preoccupations" (1915, 383). Active affiliates believe that there is a different level and quality of connection with self, others, and God when worshipping in a set apart time and place with other people.

In light of the rewards that active affiliates associate with their religious beliefs and practices, they also speak about costs that vary from friends, control over their life, fasting, giving up things during lent, time, or money. Since sacrificing time, mentioned by seven individuals, and money, raised by four active affiliates, are self-explanatory (i.e., people commit time to religious practices such as prayer, attending church, or volunteering for church activities, and people tithe money to their church), and given that these themes have been examined by Iannaccone (1997a) and Iannaccone and Everton (2004) elsewhere, I focus on the costs of friends and control over one's life. Starting with the most cited cost of relationships, which twelve active affiliates like Elizabeth Hickory mention, some speak about lost and strained friendships when they were teenagers because they had to choose between the activities of their religious and non-religious friends. Reflecting on her high school years, Pauline Inger, a conservative Protestant with a BA in psychology says, "I think it was hard for me to find my place as a Christian in a secular world ... I never drank in high school. All my friends drank. I didn't do drugs. All my friends did drugs. I wasn't having sex with my boyfriend. All my friends were having sex with their boyfriends." Others recall the odd looks and strange feelings that they received from non-religious friends and family. People saw them as deviant, strange, and part of an outside group. Gale Robbins is in her 30s and works in marketing. She says, "I think there's an element of social ... isolation ... something I've sacrificed is people, like, 'Oh, you go to church? Really.' Or 'You're one of the smartest people I know, and I can't believe you go to church.' Or 'What are doing this weekend? Oh, you're' ... And so that social awkwardness ... People outside of the church really don't know how to react to people's participation in the church." For some this led to abandoning certain relationships, while for others it strained, but did not end, friendships and family ties.

The next cost that seven participants mention – a prominent theme during my interview with Stephen Nettle – is submitting control of their lives over to God. This world view is grounded in a theological position that God is highly active in the world and that a Christian's life is no longer their own. Jennifer Reed shares that "sometimes God asks you to do stuff that doesn't make any sense ... you give up control of your life." She says that she wants to experience "God in all aspects of my life: my physical body ... my emotional state, my family ... Allowing God to be in charge of everything: finances." Anthony Harder is in his 30s and he works in the financial industry. He says that "God asks for us to surrender. He says, 'Surrender all things to me,'" and David Diamond, who holds a PhD in theology, reflects that "you don't get to make your own decisions. Your life isn't your own anymore. If you're serious about it, it's not your own anymore. So you're not ... the boss." Simply put, and this sets active affiliates apart in this study, religion is a master status that informs all aspects of their lives. Many believe that God leads people to the person that they marry, the job that they work at, and the friendships that they form, and they know it is God speaking to them because of the words they read in the Bible, the internal peace that they feel, the validation that others pass along, and their past experiences. The pursuit of religious practices such as Bible reading, prayer, meditation, and church attendance are all intended to help active affiliates to discern God's will for their life and to act obediently to what they believe God calls them to do, even if it means following paths in life that they would not otherwise choose on their own.

Despite these costs, a critical finding that raises some questions about the usefulness of Stark and Finke's assumptions regarding costs is that one third of active affiliates do not incur any costs for believing or belonging or they give up time and money, but do not see such things as a negative cost. When asked if he experiences any costs in his pursuit of religious rewards, Mark Limerick, a United Church of Canada member, says, "I don't think so ... I don't think I've had to sacrifice anything." Adam Major responds, "I don't think so ... I think it's all been a benefit, in terms of benefit to me, benefit to my family, benefit to others. I don't think that ... what I do and how I try to live my life, in a sense, costs me anything ... or deters from my life." More than this, if they acknowledge that they sacrifice time and money, they do not interpret these as undesirable or bad costs. Melanie Jenkins, an administrative assistant in her 20s actively participates in the United Church of Canada. She shares that "it costs money. Tithe ... I don't necessarily think that those are all bad things ... I don't think that the money is wasted, or anything like that." Brad Ackles extends Melanie's reflections: "I give away a lot of money, but I give it away 'cause I want to ... I never give to church because I have to, or because I should ... I support different missions unconnected to the church. And . . . so is it a cost? I suppose. But it's kinda like ... what gives you satisfaction and joy ... So I don't really see much of a cost."

Stark and Finke are correct to note that people make trade-offs when making religious decisions. Strict religious beliefs and practices do not necessarily attract active affiliates to be as religious as they are, though clearly such costs are worth it for some relative to what they believe they gain in the process. The limitation is that Stark and Finke (2000, 85) assert that weighing rewards and costs is a *conscious* process, yet individuals do not necessarily identify any costs with their religious decisions (even though someone else might readily label another's tithing or church volunteering as a trade-off). It seems that this religious decision-making process is not as deliberate as Stark and Finke assert. Further, individuals do not equally identify some things as costs and even if they do, their evaluation of costs is highly subjective, making it difficult to empirically test or compare costs between individuals. For example, giving up time and money for the sake of their religious group is understood as a bad cost for some active affiliates, while for others they joyously give their time and money. Objectively one can calculate the number of hours given to religion relative to other activities and relative to what others do. But such calculations are only meaningful if the individual sees the forgone activities as some kind of sacrifice (and attaches the same level of significance or loss to that sacrifice as others do), and people evaluate the quantity and quality of these "sacrifices" differently.

Simply put, there is no single criterion for measuring religious rewards and costs, and even if there were, the term "cost" raises undue assumptions that costs are negative or bad (i.e., the term "cost" is not as neutral as is assumed by Stark and Finke). Stark and Finke would readily agree that rewards and costs are subjectively understood and they likely did not intend to imply that a trade-off is understood as "bad," but one has to wonder how useful their axiom is in light of the aforementioned observations – a conclusion that I reinforce in subsequent chapters. Taken together, these findings support Bruce (1999) and Bryant's (2000) criticisms levelled at Stark and Finke, and provide some empirical evidence with which to move the theoretical conversation about costs and rewards forward.

A DEPENDABLE GOD AND CONGREGATION

Stark and Finke (2000, 96–102) theorize that in addition to weighing rewards and costs, people's past exchange experiences with the gods shape their current and future religious decision-making processes. If humans believe that the gods are dependable, responsible, and of great scope, then they are more likely to make extended and exclusive exchanges with the gods. From the data presented to this point I would expect active affiliates to respond favourably in their perception of the gods. Going beyond Stark and Finke and exploring people's level of involvement in a local congregation, one might equally expect active affiliates to find those in their church to be dependable and responsive, resulting in extended and exclusive exchanges with that local church. If all of these things are true, which the following data support, then active affiliate exchanges with the gods and their local congregation are less risky than if they held negative views about how dependable, responsive, or of great scope the gods or their local congregation was.

Two active affiliates, the only two who are unsure about God's existence, do not believe that they can depend on God, while most that I interviewed, like Stephen Nettle and Elizabeth Hickory, shared countless stories of successful attempts to depend on God in the past. In a similar fashion, nearly all active affiliates maintain that God is responsive, that He is concerned about and acts in the best interests of humans. Interviewees offer many accounts of how God assists them at work, school, in times of need, or with their relationships. Doris Sanderson's narrative on a near car accident showcases how active affiliates believe that they can depend on a God who is actively involved in their day-to-day activities: "I couldn't move right, and I didn't want to go down this cliff. Well, all I could call is on the name of Jesus ... you would not believe what happened ... The Lord took me off the street, off the road, and I flew through the air like in a movie ... I lifted off, and I went through the air ... on that embankment, and then I landed ... the Lord put this snow bank there, like a huge snow bank ... I just hung behind the steering wheel and just thanked the Lord that I'm still alive ... I couldn't explain it. I didn't do anything ... I believe the Lord heard my prayer, right then and there ... And nobody can talk me out of it. And people ... when I share with unbelievers ... 'Oh, that was just a coincidence.' No, it wasn't. Not for me."

For 25 of 30 active affiliates God is very active in the world and they can depend on Him, though some are quick to comment that humans also have a role to play in life; God helps those who help themselves. This was particularly noticeable when I asked participants about good and bad events in their life. Active affiliates credit God for the good things in their life, but shoulder the blame for bad events that could be explained by human error, such as a failed business venture or marital relationship. Max Weber (1963 [1922], 32–3) makes a similar point when analyzing the relationship between gods, priests, and worshippers. When the gods do not satisfactorily respond to human prayers, priests rationalize this so that "the responsibility falls, not upon the god or themselves, but upon the behaviour of god's worshippers ... the problem of why god has not hearkened to his devotees might then be explained by stating that they had not honoured their god sufficiently, that they had not satisfied his desires for sacrificial blood or soma juice, or finally that they neglected him in favour of other gods" (33). Anthony Harder who owns his own business says to me, "If I made a decision that was wrong or I did something that was ... questionable by ... ethics-wise, then I would blame that aspect on me. It had nothing to do with God ... I don't believe my business will fail because God is with me, and if there's anything that does fail because of it, it would have had to do something with the aspect of something that I did on the side of things." Conversely, active affiliates rationalize the death of a loved one on grounds that everything happens for a reason (a stark contrast from marginal affiliates and religious nones). They offer similar explanations when losing a job, as Gale Robbins' story demonstrates: "I lost my job on Tuesday ... it was an action of one person, the choice of one person against, literally, a hundred others that caused me to lose my job, and I feel like God's will was in that, like God's blessing in that ... that's actually God's desire, that God is going to renew me and take care of me ... I have something overwhelming that I know like peace. Am I upset? Absolutely. Do I have millions of dollars saved? No. But I'm not worried ... that's, to me, an example of depending on God." It was clear from the bulk of these interviewee's stories that they were socialized at home and church to adopt these legitimations. They were taught that God wants individuals to submit their entire life to Him and if they do so, they will find religious meaning in all circumstances, especially negative ones.

This finding is a clear illustration of Peter Berger's (1967) discussion of anomie and alienation. Briefly, Berger works from the social interactionist assumption that humans are co-creators of their social worlds (3–4). Humans create culture and culture shapes humans. In this dialectical process humans strive for stability in their social worlds, particularly because of the anomie, or meaninglessness, that they experience in the face of chaotic and uncontrollable events in life, like death. However, this quest is an arduous one given the central role of humans, who are unstable, in the process (4–6). One way of staving off anomie is to provide socially constructed explanations as seen above, that God is in control and everything happens for a reason (22, 44, 53). Doing so provides a framework of meaning for individuals to interpret their social worlds. Berger suggests the problem that arises with this response is that humans incur the cost of alienation; they forget that they are the co-producers of the social world that they live in (81–101). As soon as individuals claim that God is the producer of their world, they abandon control over that world. According to Berger, the prospect that humans have no agency or control over their surroundings is scary because this sense of control gives people a feeling of stability. However, this is a double-edged sword – they cannot manage the uncontrollable facets of life, and yet they give up power if they project control of those events on to God. In this, anomie and alienation are constantly held in tension against one another. Writing about individuals who give up control of their life to a higher power, Abby Day (2011, 121) notes, "A sense of powerlessness ... is only ameliorated by believing in and subordinating themselves to a more powerful agent that acts for them." From my interviews it is clear that most active affiliates are willing to welcome alienation to stave off anomie, while, as depicted later, marginal affiliates and religious nones overwhelmingly incur anomie in order to stave-off alienation.

One qualification to the above should be made regarding active affiliates in the United Church of Canada. A few such individuals indicate that they do not believe that God is active in the world and that humans control everything. In a related manner, these individuals are ambiguous about whether God exists, they do not pray, and they are less likely to believe that there is life after death. When asked if he believes that God is dependable, Adam Major responds, "I'm not sure that there is a God or is not a God. If you accept the fact that there is a God, I believe that God gave us free will and gave us the ability to use our brains and to do what's right. And that's why I think that God does not interfere in day-to-day activities of people." His final statement suggests that he might believe in God, so I push him further and ask whether this means that he does believe in God. He clarifies his response by saying, "I'm not sure. I don't know … I struggle with that, and, I guess, if I had to … if I had to make a choice, a definitive choice, I'd say no."

Following Stark and Finke's logic that individuals are more likely to enter extended and exclusive exchange relationships with the gods if they are believed to be dependable and responsive, I tested this idea in the context of religious congregations. In theory I expected that people are more willing to make sacrifices such as time to attend church regularly if they believe members in that congregation are dependable and responsive. To this end I asked active affiliates about whether they could depend on others in their congregation and whether their congregation is responsive to people's needs both inside and outside their congregation. Similar to Elizabeth Hickory's experiences, the majority of active affiliates (23 of 30) believe that they can depend on people in their congregation, and that people in their congregation demonstrate an authentic concern for its own members and people at large. For some they have successfully asked others to pray for them, to help them in a volunteering capacity in the church, to babysit their children, or to help them move homes. Others indicate that they can depend on people in their church, though they are more likely to turn to others outside their congregation whom they know better. Some suggest that they are not the type of people to ask others for help, though if push came to shove, they can turn to people in their congregation in a time of need. Looking beyond their own needs, active affiliates offered several examples of ways in which people in their congregation demonstrate care and concern for others. These ranged from serving the ostracized in society, such as the homeless, drug addicts, and mentally ill, to providing for fellow congregants' financial, emotional, and spiritual needs. While active affiliates are optimistic about how dependable and responsive their congregations are, some also comment that their congregations act with good intentions, but do not always successfully meet other's needs. They note that every group in society has people who deviate from the groups' ideals, including politicians, educators, business executives, and social service providers. Sometimes people in church groups are too judgmental, other times they fail to respond to the needs of the homeless, and on some occasions they are too selfish to pay attention to another's physical, emotional, or spiritual needs.

THE AFTERLIFE ON THE PERIPHERY

In chapter 1 I summarized the view among many scholars, including Reginald Bibby, that people have an inexhaustible demand for religion, particularly for life after death, and that people are more willing to join "high cost" religious groups if the rewards that groups offer are worthwhile and desirable. With these things in mind I explored whether most people do believe in and desire the afterlife and whether this belief is central to their religious decision-making processes. Stark, Finke, and Bibby's response to this question is "yes," but these claims, which underpin their entire theory, lack empirical verification.

Nearly all active affiliates (27) believe in life after death. But belief and desire are two different things and thus I asked interviewees about their desire for the afterlife. Is there anything to indicate that individuals have a strong desire for life after death, so much so that it drives their religious decision-making processes? Life after death is not a strong desire for most. Active affiliates do not want to escape this life in anticipation of a much better next life, and most suggest that life after death is not *the* motivating factor for being religious. Instead, some say that life on earth is more important, either in the rewards that they receive right now, or in the possibility of bringing about "God's Kingdom on earth as it is in heaven." Kathy Mavis, a schoolteacher and a Roman Catholic, says, "I don't think I desire it. No ... I look forward to a time to ... figure out what it would be like to be in heaven with God. But ... I don't desire it. I'm not just waiting for it." When asked if she desires life after death, Gale Robbins replies,

"Sure. If it's good, sign me up ... if it sucks, keep me out. I just ... do I go there sometimes? Sure, I go think about all the angels singing and thinking about it, and maybe there's still just a begrudging of my charismatic days where I refuse to let that be the driver. I believe *more* strongly on 'Your Kingdom come. Your will be done on earth as it is in heaven,' meaning that God's kingdom is here with us, and the power of Christ is effective in my day today."

Findings about the afterlife develop when respondents speak about what is required to obtain life after death. Over half of active affiliates, mainly from Roman Catholic and conservative Protestant backgrounds, believe that proper belief and practice are necessary to move on to the next life. These active affiliates, similar to Elizabeth Hickory, assert that individuals must believe in Jesus Christ, that He was crucified on a cross for people's sins, and that people need to repent and ask Jesus for forgiveness for their sins. They also need to proclaim that Jesus will guide their life, so that their entire world view is shaped by the "Godly" things outlined in the Bible and learned at church. When it comes to practices, active affiliates, especially conservative Protestants like Elizabeth Hickory, are hesitant to say that one can earn their way into heaven by performing religious practices – a belief that several interviewees associate with Roman Catholicism, such as Kyle Kerry who says "I knew I didn't want to become Catholic, because ... I don't believe that ... going and confessing your sins to a priest will help or ... doing any other rituals or doing any other sort of performances ... you can't buy your way into heaven. You can't be good enough ... I don't think that there's anything that ... I can do ... to obtain that." Active affiliates instead point to God's grace that is extended to humans who earnestly desire to "have a relationship" with Him. In other words, church attendance is not a prerequisite to go to heaven. Yet, they maintain that true and proper belief inevitably leads to proper practice too. These include spiritual practices such as praying, reading religious texts, and serving the less fortunate as well as moral practices like being kind and loving and honest in all circumstances.

The remaining active affiliates, disproportionately from the United Church of Canada, either indicate that they are unsure of what is required to obtain life after death or do not believe in the afterlife. Also, a couple of others, surprisingly from Roman Catholic and conservative Protestant traditions, hinted that one does not need to be Christian to go to heaven. One just needs to believe in God, whatever that god might look like and pursue a connection with this transcendent being.

As Zach Tuttle says to me, "I do believe it's a gift of God, and I believe that God pulls people to ... the afterlife when they die ... regardless of faith or religion ... I believe God speaks to all people. I believe God's breath of life is in all people ... I believe there's a small percentage of people in all kinds of religions that are deeply connected to the spirit of God."

One observation stands out: life after death is not as important a variable for active affiliates as Stark, Finke, and Bibby might have us believe. Yes, active affiliates overwhelmingly believe in the afterlife, but they do not earnestly desire it nor do they necessarily believe or behave here on earth in ways that directly influence their chances of attaining life after death. The afterlife lay at the periphery of people's religious lives and this conclusion becomes even clearer among marginal affiliates and religious nones. This observation does not necessarily entail dismissing claims of an unending demand for religion, however a desire for the afterlife may not be the important piece to the "religious demand" puzzle.

RELIGION AIDS MORALITY

I return to my conversation with Elizabeth Hickory who believes that religion is positive for society. Twenty-three active affiliates agree. Brad Ackles has two graduate degrees and he converted to Christianity late in life. He confidently declares, "If you go back, let's say to 1960 or 1970, and you look at all the orphanages in the world, most of them were started by Christians. If you look at all the higher institutions and universities back in the fifties and sixties and before, started by Christians. If you look at the hospitals, started by Christians. So how you can argue against that? I don't think most unbelievers recognize how the world is a much better place because of people who call themselves Christians." Doris Sanderson says "it is because when you have a church, which, of course, is the people in a community, it has a ripple effect on the people around you. You place a standard, and people see the standard you have, and they will be affected by it ... in the community that the church is in. Like, I'm thinking, a porn shop won't open next door to a church ... people still have a bit of a respect when they see a church and a steeple ... in the community, you have an influence, I believe." Kathy Mavis says that religion is good overall "because of what is at its core and at its root. And this is sort of regardless of the background of the faith. There's love and caring for others." Actively involved members in other religious traditions concur. In his study of Muslim, Hindu, and Buddhist youth in Canada Peter Beyer (2013d, 55) states, "Very few expressed the idea that the world would be a better place without [religion]. The vast majority declared not only that religion was a good thing but that there were no bad religions."

An additional six active affiliates maintain that religion is both positive and negative in society, referring to examples where religion is the source of evil such as during the Crusades or religious terrorism with many citing Islamic extremism. Harmony Oswald says, "I think it's an extremely positive force when it's not used for bad things, like religious wars, or persecution, or demoralizing, or demeaning another race, culture, creed, sex ... I think it's both good and evil. It's good when it's used for good, and ... of course it's ... bad when bad people use it for their own personal reasons." Norman Harper, another Roman Catholic, says "it totally depends on what religion and in what context. I think that, if you took religion out, you would have a true disaster ... That being said, look at Al-Qaeda, you know? You've got religion steered by the wrong people, and it's very dangerous."

As active affiliates lead the charge to praise religion for the good that it does in society, they are less inclined to say that religion is necessary for people to be moral or ethical (only three active affiliates claim this). Still, nearly half of active affiliates are like Elizabeth Hickory who believes that religion still helps in this regard. I received responses like the following: "I think that everybody is probably born with a set of morals, but they can get corroded by the lack of religion"; "I don't think you totally need it, but I think it certainly heightens your awareness of it"; "I have met people who aren't really religious that are moral and ethical. But I ... do think that most people do need it. Like, I'd say it's rare. I'd say most people need religion to help them to be moral, and ethical, and to make the right decisions in life."

FULLY CONFIDENT IN MY RELIGIOUS WORLD VIEW

Recognizing that religious decision-making processes entails risk, Stark and Finke (2000) explore factors that might reduce the level of risk involved. They theorize that an individual's confidence in religious explanations is strengthened to the degree that others express confidence in the same explanations, that individuals participate in collective religious ceremonies, and that people conserve their religious and social capital (2000, 106–38). In other words, people have greater confidence in their religious beliefs and practices if people around them share similar beliefs and practices.

To test Stark and Finke's assumptions I asked interviewees a series of questions about the social aspects of their religious lives. I asked whether they believe religion is primarily an individual or a social journey and how that is reflected in their religious life. I also queried about how influential religious groups should be in shaping people's religious beliefs and practices, and how influential their group is in shaping their religious world view. I asked about how many of their close friends participate in the same congregation, another congregation within the same religious tradition, another religious group, or no religion at all. Finally, I solicited their level of confidence in the religious explanations that they adopt. If Stark and Finke are correct, I expect that active affiliates are highly confident in the religious explanations that they adopt, more so than marginal affiliates or religious nones, given their regular involvement in a local congregation and the anticipated social side to their religious life.

When asked about whether religion primarily is or should be an individual or social phenomenon, twenty-nine active affiliates indicate that religion is primarily social in nature or that it is a combination of an individual and social activity. Edward Drew, a Roman Catholic who works for the government, expresses it this way:

> I think it should be shared with others because ... it's a good process ... and it's sort of like Alcoholics Anonymous ... if somebody just threw a book at you and said, "Stop drinking" ... I don't think you'd be successful ... But if you had a bunch of support people and said ... "*We're* going to do this" ... And I think that's why you go to church together ... at certain hours ... because you're all together, and it's reinforcing each other's behaviour ... rather than, if they just opened up the doors of the church and said, "Everybody come by for a few minutes a week" ... and then people probably wouldn't do that because ... we're social animals, and we ... suffer from the herd instinct, and we flock together ... and that's the support we derive off of each other. We take ... kind of, on the days I don't really feel like it, well, I will because I can see that the others are there, too.

Others expressed similar things. Adam Major states, "I think it has to be shared with others ... I think humans are made to be in relationship with people, and any time you try and go solo ... it's too small. Like, you need to talk to people and, I think, get other people's opinions and perspectives, and you need to love, and you need to be loved." Jennifer Reed says that "as an individual, you make a decision, but when you make that decision ... you make a commitment ... to a group of people ... to be a part of their family ... and family's not something you just abandon ... you're stuck with them. So both. I think we all have responsibility to each other, but we also have a responsibility to God individually." Overall, active affiliates believe that they model these beliefs in their life.

I proceed to ask active affiliates about their religious group's role in shaping their personal beliefs and practices. Is their group very influential, not influential at all, or somewhere in-between? Not surprisingly active affiliates largely believe that their religious group should play a prominent role to shape their religious beliefs and practices. Most active affiliates believe that their religious group, particularly the church leader's teachings, should strongly influence their personal religious world view. Zach Tuttle puts it this way:

> I think they should be fairly influential because, as much as I believe the individual faith experience is important, if we're all just left to our own devices, it's very easy to be led astray and deceived ... our sinful fallen nature is sort of wired to just go down the selfish route, so it's very easy to get selfish and ingrown ... and that's not a Christ-like way to live ... I think one way to counterbalance our fallen nature is to submit ourselves to a larger community of people and a larger authority ... whether that's church or Scripture or denomination. Whatever larger authority outside of yourself so that you're not just doing your own little thing ... it's a choice to acknowledge that ... life's not just about me, and faith's not just about me. And it also takes trust because you have to have a certain amount of trust in your church, your denomination, your pastor, your community in order ... to buy into what they're saying. If you don't trust them, then, you're obviously not going to be able to ... and it's not about blind trust because you need to think for yourself, but you do need some trust because you're not always going to ... believe

everything, or you're not always going to agree with everything, but sometimes you just have to trust that these people leading are spirit filled, and these people leading you do have your best interests and the church's best interests in mind, even if, at this particular junction, you might not understand or agree with everything they're saying.

As active affiliates give significant authority to their religious group, they, especially those with some experience in a conservative Protestant setting, also say that the Bible should inspire what their church teaches and what they believe as true.

When asked about how influential their religious groups *actually* are, fifteen active affiliates continue to say that their group is important, nine say that the individual is more important, three say that their church is one of many important voices, and three say that the Bible is the most important influence on their religious attitudes and behaviours. On the surface it appears as if half of active affiliates place great importance on their religious group, and they do, but some, like Stephen Nettle, qualify this, saying that their religious group was very significant during their younger years, however as they aged and developed a mind of their own, they take more ownership over their faith. Once their beliefs and practices are cemented active affiliates generally seek churches that endorse their way of thinking and behaving. As such, interviewees in this study maintain that social influences do affect their approach to religion, but in the end they are responsible for their religiosity. In practical terms this means that they might (and sometimes do) disagree with various church teachings (e.g., on homosexuality or women in leadership), still confident that they belong to and endorse the group's overall world view. Points of disagreement stood out among Roman Catholic interviewees in particular, such as Georgia Ainsworth, a schoolteacher, who says, "I don't agree with everything, for sure. But I think we just kind of live by the guidelines of being helpful ... people, and giving people ... we just take the positives. We don't live by everything, for sure." She goes on to single out her disagreement that priests are not allowed to get married. Harmony Oswald, a Roman Catholic, agrees with Georgia and goes even further to say, "I think I follow ... Christian beliefs. Roman Catholic beliefs ... it's being a bad Catholic to ... what do they call it? ... Shopping cart Catholics. You can't choose your ... menu ... I'm way too much of a libertarian to ...

allow my views on somebody else ... the big ones are abortion ... Premarital sex. I mean, I'm such a ... hypocrite. So I mean ... they're fine for some people ... I wish priests could get married. I think that that would alleviate ... a huge problem that they have in terms of getting really good ... people to go into ... the ministry."

When disagreement with their religious tradition ensues active affiliates do one of two things. Either they continue to attend a congregation within that tradition believing that their beliefs and practices trump those of their religious group as in Georgia and Harmony's case, or people seek congregations whose values conform to what they already believe to be true. In the latter case this tends to be a shift from theologically conservative to theologically liberal denominations. Both responses, however, reveal a move toward an individualist faith amidst ongoing participation in a religious group, manifested sometimes in resistance to even their religious group imposing certain beliefs on to them. Andrew Grenville (2000, 218) identifies churchgoers like these active affiliates as "privatistic churchgoers" who claim that private beliefs are more important than their church's doctrines; the church plays a role in reinforcing world views, but it is ultimately the individual, not their church or its leader, who is the final authority of what they believe and how they behave. Peter Berger and Steve Bruce predicted heightened individualism as the natural result of growing pluralism and diversity in society, and Reginald Bibby (2006) more recently accounts for shifts from dominance to diversity and deference to discernment in Canadian religious sensitivities. The findings among active affiliates appear to verify these earlier projections, more so today than in past generations (see Hervieu-Léger 2006; Dillon and Wink 2007; Smith and Snell 2009).

One of the most direct measurements of how "social" one's religion is involves their friends' religious identification and involvement. Akin to previous research findings on members across different faith traditions who are actively religious (Olson 1989, 1993; Nemeth and Luidens 2003; Wuthnow 2004; Ramji 2013; Madge et al. 2014), active affiliates are close friends with those who are similar to themselves, religiously. Twelve active affiliates have at least one close friend in their congregation, while another ten are good friends with someone involved in another Christian congregation. In many of these cases nearly all of their closest friends are actively religious like them. One-third of active affiliates, predominantly those who had no religious upbringing or who participate in conservative Protestant traditions, are close friends with those who are not particularly religious. Two explanations for this discovery are helpful. First, for some active affiliates in less strict denominations such as the United Church of Canada, they are not discouraged to separate themselves from the "outside world" and thus social ties with less religious individuals is normal and acceptable. Some of those who converted to Christianity joined these less strict groups because they did not need to abandon their non-religious life and social ties altogether. Second, conservative Protestants form meaningful relationships with non-religious folk mainly with the theological hope to evangelize "outsiders" (see, e.g., Bebbington 1989; Reimer 2003; Wuthnow 2004). This was on display in Elizabeth's story, and here in Anthony Harder's account. As he discusses his relationship with non-Christians and declares that there is only one way to heaven, through Jesus, Anthony offers the following comments: "We're supposed to be a light to the world. However, it hasn't been that I haven't shared the love of Christ with them. It's just that they have denied it and have decided to believe in what they want to believe, so that's a point where you've just got to leave it, and then you've just got to keep praying. And, through your actions and through the way we live our lives ... that's what needs to draw them in. Whatever ... drew people into Christ was because of everything that He did and everything that He represented. So the same for us ... we can never give up. But, ultimately, it always comes down to the people and their choice."

On the whole active affiliates seem to conserve their social and religious capital by surrounding themselves with people who are like themselves religiously. They are more individualistic in how they approach religious belief and practice than past generations, yet they do believe their religious group should influence their attitudes and behaviours. As such, I expect active affiliates to be highly confident in the religious explanations that they hold on to – and they are. The majority of active affiliates (28 of 30) indicate that they are very confident in the religious explanations that they adopt with many saying they are "100 percent confident." Active affiliates' assessments of rewards and costs and positive experiences with God and their congregation strongly inform their level of confidence in their religious world view and it is unlikely, based on my interviews with them, that they will turn their back on their religious faith (see Hunsberger and Altemeyer 2006, 61–3).

AN EMERGING DIVERSITY

My concluding reflections surround what appears to be an emerging diversity between active affiliates and their approach to faith. At the core active affiliates do share more in common than not on the themes explored in this chapter. Their faith anchors them in life and gives them meaning, purpose, and direction, to the point that they will incur a range of costs in the process – above all to give up control of their life to God's will. This approach to faith and life is possible because of repeated personal experiences where they assert God and others "came through" for them. Attending church each week is a necessity, as Elizabeth Hickory believes, because it ties active affiliates to others who share a common faith. Church attendance also helps to remind individuals and the collective to believe and behave in ways consistent with what they consider are fundamental Christian beliefs and practices.

Yet, some active affiliates are embracing a widening gap for different beliefs about the afterlife, religion's place in society, or morality, sexuality, and gender. Characteristic of modern society where individuals frequently encounter diverse world views that yield more complex and subjective perspectives, nearly half of active affiliates like Stephen Nettle and Brooklyn Strait resemble Andrew Grenville's category of "privatistic churchgoers" – they sometimes elevate their personal beliefs and practices over their church or pastor or religious tradition. A clear example of this is when regular attenders compare what the minister says against what they already believe to be true. If the two perspectives do not align, as is the case for several Roman Catholic interviewees on matters of gender, the body, and sexuality, individuals tend to elevate their personal views over the minister. Granted, active affiliates are less selective of religious beliefs and practices compared to marginal affiliates, but active affiliates are more selective in comparison to previous generations. The result is increasing diversity within congregations and denominations, which Gerardo Marti and Gladys Ganiel (2014) single out as a key area to pay attention to in the years ahead.

Why is diversity emerging between active affiliates in this study? It largely has to do with being embedded in a Canadian narrative that prizes individualism, choice, and tolerance amidst the cacophony of diverse perspectives around. This social context is magnified in a technologically advanced and global age where individuals actively construct and express the "self," encountering multiple ways of "being" and "doing" in the process. Here God, others (i.e., family, religious leaders, fellow congregants), and one's self converge to shape religious belief and practice for active affiliates like Stephen Nettle, Elizabeth Hickory, and Brooklyn Strait.

3

Marginal Affiliates: Cherry-Picking Religious Beliefs and Practices

Someone familiar with my research on marginal affiliates gave me an Easter card. On the front it read "Today's Easter Sermon Is …" and on the inside, "Where the Hell have you all been since Christmas?" A church leader is unlikely to make this statement aloud, though it is a question that undoubtedly crosses the minds of church leaders and weekly attenders, who suddenly struggle to find a parking spot or a seat in church each Easter or Christmas. Most who raise this question could likely offer a response in return – marginal affiliates were at home sleeping or taking their kids to hockey practice or grocery shopping or doing laundry or watching the National Football League or enjoying some leisure time before work and life demands resume on Monday morning. These are plausible responses that are no doubt accurate in many respects, but very little is at present known about the religious background, beliefs, practices, and experiences of the 40–50% of Canadians who are marginal affiliates (Bibby 2006, 192).

Only a handful of studies give passing attention to this group worldwide (e.g., Walliss 2002; Lamoureux Scholes 2003; Inglis 2007; Zuckerman 2008; Day 2011; Bibby and Grenville 2013). One of the most common findings is that few turn to religious groups for religious holidays or rites of passage with religious motivations in mind. John Walliss (2002) reveals that people mainly get married in a church out of respect for tradition, because it is the "proper" thing to do. His interviewees identify parental or other social pressures to get married in a church or beautiful church aesthetics that fulfill fairy tale wedding images. None of his interviewees concede any inherent religious significance to these rites of passage. Laurie Lamoureux Scholes (2003, 36) surmises that Canadians turn to church leaders and church buildings for funerals because "the traditional religious identity facilitates access to a convenient, ready-made ritual through which social obligations to the deceased and the bereaved community can be fulfilled." When discussing baptism in Sweden and Denmark Zuckerman (2008, 161) emphasizes that "the majority of Danes and Swedes participate in the ostensibly and historically religious ritual of baptism for a variety of reasons – from pleasing the in-laws, to enjoying it as a nice tradition. But very rarely do they celebrate it with any beliefs about God swelling in their hearts, or deep otherworldly concerns" (also see Palm and Trost 2000). More recently Abby Day's (2011, 55–6) research in England deals with "natal membership" or those who are members of a religious group from birth to death and who occasionally turn to religious groups for rites of passage. She claims that this growing population in England believes their religious identities are ascribed from birth. They did not choose nor do they believe they can abandon their religious identity, and they maintain they ought to pass their religious identity on to their children. In turn, religious belief and practice is not an important part of their life even when they turn to religious groups for rites of passage. Rites serve as a cultural custom more than a religious one for marginal adherents (also see Demerath III 2001, 43, 49 for a discussion of "cultural Catholics" in Poland and Northern Ireland, Dencik 2007 for a summary of ascribed religious identity among Lutherans in Denmark, and Inglis 2007 for research on Catholic identity in Ireland). In a study of "unsynagogued" Jews in the northeastern United States Lynn Davidman (2007) reveals that Jewish traditions are observed mainly to rekindle family memories, not to elevate any particular religious aspect to their Jewish identity. These findings stand in contrast to Reginald Bibby's assertion, based on religious leaders interpretations (1993, 147–51), that people are "there and something is happening. Identity is being reaffirmed; life is being given meaning; memories are being constructed" (168), or Stark and Finke's (2000, 103) claim that "people may participate in religious organizations for all sorts of secular reasons (fun and friendship are common motives), but the raison raison d'être of all organizations to be identified as religious has to do with relationships with a god or gods."

My interviews with Larry Masters, Matthew Walter, and Rose Eskin extend beyond these studies as I explore some of the central religious beliefs and practices that marginal affiliates hold on to. Why do marginal affiliates attend "religiously" for religious holidays and rites of passage and what other rewards and costs factor into their religious decision-making processes? Keeping in step with the other axioms in Stark and Finke's work, how do marginal affiliates make sense of their exchanges with the gods and their congregations, what are their beliefs about the afterlife, how do they interpret religion's role in society, to what extent is their religious life "social," and how confident are they with the religious explanations that they hold to be true? I defer two important questions regarding marginal affiliates to chapter 5: why do marginal affiliates no longer attend religious services regularly (as most once did in the past) and what are the chances that marginal affiliates might pursue greater involvement in their religious group in the future?

LARRY MASTERS

I will never forget Larry Masters – the first individual that I interviewed in this project, and the first that I introduced at the outset of this book. Larry is a physically fit, dynamic, charming, and forthright individual who grew up in England. His dad sold bicycles for a living and his mum stayed at home to care for Larry and his older brother and younger sister. Now in his 50s, Larry eventually migrated to Canada, working in various technology and electronics-related industries. He has been married for over thirty years and he has two children in their late 20s.

I ask Larry if he was affiliated with a religious group when growing up. His response is a telling indicator that sets the context for his marginal affiliate status in the Anglican Church: "No, not affil ... well, by affiliated ... most people in the UK are Church of England, okay? And so my ... mother was ... Church of England, and my father was Church of England because, for that generation, it was just the way it was. Everybody had a religious affiliation in those days in the UK. And you *were* Church of England." They never attended religious services, aside from what was necessary for the kids to receive confirmation in the Anglican Church, and for services tied to the local Anglican Church school that Larry attended growing up. Larry attended Sunday school weekly (linked to his school) with a friend down the road, which did not trouble Larry's parents. Larry believed that he received a good education and a faith-based "grounding and anchor" for life – to be a good, moral person – though he lamented that he attended all-boys schools. In turn, Larry and his wife sent their children to Sunday school, believing that they would benefit morally in the process.

In his young adult years Larry questioned his religious beliefs and practices, though not enough to abandon his religious affiliation. He continues to identify with the Church of England (i.e., the Anglican Church), attending each Christmas and Easter, and when his mum visits from England. Interestingly, his mum started attending church regularly when her husband died, and Larry attended regularly for a period of time when his wife was very ill. For Larry, religion is a "crutch … Sometimes in times of trouble … you go back, you revert … to what you were indoctrinated in … You go back to where you feel a little bit more comfortable … About twenty, twenty-five years ago my wife was very sick, and I would go to church … and it made me feel better. And whatever gets you through the night … makes you feel better." Larry loved, and still does, the prayers and songs at church, but not to the point of attending regularly beyond his wife's illness; when she was better, so was Larry's need for this religious crutch. He is very content with his current level of involvement once or twice a year, and does not desire greater involvement in the Anglican Church. He simply attends each Christmas and Easter because of "the ritual of the songs … the carols. The rituals … Being all there with family on Christmas Eve." This said, Larry later bemoans that his daughter did not have a religious wedding because "I wouldn't have felt married unless it would have been in a church and the vicar would have the … 'till death do us part' and 'to have and to hold, to love and to' … the actual ritual of the words 'Do you take this man to be your lawful,' and all … that ritual … beautiful words … I wouldn't have felt married if I hadn't have had those words said before God … like now before my family and friends and before God."

Larry's Church of England identity remains very important to him. Why? He states, "Background and brainwashing … It's what I'm comfortable with. It's what you've been brought up in … I like the Church of England because there isn't the dogma of the Catholic Church … and there isn't all the ritual you have to go through and all this kind of nonsense. It's very much an easy-going church. They don't mind if you lapse a bit … It suits me." I pursue further the cultural aspects to his affiliation. Larry articulates that "for me it's a cultural thing … your folks were like that, your grandparents were Church of England, going back to the blinking Reformation … going back to the dissolution of the monasteries … that's what you're …

brought up with, and you're comfortable with it now." I probe further about whether he would ever consider changing his religious affiliation, even to another Christian denomination. He quickly and adamantly replies, "Nope. Never ever ... couldn't possibly do that."

In addition to showing up to his church a couple of times a year Larry helps the Salvation Army raise funds each Christmas. He admires their compassion for people, recalling how they provided "cups of tea for the people who had been bombed [during the war] ... They get the guy off the street. They help him with the rehab. They're doing the practicalities ... before they start thinking about ... banging the tambourine ... they tend to get the practicalities: get the guy fed. Get him off the street ... those kind of things." Larry also volunteers by running or cycling in fundraisers for cancer and heart and stroke.

When I inquire about other religious or spiritual beliefs and practices that are part of Larry's life he initially responds that this is a tough question. After pondering for a few moments Larry expresses in a somewhat scattered way that "I don't wake up thinking about religion all and every day ... I'm very wary of organized religions and all this kind of stuff ... life's a whole journey ... I don't give much thought in my day-to-day life about religion ... I say my prayers ... I could be out on my bicycle, and ... I will say a quick prayer, or ... I'll feel my father with me ... on my bicycle ... I'll ask him for a push up a hill." Larry believes that God is involved in human affairs, yet attributes a degree of luck and chance to earthly events too. He continues on to point out that he has a few Bibles in his home and from time to time he will pull one out if a scripture passage comes to mind. He also stresses his belief in the Ten Commandments and treating others well.

Picking up on treating people well we discuss if religion is a positive or negative force in society. Larry responds in the following way:

> I think overall, if you take away the Inquisition and all kinds of things like that ... if you take away all the hate in the world and all the religious conflict ... that's going on to this very day, I have hope. I still think it's a positive ... I think it's the extremists that ... go off crazy, half-cooked. And you get extremists on the Christian right down to the Muslim Islamics ... I would like to think it's a positive ... I think the tendency of most religions in the world ... there's not many that go around telling me to kill people and stuff like that. Islam gets a bit borderline ... with the Qur'an, but I still think the basic tenets to try and be good, to try and help each other ... So I think it's a positive thing.

At the conclusion of our interview I ask Larry, as with all other participants, if he had anything he wanted to add. He summarizes his reflections: "I've enjoyed this. I don't get to sit and talk about religion very often ... I always think that religion is ... a very important thing to have as ... a prop to your life. It's more like a prop. It's sort of one of those sort of things like on a wigwam ... you've got all these wigwams that keep it ... coming up. And one of those is religion ... The other ones are like your family or your job, the way you think about stuff or whatever. But it's one of the props that keep you up ... Yeah, it's important ... I enjoy going to church occasionally. Just singing the songs, and just listening to the words ... I always come out of it thinking, 'Hmm. I've enjoyed that.' Yeah, not feeling holier than thou, but thinking ... it's like a very gentle, low-key type of thing ... but that doesn't take away from your spirituality."

MATTHEW WALTER

It was a cold March morning and the bitter Calgary winter had not yet subsided when I walked downtown to meet Matthew Walter in his high-rise corner office. We tried to schedule an interview for a couple of months, so I was hopeful that nothing would come up at the last minute that would take him away from our appointment. Thankfully he was there when I arrived and was welcomed into his office. Matthew, age 33, has a Bachelor's degree in geography and currently works as a director of a financial services firm. He is married, with one daughter and twin boys on the way.

The second of four children, Matthew grew up in Montreal where his father was an engineer and his mother stayed at home. His father has a Roman Catholic background and his mother was raised in the United Church. Though he does not describe his father as a devout Catholic, he characterizes his mother's parents as actively religious. His mother was also a Sunday school teacher in the United Church. When recalling his family's church involvement, Matthew indicates that it was limited to the United Church at Christmas, Easter, and when they visited his grandmother. Asked if religion was important to him or his family, he replies, "We're not atheist non-believers or anything like that, but ... it doesn't make up ... a big part of what we do or who we are." They did not pray, read the Bible, or talk about God or religious things.

Matthew has maintained a consistent level of church involvement throughout his life. Today he identifies with the United Church of

Canada, though his affiliation with this denomination means "nothing" to him because he knows almost nothing about other denominations. This is all he has ever known. Matthew and his wife were married in the United Church and they attend almost every Christmas. They do not really practice their faith in the home, and he is uncertain when I ask him about his belief in God: "I think I do. I believe in something. I don't know if that's just been instilled ... I don't know what side of the fence ... I sit on ... I have no reason to, but I ... but you do ... I don't know if I believe in a big bang theory any more than I believe in God ... it's comforting to believe in God ... But, probably, I believe more in the science ... but God provides comfort." He shows a similar apprehension toward life after death, unsure of what exactly happens after life on earth.

I ask Matthew about the appeal of attending religious services selectively and to identify as a Christian while not subscribing to definitive beliefs about God or the afterlife or observing any religious practices in the home. For him religion is a source of good morals and principles in society, though he admits that religion is also a source of immense evil in the world. He says that he tries to do unto others as he would have them do unto him. He wants his children to subscribe to this belief, but he does not believe that he and his wife can suitably provide the framework for their children to live this out. He acknowledges that this is where the church and a trained specialist (i.e., a religious leader) may have more of a role in his family's life: "Moving forward, we'll have ... I don't want to say we'll have more influence, but ... We'll expose our children ... to it just so they get, sort of ... a basic understanding ... I don't think I'm capable ... of conveying it properly to them ... I'm not an expert, you know? But I think it's good for them ... I had that basic knowledge that I feel like some degree ... of desire to convey that to my children." For those who are hopeful that individuals like Matthew might pursue greater involvement in their church, he qualifies the above statement later in the interview: "I'd say I'd like for that to happen, whether or not I ... am willing to be up at ... I don't even know what time that starts on Sunday. Eleven? Ten? ... We look at that as our day of rest ... Like, we're busy the rest of the week ... But, again ... I think it would be more along those lines of ... to expose them that way."

On top of Matthew speculating about his future beliefs and actions, I pose some questions about his past and current beliefs and practices. I ask him, "What draws you on Christmas?" "Custom," he replies. Each Christmas his family goes out for Chinese food, they attend a Christmas service, and they watch *A Christmas Carol*, and the Chinese food is as important as the church service. Denying that he gains any religious significance when attending, he stresses that Christmas services are an opportunity for his family to spend time together. Not unlike sitting around the fireplace and talking, the Christmas service is another social event. He even leaves money in the offering plate, comparing the church service to watching a live show. He pays for the services that others offer for his enjoyment. When asked about the benefits of attending, he says that he feels good when he leaves; "it's nice to be there." It also helps remind his family that Christmas is not just about exchanging gifts.

Changing directions slightly I ask Matthew why he got married in a church. Matthew quickly comments, "We wanted the ceremony ... I didn't want to do it in a field or this or that with a justice of the peace or anything like that ... I wouldn't say it was overly religious ... there were some ... undertones, but there was no readings ... we didn't look and say, like, 'Do this.' Like, it was, probably, 'whatever one that everybody does.' He said, 'Pick one of these three.' It was like, 'Pick a box.' And so we had somebody do that ... in my mind, that's where you get married: you get married in a church ... and whether it's overly religious or not, we like to do it in a church ... in that forum ... we wanted people sitting in pews ... we were up ... on stage and that sort of thing, and ... that worked for us." I ask Matthew if there was "any sense of religious significance" in the ceremony. He responds affirmatively, seeing marriage as a sacred union between a man and a woman. He rejects gay marriages and opposes polygamous forms of marriage on religious grounds. He acknowledges that he does not understand the religious meaning, significance, and justification for Christian wedding rituals, but holds firm in his conviction that marriage is a practice instituted by the Christian church that should be observed and respected.

Some, like Kurt Bowen (2004), posit that religious belief and practice is more consequential for daily behaviour the more a person attends religious services. So I ask Matthew if getting married in a church had any impact on the quality of his marriage. He responds, "No, I don't think so ... But being married in a church and stuff like that? That was more ... I don't want to say pomp and circumstance, but it was something that ... we felt strongly about doing. I just can't tell you why ... I don't want to say the perception and perspective or anything like that, but ... it was the place where the ritual is conducted, and that's what we wanted to do."

Curious about the United Church's influence on Matthew's everyday activities, I ask him about whether religion is mainly an individual or social phenomena and how influential his own religious tradition is in shaping his beliefs and practices. Here is where a defining feature of the marginal affiliates (and religious nones) that I interviewed, relative to active affiliates, appears. They believe that religion is primarily an individual phenomenon. Matthew claims that "it's more individual ... You've got a belief. That's yours ... and that's your journey, in terms of where you want to go with that. And I believe everybody else is entitled to their own [beliefs]." Matthew justifies his response by pointing to individualism as a cultural value where individuals are entitled to choose their own belief system. He is especially adamant that groups not force their way into an individual's space to convert them, such as Mormons or Jehovah's Witnesses, who have a negative reputation among interviewees for their door-to-door proselytizing – this was the most cited negative image of a religious group (followed by Muslim terrorists) that interviewees referenced (see Madge et al. 2014, 52–5). Matthew agrees that churches have a role to influence members of their congregation, though he admits that his church has little say in his personal beliefs and practices: "They probably would prefer me to be more engaged et cetera, but ... as long as I show up and bring a cheque ... I appreciate what they do, and there's people who want to be much more involved and who can agree to exist on those terms."

To summarize, Matthew had some religious exposure growing up, he continues to attend at Christmas because it is a traditional custom, he was married in the church because that is where weddings should be held, and he wants his children to be exposed to church to gain good morals and values. Matthew is uncertain about God's existence or life after death, his views about religion are unapologetically individualistic, and he has little desire for greater church involvement. He is not alone.

ROSE ESKIN

Rose Eskin is a single, 28-year-old who identifies as a Roman Catholic. She is the second of four children born to an Italian-immigrant mother and father from the Canadian Army. We conversed over cold drinks at Starbucks as she shared her strong religious upbringing in the Roman Catholic Church. Rose's family attended Sunday mass each week, her parents were Eucharistic ministers and readers, she regularly attended Sunday school, and she went to a Catholic school where she interacted with many friends who attended the same church as she did. Reflecting on weekly religious rituals with her family, Rose says, "we're a really close-knit family … it was nice to have a designated period of time where everyone gets dressed, goes out … there was kind of a ritual behind it. Like you'd put on your nicest clothes, my dad used to put on country music … and it was like a whole Sunday routine that my family would do. And if we were good in church, we would get to go to Moxie's after." Throughout the week her family said grace before meals and prayed before bed, and they faithfully observed lent and advent each year.

Religious involvements changed for Rose and her family when she was in high school, following her grandmother's funeral that was sorely "bungled" by the priest:

> When my dad's mom passed away … we had a service for her at our church and … some people have bad days and I'm sure the priest was having just a bad day. Anyways, he completely bungled up everything about the service. Like, said that my dad was married to his sister, like got the names wrong, the dates wrong, the relationships from and that was kind of a turning point in our family because I actually don't think my dad has gone back to a church since. And you know, I mean it's one of those things where it's like, I understand for him how upsetting that would be because you're a part of this community and he could probably name every single choir member's parents, right? And so for someone to mess up something like a funeral service for your mom, he just felt really let down by something he had so heavily invested in. Then it was kind of up to us if we wanted to continue to go to church at that point. So my mom and her mom continued to go together, but the rest of us not so much.

Despite no longer attending Sunday mass each week, Rose continues to attend for major religious holidays like Christmas and Easter and she insists that her Roman Catholic identity remains very important. She has never considered affiliating with a different denomination or religious group. If she does eventually marry she would like to get married in a church and if she ever has children she would like to raise them in the Roman Catholic tradition. I ask her why turning to the Church for these occasions are important. She responds in the following way: "It's for my grandma mostly. It's for my Nana. I mean it still is really important to her ... I attend because it makes my mom and my grandma happy, and I like to sing the songs." When discussing a Christian wedding Rose states, "again, it's so important to my mom ... My brother didn't get married in a church and I just know it broke her heart. My sister-in-law is an atheist and yeah, it just broke my mom's heart. So for her, I would absolutely want to do it. And again, I do think it's one of those things that is really special in the Catholic Church, is marriage. And I would hope whomever I choose to marry would either be Catholic or would consider changing to be Catholic, because again like, should down the road there ever be kids, I'd want them raised the same way I was raised." I inquire about whether there would be any religious significance to a wedding ceremony in a church:

> Just the kind of usual stuff: you know, the Eucharist, going through the passages, lots of prayers, lots of songs ... Not that I need the blessing of the priest per se, but just to, in God's house, have that part of it would be really nice ... As a little kid, all your important milestones are in church, right? It's just so beautiful in there and it really is relaxing, and you just feel special, and I would want all of my special occasions, including my death, to be marked in such a beautiful place ... It's just a feeling when you walk in. Like I remember even in school they had a chapel. When you walk in there, there's just a real calmness and a real serenity ... there's like a smell to it almost that just feels very like home to me ... That's a really special connection and that feeling of being in the church is really nice.

Amidst her long-standing devotion to the Roman Catholic Church, Rose has developed a strong disdain toward some of the highly exclusive and discriminatory beliefs and behaviours connected with the Catholic Church. Namely, views on homosexuality or birth control trouble her, and she is well aware that many of her friends look down on those associated with the Roman Catholic Church for this reason. Rose begins this conversation point by speaking against those who force their beliefs on to others: "Personally, I follow quite a few teachings, but I think the difference is that I don't really judge what other people do – at all! Like, it doesn't impact me. You're not trying to be my religion at all so I'm not gonna sit here and force anything that I view on you because I would super not appreciate it if you did it to me." She carries on speaking of specific issues on which she disagrees with the Roman Catholic Church, along with providing suggestions for the Roman Catholic Church:

> Homosexuality ... obviously I'm not born gay so I can't really say. I've never been this way. But again, it's not my choice. Like, you do what you gotta do to be happy and be a good person. I think it gets grey though when you talk about trying to come into someone else's religion that does have set beliefs. I think it's unfair to expect either side to bend. So why not just create something new that is an offshoot of Roman Catholic that accepts these things instead of trying to force something that I don't think is ever going to change ... that's the kind of church that I'd go to ... You do what you gotta do to be happy. Contraceptives, I think, is just stupid. I mean, I don't think that science and the medical backs up the decisions being made ... But you're focusing on the wrong things. I mean teach people why it's important to keep certain things for marriage and show them ... work on the self-esteem part of it. Don't ban them from things that are inevitably happening right now. Like, keep them safe, you know? It's ridiculous actually ... And that's the kind of stuff in the media that makes people side eye you when you say you're Roman Catholic. Like how diluted are you to think that banning this is going to stop people from having sex ... Teenagers are teenagers, and they're either given the tools from their parents to deal with that, or they're not. I mean it's not going to matter what religion is. It's not going to matter if they have access to an HPV shot. They're gonna do it. You just have to give them the tools to decide not to do it.

Laced within this narrative is Rose's willingness to pick and choose which aspects of Roman Catholicism she will keep or reject, a point that she makes when discussing her faith with others who struggle with Roman Catholicism's conservative stances: "they think just because the church says so, that speaks for all Catholics. I don't know. Maybe those are the actual rules. I'm not sure, but that's just not how I identify and that's not how I think. I mean for me, anytime those topics are open, I embrace them because it gives me a chance to say, I identify as a Catholic and I don't agree with the church on certain things and this is why, and you can still be religious ... Like, it's not a set of laws that you have to follow or else you're going to jail. You can take what you want and you can do what you want. I'm sure the church disagrees with me, but it's working out okay for me."

Rose's current religious practices involve yoga and sun salutations each morning, directing her thoughts and prayers to God in the process. She also observes lent each year because "it really does make you stop and think ... I am so lucky and so blessed and there's that whole thankfulness again and gratefulness again. It's nice to just check in once a year and take stock of what you need to be grateful for." When asked how important her religious beliefs and practices are to her, Rose says, "I try to live my life honestly, morally, and kind. Above all, I just try to be kind. So, it's always in the back of my mind, particularly if I've done something that I don't think is very in line with that stuff. I mean it's always in the back of my mind. I can't say that I ever make any solid decisions based solely on that, but it is like a little guiding thing."

At various points in our conversation Rose speaks about past attempts to attend religious services more regularly as well as the possibility to attend regularly again in the future. She shared her efforts to find a church in her neighbourhood at a point in life when she had been home for a few years after traveling the world, she was restless with her job, and she was looking for something to ground her a bit. She relied on Google as well as her bike to locate churches in the area, but no church satisfied her. She felt like an outsider as a single female in congregations that were dominated by young families, she did not think the preaching was relevant or current, the priest was not inspiring or charismatic enough, and/or the church's theology was not progressive enough. This final reason was ultimately the sticking point for Rose and will likely prevent her from attending religious services regularly again in the future. Nonetheless she plans to continue to turn to the very church that she disagrees with in some respects, yet links her in important ways to her childhood roots.

Rose concludes our interview with this final reflection: "I guess it probably sounds pretty wishy washy, but in my head it makes total sense. I guess, my big thing is ... I think the God that I knew growing up and the guy I formulated a relationship with in my head, is one that's super open, super forgiving, and just wants us to be good to one another ... So that's just how I try to live my life, and I try not to sweat all the other stuff."

TRADITION, FAMILY, AND SACRED SPACE

From Larry Masters, Matthew Walter, and Rose Eskin's narratives we learn of some of the rewards and costs that marginal affiliates associate with their religious life. Based on my thirty interviews, over twenty rewards associated with church attendance in particular emerged ranging from a few moments of quiet and solitude away from the busyness of life, to gathering with like-minded individuals around common religious values, to attempts to avoid going to hell if they did not attend for important religious holidays, to keeping ongoing membership standing in hopes of reduced funeral and burial rates. The three dominant rewards and reasons associated with faithfully attending church for religious holidays and rites of passage include tradition, family pressures, and sacred space (also see Thiessen 2012).

Similar to the dominant finding from John Walliss (2002) and Phil Zuckerman's (2008) research on why people turn to religious groups for rites of passage, half of those I interviewed say that they turn to their church because of tradition; it is "just what you do." Like Larry Masters and his roots in the Church of England or Matthew Walter's comparison between attending church and eating Chinese food each Christmas Eve, Rose Eskin says, "It's nice on Christmas cause I went to church forever, you know all the songs by heart and so there's that sense of tradition." Howard Davis is in his 70s and belongs to the Roman Catholic Church. He says, "It's just a tradition. We've done it for a lifetime, and I'm not going to discard it." Marcus Cooley is in his 20s and he states, "There's just something about getting married in a church as opposed to going down to the courthouse. Getting married is a ceremony. It's a tradition. It just seems right to me to do it that way." In some respects this bond to tradition is because some see their religious identity as an ascribed status from birth that they feel obliged to observe throughout their life, and to pass on to their children (see Demerath III 2001, 43, 49; Dencik 2007; Inglis 2007; Day 2011). Similar findings of ascribed status emerge in studies on religious minority groups in North America where individuals continue to identify as Jew or Buddhist or Hindu mainly for cultural and familial reasons rather than inherent religious reasons (Eck 2001; Bramadat and Seljak 2005; Beyer and Ramji 2013).

Family pressure is another dominant motivation for why just over half of those I interviewed attend services for rites of passage and religious holidays (see Durkheim 1915, 190; Sherkat 1997, 73; Walliss 2002; Zuckerman 2008, 9). Marcus Cooley, like Rose Eskin, says that he attends church because "it's important to my mom. She likes to have the whole family there." George Francis says that his wife "wanted to get married in a church ... more to appease my parents, my family – my mom, especially – than anything else." Chantelle Sine is in her 30s and she echoes this sentiment: "my parents would definitely like for me to be married in a Roman Catholic Church." Chantelle, like others I interviewed, goes on to say that huge problems would arise between her and her mother if she did not have her wedding in a church and that it is not worth the fight. She is quick to point out that she would not have her wedding in a church if her family did not pressure her into it. Clearly interviewees value good family relations and will avoid straining those relationships by marrying in a church or going each Christmas if it keeps the peace in the family. As Sherkat and Wilson (1995, 998) state regarding religious choices, "consumption choices are not, however, simply the expression of personal desire: we consume not only to maximize our own utility, but also to please those around us or avoid their wrath."

Some, like Matthew Walter, also appreciate attending Christmas and Easter services because of the opportunity to spend uninterrupted time with family, especially when families are so busy throughout the year and many are geographically separated. Janet Curtis explains her attendance patterns in the following way: "I don't always see my family very often, so when we get together, I think it just kind of is good for us to all be there to kind of come together as a family and show that to each other and to God that we still all believe." Incidentally she does not attribute any religious significance to the church services that she attends.

The third motivation for marginal affiliates to attend is because they connect to a higher power in a more profound way in a sacred place (for a more detailed examination of the role that sacred space plays for marginal affiliates, see Thiessen and McAlpine 2013). For some people their connection to God is enhanced because they are surrounded by others who share the same basic beliefs about God, for others this connection to God helps them to better centre themselves, and for some they feel that their rites of passage are more legitimate because they are performed in front of God in a sacred space. Rose Eskin comments on her church involvement by saying, "That's a really special connection and that feeling of being in the church is really nice." Margaret Cameron is in her 30s and identifies herself as Lutheran. She reflects, "It's the one time of year I'm in church, so I feel like I walk through the door, and then all of a sudden, you're in the presence of God somehow ... you don't feel like that anywhere else." Thinking ahead to where she wants her funeral to be held, Gwen Sellers says, "It just seems ... more of a connection with God ... when you worship in a church than when you're just ... Funeral homes are, are good but they're not ... it's just not the same feel." Though most interviewees believe that they can connect with God anywhere, Fran Wright's sentiments resonate with many in this study: "I feel a closer connection ... when I'm actually in the church ... or a chapel or whatever ... It might sound funny, but it just feels more holy, a little bit more ... stronger ... a closer connection. You know, it's the house of God."

Without discounting their experiences of closeness to God in a sacred space, one question that consistently arose for me throughout this study was how significant this sacred connection was for marginal affiliates. A similar question surfaced for me in light of a 2013 report where nearly 80% of Christmas-only attenders attribute religious significance to the Christmas services that they attend (Bibby and Grenville 2013). If these religious services are so religiously significant for individuals, then why not pursue greater involvement to experience that closeness to God in a sacred space on a more regular basis? I deal with this question of greater involvement in chapter 5, but one has to wonder whether such connections are as impressive as some marginal affiliates think them to be. When this discussion is extended to include tradition and family pressures as motivators for attending church it is difficult to conclude that marginal affiliates attendance patterns are strong indicators of religious vitality in Canada, or even of the possible chance of future religious revitalization for that matter. For the most part non-religious and "this-world" reasons help to explain marginal affiliate levels of involvement and though on the surface their attendance reveals one aspect of their religiosity, the meaning behind such actions reveal a telling story of what might actually be taking place here.

When it comes to costs more than two-thirds of marginal affiliates advance one of the important observations found among active affiliates: they do not think in terms of costs or they do not subjectively associate any costs with the rewards that they are after. Typical of others' responses, Larry Masters says that "there's been no costs as far as I'm concerned. No sacrifices. No sacrifices. It's all been ... I want to do it ... nobody's forced me to do anything. Nobody said, 'You've got to go to church on a Sunday. You've got to be there.' No." I ask him whether he believes that attending church for religious holidays is a cost in order to receive some type of benefit. He replies, "No. I don't think God gives a toss whether I go and sit there on Sunday or whether I say a nice quiet prayer running on Sunday in the half marathon." Opal Lackey, a legal assistant in her early 50s and from the Roman Catholic tradition, says, "I never felt like I was sort of giving up anything for the way that I ... sort of worked on my spiritualism. Nope. I don't feel like I've really sacrificed anything in my relationships or anything like that." When I ask Rose Eskin if she has incurred any costs she replies, "Not really. I mean, I do have a couple friendships that get heated when we talk about things like this, but I don't know that it's a sacrifice. I mean it's just because I'm trying to explain my views and someone's already made up their mind about them. But no, not really. I've never felt like I can't do something or that I had to give something up."

A few interviewees jokingly say that they are unwilling to incur the cost of leisure time on Sunday mornings to attend church more regularly, while a few marginal affiliates indicate that if they take their faith more seriously, then they would probably incur costs of submitting control of their life over to God. But as Richard Horton, a 32-year-old, highlights, this is a fearful step that people are not willing or desire to take: "I can imagine for some people ... if you really took the rules and ... actually tried to truly live up to them, I do believe there would be a lot of costs associated with it ... I believe that, and I kind of fear that in the back of my mind ... that if I truly, like, gave my life over to God completely and did what he truly desired ... I imagine there would be a possibility of ... some significant costs. Definitely."

On the whole then most marginal affiliates do not subjectively attach any perceived costs or trade-offs with the rewards associated with observing religious holidays or rites of passage in religious settings. As I noted in the previous chapter, one might challenge interviewee's own assessments that there are no perceived trade-offs in their religious decision-making processes, for example that they are giving up time in order to observe tradition or to please family members. However, I reassert in a Weberian vein that an individual's subjective understanding and motivation for action is of utmost importance to accurately understand the dynamics at work here. Based on marginal affiliates' subjective evaluations, it does not appear that individuals consciously think of costs to the degree that Stark and Finke suggest, or if they do, it is done in a highly subjective manner that makes it difficult to measure or compare costs between individuals. Moreover, some equate "cost" with "bad" and as evident among both active and marginal affiliates, they do not associate trade-offs with something undesirable.

A LESS DEPENDABLE AND RESPONSIVE GOD AND CONGREGATION

Active affiliates on the whole believe that God is dependable, responsive, and of great scope, and that those in their congregations are also dependable and responsive. Based on Stark and Finke's theory (2000, 96–102), I anticipate marginal affiliates to be less inclined than active affiliates to view either God or their congregations in the same manner, evident in their reluctance to enter into extended or exclusive exchanges with the gods or their congregations.

Two-thirds of marginal affiliates believe in the traditional monotheistic Christian God and three believe in a generic spiritual being or a higher power. The remaining marginal affiliates are agnostic or atheist on the existence of God. Marginal affiliates are less likely than active affiliates to believe that they can depend on God or that God cares about people, but approximately two-thirds do believe that they can depend on God and about half think that God is concerned about humans. Some pray to God during difficult times, such as when a family member dies or when life is stressful, believing that prayer makes a difference. God helps them to cope, to experience comfort and peace, and to find new friends at different stages of life. In this, marginal affiliates are not any different from active affiliates. Rose Eskin reflects on God's dependability in the following way: "I've been so blessed. Like I've had a lovely, lovely life. And even when bad things have happened, they've always turned themselves out. I mean there's no way in a family of six that we've all just gotten by on luck. There's a bigger force there, and I think it's because we're a strong family unit and we love each other and love God. He's always going to help guide us through even the bad parts. I've had a very charmed and very blessed life." Larry Masters shares, "I do believe that God or somebody looks after me. I do believe He's got his eye out for me. A few things have happened where ... had some very close calls ... and somebody somewhere has been looking after me."

Still, several marginal affiliates believe that they cannot depend on God, often because they hold a primarily humanistic outlook on the world. When I asked Matthew Walter if he could depend on God, he states, "I don't know if I can say yes or no to that ... I've always been sort of a believer in ... put your head down. You can work through any problem or that sort of thing." Howard Davis asserts that "you have to depend on yourself."

Others cannot depend on God because they believe God has failed them in the past. Cynthia Schellenberg cites her husband's death at a young age as an example where God could have intervened, but for one reason or another, did not. For individuals with these experiences, they fear that God will let them down again if they risk depending on Him. In Max Weber's (1963 [1922], 138–9) discussion of monotheistic religions he states that "the more the development tends toward the conception of a transcendental unitary god who is universal, the more there arises the problem of how the extraordinary power of such a god may be reconciled with the imperfection of the world that he has created and rules over." He goes on to highlight findings from an early twentieth-century questionnaire with German workers who did not believe in a god because of "their difficulty in reconciling the idea of providence with the injustice and imperfection of the social order" (1963 [1922], 139). Weber's findings resonate with some that I interviewed, speaking not only to Stark and Finke's axioms about God's dependability but also about His scope of power and influence.

It is hardly surprising that marginal affiliates, some of whom already possess a low level of confidence in the gods, would want to pursue any extensive involvement in a religious organization, the supposed place where exchanges between humans and the gods are encouraged and supervised. I wanted to find out if this was definitely the case, and also whether any past experiences in a church influenced marginal affiliates' current levels of involvement in their congregation.

When I asked marginal affiliates if they could depend on people in their congregation, they were far less positive than active affiliates (15 marginal affiliates responded affirmatively to this question). For some this was because they did not know others in their congregation. Personality and gender also factored into people's explanations.

Some were more independent in life and did not turn to anyone in times of need. Some males indicated that females are more likely to turn to friends, thus church or no church they (males) were less inclined to ask anyone for help. For others their apprehension to depend on others in their congregation was connected to bad experiences in the past where people in the church let them down, making them hostile to the thought of turning to their congregation again. Similar to Rose Eskin's experience, Opal Lackey shared several negative experiences in different congregations. One experience especially stands out after she missed a few services: "I missed a few Sundays, and I was shopping, and I ran into this lady, Jane, I think her name was. And I saw her, and I said, 'Hi! How are you?' And she looked at me. She said, 'I don't have time to talk to you.' And I thought, 'There you go. She thinks that I don't have time for them. I don't have time for church. I don't have time for Sister Mary … and to help anymore, and she's just going to give me the cold shoulder.' So, like, that's really hurtful." Later in the interview she describes the lack of dependability among those in her congregation in this way: "I felt … as long as I was saying the right things and doing the right things, showing up when I was supposed to, that I would be accepted. But if I made a mistake or, you know, any one of the human conditions, you experience from time to time, I was out. And that, in fact, is what happened." Ronald Darling who is in his late 40s from an evangelical Protestant tradition shared this experience: "There was, I guess, a lot of emotional turmoil in my life, and I sort of reached out to the church for support and got nothing back. In fact, I got chastised several times by the pastor for my lack of strength in the face of those things and was completely taken aback by it, shocked by it, very hurt by it … I was coming to terms with a lack of outreach by my church, and it was just, like, 'Okay. Hold it. Enough is enough.'"

Still, two-thirds of marginal affiliates believe that their congregations are responsive to people's needs in their church and broader society. Overall they believe that churches genuinely desire to love and care for people, and they provided countless examples of how their church or other churches have done so (e.g., caring for the homeless and for immigrants). Yet, the negative things that churches are responsible for, such as sexual or financial scandals, wars, or corrupt leadership remain on marginal affiliates' minds. Howard Davis highlights the perception of several others that I spoke with:

I have a real thing with these Benny Hinns and other zealots out there pushing people over and you're cured. I mean, "God blessed me with this"; "God told me this." And the people that just buy into this looking for something. Looking for a cure. Buying a vial of whatever-the-hell water they call it. Magical water ... and the people who buy into it. We had a friend ... he had been sending thousands of dollars down to Jimmy Swaggert ... it behoves me to say that some people get sucked in ... so much of that goes on ... and, with all the promises of wealth ... I mean you're in credit card debt when you send us a payment, and you're just going to disappear shortly thereafter. So they'll make their fifty dollar payment on this month's Visa card, pay the eighteen percent increase, which will keep accumulating, and think that the miracle spring water may bring this to an end. Do I have some issues with religion? Yes. Charlatans.

Though not exclusive to agnostic and atheist marginal affiliates who strictly attend church services out of obligation to family members, they stress this negative side of religious organizations as a leading explanation for why they do not desire any further involvement in church life.

These findings resonate with Kinnaman and Lyons' discoveries in *unChristian* (2007). Through survey and interview data in the United States they document six leading perceptions that relatively irreligious folk have of Christians, particularly evangelicals: hypocritical, homophobic, sheltered within a Christian subculture, too political, judgmental, and motivated to make friends with non-Christians only because they wish to convert them. Christians are known not for what they stand for, but what they stand against. They are perceived as closed-minded, arrogant, and highly exclusive relative to the surrounding culture. Such perceptions are based in large part on people's first hand experiences, like those of Rose Eskin and other marginal affiliates with Christians (also see Hunsberger and Altemeyer 2006, 15; Clydesdale 2007, 196–7; Baker and Smith 2009; Putnam and Campbell 2010, 499–501; Kinnaman 2011; Zuckerman 2012).

Framed in the context of rational choice theory these signs of strictness are a barrier for marginal affiliates to believe and belong more fully in their religious group. I am not surprised that these findings challenge rational choice assumptions about strictness given that inclusivity and tolerance are prized values in a socially and religiously diverse Canada. Strictness might lead to heightened levels of religiosity in some situations, but this is not a linear relationship and, at least in the Canadian milieu, strictness poses significant challenges to increased religious belief and practice. Dillon and Wink (2007, 34) conclude that "although religiously strict churches are effective in attracting and maintaining new members ... our data suggest that the aggregate logic behind this does not necessarily persuade all individuals, nor is it transmitted intact across generations."

GOOD PEOPLE GO TO THE NEXT LIFE

Marginal affiliates are less likely to believe in the afterlife than are active affiliates (see Inglis 2007, 217), but just over two-thirds of marginal affiliates do believe in the afterlife. Agnostics and atheists who attend religious services out of respect for family members are the least likely to believe in an afterlife, followed by those who tragically lost a loved one. For this latter group, believing that God did not stop someone close to them from dying contributes to their lack of belief in life after death.

Like active affiliates, fewer marginal affiliates show a desire for life after death than those who actually believe in the afterlife. Aside from the third who do not believe in life after death, another third desire life after death, and an additional third indicate that life after death is inevitable or that they are unsure of what life after death looks like, thus questions about desire are irrelevant. For those who desire the afterlife I did not get the sense that there was a strong longing for it, except for a couple of individuals who wanted to resolve issues with deceased family members or spend eternity with departed family members. Kevin Cheal, who was raised in a Baptist congregation, says, "I have a lot of unresolved issues with, I'm going to say, God, family members ... both my parents are deceased, but I have a lot of issues I would like to be able to get through to them, I guess, face-to-face rather than me talking to the air. I'd love to go and see them again, to tell them why I feel the way I do, again, rather than just laying in bed saying it to whatever." This finding resonates with Abby Day's (2011, 119, 167–8) research that desire for the afterlife is largely about connecting with loved ones. Among those who believe that life after death is inevitable there is a general opinion along the lines of Sasha Unger, who says, "I don't have any questions about death. I never question death, so when that happens, I think that's going to be awesome, but I don't have a desire. I just have a knowing ... that's what it's going to be."

What is required to obtain the afterlife? Marginal affiliates do not consider definitive belief in a god or a supernatural being, extended or exclusive exchanges with the gods, or active involvement in a religious group as necessary requirements for obtaining life after death. People of all religious faiths or no religious faith at all can move on to the next life if they are good, upright, moral people (see Putnam and Campbell 2010, 534–40). For them this entails following the Ten Commandments and being generous, friendly, cheerful, and honest, while avoiding the major sins such as murder, rape, and stealing (see Day 2011).

In his book *Sex in the Snow* (2006), Environics president, Michael Adams, plausibly argues that a relationship exists between Canadians' increased orientation toward "this-world" and declining desires or fear of the afterlife. Commenting on the impact of technology and the resultant sense of urgency and immediacy for many Canadians, Adams (2006, 31, 124) states: "[Canadians are a] population that is unwilling to defer gratification to the next life, that wants to 'have its cake and eat it too.' What is the point, after all, of having a cake you don't eat, or waiting till it's stale? Canadians are increasingly focused on immediate gratification, and have pretty much given up on the promises – and *threats* – of an afterlife ... Canadians are no longer willing to wait for gratification until death's door delivers them into an afterlife they're not even sure exists." Adams' ideas ring true on two fronts. The first is that several marginal affiliates and some active affiliates do not believe in or desire life after death, and even among those who do desire life after death the intensity of that desire is rather small. Second, that every single person that I interviewed mainly offered "this-worldly" rewards for maintaining some level of religious belief or practice indicates the limited role that "other-worldly" rewards play in Canadian religious decision-making processes. Put differently, the reward of life after death is not a critical variable that many consider when deciding to be religious, or deciding how religious they will be. This conclusion echoes Marx (1970), Norris and Inglehart (2011), and Zuckerman (2008) who believe that advances in modernity and material security leads to lower levels of religiosity that in this case could mean that people attach less "other-worldly" significance to their religious beliefs and practices.

These findings suggest that maybe there is a lack of demand for the things that religion has to offer in terms of the afterlife. Perhaps a belief in or desire for the afterlife is not as central to people's approach to religion as once thought.

MORALITY AND RELIGION

On display in the opening vignettes are Matthew Walter and Rose Eskin's concerns over religious groups going door-to-door to proselytize or advancing exclusive and discriminatory positions toward homosexuals or women. Similar to other marginal affiliates in this study they are less likely than active affiliates to overwhelmingly conclude that religion is a positive force in society (10 arrived at this conclusion), but they are not willing to outright say that religion is bad for society either (6 indicated this). Instead, about half of marginal affiliates say that religion has both a positive and a negative presence in society. Marcus Cooley thinks carefully before saying, "I think it's positive when it contributes to helping the community and helping people. I think it's negative when it contributes to excluding people and discriminating against people." Fran Wright answers, "I think it's both ... it has a lot of good about it, and I think it does a lot of good for people, but I also believe that ... going out there and trying to recruit or push ... I don't believe in, and I don't think it's right. Only if someone so desires to go that route." Lesley Alford, a stay-at-home mom in her 30s, is connected to the Roman Catholic Church. She expresses, "I think it depends. I mean, obviously, there's some wars fought for religion ... Generally, I think it's good because I think the message is inherent and the morals in religion are great." Bernie Pickles, a conservative Protestant in his 30s, reflects, "It's both ... at extreme ends ... I think a positive is ... the support that it gives different groups. But, at the same time, that becomes a negative ... You can have yours, just don't shove it down my throat. But I'll leave you lots of space to believe whatever you want as long as you aren't going to create a bomb to kill us all because you think that's what we all deserve, right? And that scares me that, especially in the Middle East ... that some quacks can get a hold of the big bomb and decide that that's a religious thing to do." Collectively marginal affiliates assert that religion provides good morals and community to religious adherents and religious groups do good things in the community, yet interviewees are apprehensive about the tension and conflict that ensues when religious extremists act violently in society (Muslims were repeatedly referred to) or when religious zealots force their faith on others to convert.

Marginal affiliates are more likely than active affiliates to claim that religion is unnecessary for people to be moral or ethical (nineteen versus fourteen), or that religion helps individuals or societies toward moral and ethical behaviour (nine versus thirteen). Many, like Quinton Sylvester, shared stories of personal friends and family members who are not religious, but who are good contributing members to society and to those close to them. Quinton, a conservative Protestant in his 30s recalls, "a woman I worked with up in Edmonton ... she's a lesbian ... she's married to this, another woman ... they adopted two kids. They're active in their community. They love their kids. They're very good people ... No, I don't think, I don't think you need religion to be moral. I think there's rules in place in society that have been established." Margaret Cameron shares, "I look at my husband, who has no religion, and I'm obviously married to him and in love with him, but I think he is an outstanding, contributing member of society. And he has no religious background. And I think there's people that are, like my good friend who is at church on Sundays, in the church group. All her friends are from church. Like, very, very religious, and she is a very moral and ethically revered member of society. And she is one of my closest friends." Rose Eskin says, "No I don't think so. I mean, you either grew up right and made good choices and you continue to make good choices. But I know just as many awful people that grew up religious as I do ones that aren't."

The differences between active and marginal affiliates are not that surprising. But a paradoxical belief to emerge in my interviews with marginal affiliates and religious nones is that while they do not believe that people need religion in order to be moral or ethical, many of them still wish to expose their children to religion by sending them to Sunday school or a religious school to strengthen their moral footing in life. I explore this ironic dichotomy in the next two chapters, but wonder here whether marginal affiliate beliefs about religion and morality are as separate as they make them out to be. Do they really believe that people do not need religion in order to be moral, and if so, why are they compelled to expose their children to religion for moral reasons, particularly when they are not that involved in a religious group themselves?

RELIGION IS A PRIVATE MATTER

Recalling Stark and Finke's (2000, 106–38) axiom that people's confidence in religious explanations is strengthened the more they participate in religious rituals and interact with others who think and behave as they do, I asked marginal affiliates various questions about the "social" side of their religious life. Unlike active affiliates, marginal affiliates view religion as a solitary and private affair. Opal Lackey says that religion is "definitely an individual journey," while Larry Masters states that "it's individual. From my point of view, it's an individual journey ... I don't care if someone shares it with me, to be honest." Similar to Bibby's observations in 1987 and 1993 and Michael Adams' (2006) observations of Canadian life, most believe that religion is a private matter where they can create, customize, and arrive at whatever set of religious beliefs they want. In particular, marginal affiliates do not believe that others should force their faith on to another person, and they admit that they do not talk about religion with their friends nor do some of them even know their friends' religion. Fran Wright says to me, "I don't believe pushing anything onto anybody, I guess. I can talk about how I feel. I can talk about ... what I believe and what I do, but I don't think I would have a right to push it onto somebody else ... I think it's a very personal thing. It's a personal journey." Matthew Walter speaks strongly against forcing one's faith on another: "I'm not a big fan of the Church of Jesus Christ of Latter Day Saints sending people through my neighbourhood every couple weeks ... and then showing up with their whole family on my doorstep. I don't think that's fair ... I think everybody's entitled ... to believe what they believe, and, granted, they have to be exposed to it somehow. But I think people on their journey ... will be drawn towards something ... And there's enough influence out there that they'll gravitate towards something without people have to show up ... and ... they'll stand there all day ... I understand that they're making a pitch, only with God ... I appreciate that. I'm the wrong guy, but I appreciate the gesture." Once more the impact of living in Canadian society on religious belief and practice is evident among those in this study. Most subconsciously subscribe to Canadian values of diversity, pluralism, and tolerance that yields a strong aversion to pushing one's religion on to another, instead keeping faith to one's self.

A handful of marginal affiliates indicate that religion is social or that it is both individual and social. Unlike active affiliates, marginal affiliates define "social" as sharing their faith with others by modeling what it means to be a "good" Christian – be kind, generous, and loving toward others. None of them gave the impression that this means regular participation in rituals with fellow believers or that they need to actively proselytize the "unsaved."

The marginal affiliate emphasis on individualism is heightened when just over half believe that the individual, rather than one's religious group, should have authority over shaping a person's religious beliefs and practices. Participant after participant reinforced Matthew Walter and Rose Eskin's beliefs, including Larry Masters as depicted at the outset of chapter 1: "Sometimes I don't agree with them. Sometimes I agree with them. Sometimes you cherry-pick, like everything in life ... There's not a lot of black-and-white ... You pick what you like: 'I like that. That one would be suitable. I'll keep that.'"

Marginal affiliates are less likely than active affiliates to have close friends in their religious group. Less than a quarter of marginal affiliates are good friends with at least one person who regularly attends the same congregation that they drop in for a few times a year, plus less than a quarter of marginal affiliates are close with someone who attends another congregation. Most people that marginal affiliates are good friends with either attend religious services to the same extent that they do, do not attend at all, or marginal affiliates have no idea because they do not talk about religion with their friends.

In theory, I expected marginal affiliates to be less confident than active affiliates in the religious explanations that they hold on to because of their rather individualistic approach to faith. This assertion is partially true, but not to the extent that I thought. On one hand marginal affiliates are not tied "socially" to others in their religious group on a regular basis nor are they repeatedly exposed to social reinforcements and reminders of their group's beliefs and practices. On the other hand marginal affiliates tend to associate with others who hold similar attitudes and behaviours toward religion, by chance more than anything. My findings reveal that similar to those in a study in Kendal, England who had limited involvement in a religious group (Heelas et al. 2005), over 80% of marginal affiliates are strongly or somewhat confident in their religious world view. Some marginal affiliates point out that their spiritual search is always evolving, but they are entirely comfortable with this approach – this does not make the religious ground beneath them any less solid. When asked about his level of confidence in the religious beliefs and practices that he adopt George Francis says, "I'd say fairly confident, but because it's ... an ongoing ... exploration ... it's not like I can say for sure that ... the afterlife exists ... from my personal perspective, I'm ... confident that that belief works for me and is right for me in the space that I'm in right now."

FREE RIDERS

The marginal affiliate approach to religion can be summarized in the following question that Reginald Bibby has long asked on his surveys and I asked during my interviews: "Some Canadians suggest that they draw selective beliefs and practices from their religious tradition, even if they don't attend regularly. They indicate that they don't plan on changing religious traditions, but they will turn to religious groups for important religious holidays and rites of passage. How well would you say that this describes you?" Nearly all marginal affiliates in this study responded affirmatively to this question, with a handful saying that it partly described them (i.e., they would turn to their religious organization for rites of passage, but not necessarily religious holidays). Robert says it describes me "very well," Nancy responds "it's pretty accurate," and Iris claims "perfectly."

Descriptively, not pejoratively, marginal affiliates are free riders in the classic sense put forward in rational choice theory, and most of my interviewees are very content with this arrangement. Whether it is because of tradition, family pressure, or connecting to God in a sacred space, Larry Masters, Matthew Walter, and Rose Eskin appreciate that others invest time and energy to ensure that marginal affiliates can limit their church attendance to every Christmas or Easter, baptize their child, and enjoy a wedding in a church. Some marginal affiliates value that churches provide outlets for children to acquire moral training toward being a better person in society and by extension ensuring a ticket to the afterlife, all without high expectations of religious or group commitment in return; individuals can come and go as they please. The real appeal for "free riders" is the intersection with individualistic approaches to faith. Larry, Matthew, and Rose retain power to determine the nature and scope of their religiosity, mindful that a safety net remains if or when they want to benefit from the services and rewards extended through their religious group. At the same time this tactic distances marginal affiliates from "owning" the baggage and social stigma associated with their religious groups in the ways that active affiliates might.

In a cultural context such as Canada where religion is not privileged in any meaningful sense in social life and dying religious groups are often happy for any point of contact with individuals who are not regularly involved, it is relatively easy to remain a "free rider." What remains to be seen is if religious organizations will continue to make space for free riders, fearful that if they do not their membership and attendance numbers will drop even further, or whether religious groups will make it difficult for free riders to hang around in ways that force marginal affiliates to either pursue greater levels of commitment or abandon their institutional religious ties altogether. I suspect that on the whole the former is the likely outcome, but only time will tell.

4

Religious Nones: Freedom from Religion

Religious nones are the fastest growing "religious" group in Canada, the United States, and many other Western countries. Many scholars are giving increased attention to this group in the last decade especially (see Bullivant and Lee 2012). The 2011 Canadian Census reveals that 24% of Canadian adults have "no religion," up from 16% in 2001, 12% in 1991, 4% in 1971, and under 1% in the 1950s (Bibby et al. 2009, 176; Statistics Canada 2013). Reginald Bibby's research with Canadian teenagers shows increases in the "no religion" category from 12% in 1984 to 32% in 2008 (Bibby 2011, 51). Similar upward trends in the religious none category are evident in the United States as 15% to 20% currently claim no religion, up from 8% in 1990 (Kosmin and Keysar 2008; Pew Forum on Religion and Public Life 2008; Grossman 2012). The United Kingdom (Bullivant and Lee 2012) and Australia (Singleton 2007) bear analogous shifts too.

Recent research highlights that religious nones are predominantly male, young, politically left-leaning, and are increasingly found among immigrants to North America (see, e.g., Campbell 1971; Condran and Tamney 1985; Statistics Canada 2001; Kosmin and Keysar 2006, 2007, 2008; Hunsberger and Altemeyer 2006; Pew Forum on Religion and Public Life 2008, 2010; Baker and Smith 2009; Valpy 2010; Zuckerman 2012). In other ways religious nones are no different than the general population in terms of education (see Voas and McAndrew [2012] for an alternate view on the relationship between education and religious nones), socioeconomic status, marital status, and race and ethnicity (Kosmin and Keysar 2008, 2–5).

Religious nones are not a homogeneous secular group. Some believe in God, in miracles, or in the afterlife, and they attend religious services, pray, or believe that religion is important (see Hout and Fischer 2002; Kosmin and Keysar 2006; Pew Forum on Religion and Public Life 2008; Baker and Smith 2009; Lim et al. 2010; Manning 2010; Voas and Day 2010; Bengtson et al. 2013). There are different types of religious nones, from atheists to agnostics to unchurched believers, and as expected, "on all these measures atheists are the least privately spiritual, followed by agnostics, and then unchurched believers, who have the highest means on private religion and spirituality among the non-traditionally religious categories" (Baker and Smith 2009, 726).

In these early days of rigorous sociological research into them a qualitative study of Canadian religious nones has yet to take place to my knowledge. What religious beliefs and practices, if any, do religious nones adopt? For instance, do they believe in a supernatural being or power, and if they do, do they think that this supernatural entity is dependable and responsive? What are their beliefs about the afterlife and about morality? In what ways are religious nones similar or dissimilar from each other, and how are they like or unlike active affiliates and marginal affiliates? What are their thoughts on the "social" nature of religion, is their world view on religion socially reinforced in any way, and in turn, how confident are they in the world view that they hold to be true?

WHAT WE KNOW ABOUT RELIGIOUS NONES

Initial research on religious nones in the late 1960s and early 1970s revealed three main conclusions. First, to that point in time sociologists of religion neglected studying religious nones even though non-religious individuals always existed over the course of history (see Stark 1999a). Glenn Vernon (1968), in his article "The Religious 'Nones': A Neglected Category," and Colin Campbell (1971) in his seminal book, *Toward a Sociology of Irreligion*, make a case for studying the irreligious in the same way that we study the religious – by exploring people's beliefs, actions, attitudes, and experiences, looking for degrees of religiosity or the absence thereof along the religious/irreligious continuum. Methodologically they implored scholars to distil nuanced beliefs, practices, and experiences among religious nones and to pay careful attention to whether their irreligious identity was a core or peripheral aspect of their identity. It took nearly four decades, but Vernon and Campbell's appeal to sociologists of religion is finally bearing fruit.

The second observation was that the language "religious nones" had a negative connotation, normalizing religious belief and practice and stigmatizing irreligious individuals. Vernon recommended the neutral phrase "religious independents," yet religious nones is the label that most scholars continue to use today. Regardless of how religious nones were labeled they were ostracized in society, in the United States especially: "to be non-religious in the mid-nineteenth century was to risk not only social ostracism, petty persecution and accusations of immorality but criminal proceedings as well" (Campbell 1971, 4). Campbell intimated at the time that ongoing social pressure against the irreligious could serve as a catalyst for religious nones to eventually band together, organize, and actively resist social stigmatization. He was right, though much is yet to be accomplished in this regard for religious nones.

Finally, in linking religion with morality and resolving matters of "ultimate concern" Campbell reminds sociologists of the socially constructed nature of this subject. Discussions about whether religion or irreligion is good or bad for society, or whether religion more legitimately helps individuals to address "ultimate" questions is socially and contextually situated. The religious and irreligious define morality and things of ultimate concern differently and therefore one should not quickly jump to the conclusion that religion is good for society and that irreligion is bad for society.

Vernon and Campbell paved the way for scholars to systematically study religious nones. Toward this end the following three findings stand out in the current literature on religious nones. First, identifying as a religious none does not mean that one is an atheist or agnostic. Drawing on the 2001 American Religious Identification Survey data, Barry Kosmin and Ariela Keysar (2006, 45) show that 45% of American religious nones strongly believe that God exists, 22% somewhat agree with this belief, and only 12% strongly disagree that God exists. In Canada approximately half of Canadian adults and teens who claim to have no religion identify as atheists (Bibby 2011, 48–9). In the United States only 2%–4% of the entire population are atheists or agnostics (Kosmin and Keysar 2008, 5; Pew Forum on Religion and Public Life 2008, 5), including about 20% of religious nones (Kosmin and Keysar 2006, 45) (also see Hunsberger and Altemeyer 2006, 18). Kosmin (2007, 7) declares that "although the self-described secular population in the United States has doubled since 1990, it cannot be said that American society has become more irreligious or anti-religious, only that there is less identification with religious groups." Put another way, several religious nones do adopt some semblance of religious belief and practice, and Canadian and American religious nones are similar in this regard.

One caveat to the low numbers of atheists is that some religious nones are by definition atheists and say on a survey that they do not believe in God, however do not self-identify as atheists (Cragun et al. 2012). Instead they say they are humanist or secular or skeptical or agnostic (Pasquale 2007, 45). The reason for this distancing is because some are leery to associate with fundamentalist atheists (or "new atheists") such as Richard Dawkins, Sam Harris, or the late Christopher Hitchens. Religious nones are often less militant in their views than fundamentalist atheists and religious nones do not feel the need to convince others to adopt their world view. Similar realities exist for some who distance themselves from identifying as Christian or evangelical, fearful of the stigma and baggage that is conjured up for others (e.g., this is the rationale given by the lead singer of the band Mumford and Sons, who rejected the Christian label in a 2013 interview with *Rolling Stone*). The same applies to some Muslims in Canada who detach themselves from militant expressions of Islam (Beyer 2013b), notable among countless Muslim leaders across Canada who strongly and publically denounced the attacks on Canadian soldiers on Canadian soil in October 2014. To summarize, due to negative stigma associated with the term "atheist" the actual atheist population could be slightly larger than survey figures suggest, but it is not as large as the religious none population as a whole.

Second, social acceptance and stigma simultaneously characterize the religious none experience today. Beginning with acceptance, it is less deviant to say that one has no religion today than when Vernon and Campbell wrote in the late 1960s. This changing narrative contributes to more people declaring today that they have no religion. This gradual openness in society to relatively irreligious individuals is likely a function of widespread pluralism and diversity found in many late modern democratic societies, especially in Canada, where a single sacred canopy no longer exists, just as Berger (1967) projected. In the Canadian circumstance one might go as far as to argue that it is socially unacceptable to be religious, at least to be too religious in the form of exclusive, strict, fundamentalist, and/or conservative religion (e.g., just ask Stockwell Day, the one-time leader of the Canadian Alliance political party or read David Haskell's [2009]

Through a Lens Darkly or Marci McDonald's [2010] *The Armageddon Factor*). In the United States social acceptance of irreligion has grown, but nowhere near the level found in Canada. One striking example of this is that 18% of Canadians believe that an atheist is unfit for public office, compared with 32% in the United States, and Americans are less likely to vote for a presidential candidate who is an atheist (45%) than one who is a homosexual (55%), has been married three times (67%), or is a member of a visible or religious minority (Bibby 2011, 92–4).

Negative perceptions toward the irreligious persist, especially in nations with many very religious individuals. Marcel Harper's (2007, 549) findings among university students in South Africa show that people stereotype non-religious people in negative ways, describing them as "'immoral,' 'anti-Christian,' 'prejudiced,' 'hard-hearted,' and 'self-centered' ... 'aggressive,' 'arrogant,' 'empty,' 'evil,' 'freaks,' 'ignorant,' 'lost,' 'miserable,' 'sinners,' 'stupid,' and 'shallow.'" Several studies show that those with no religion compare themselves to homosexuals who need to "come out" to their friends, family, and co-workers, seeking acceptance in ways that they believe the secular community has not historically experienced (see, e.g., Linneman and Clendenen 2010; Cragun et al. 2012; Niose 2012; Williamson and Yancey 2013).

Interestingly, research conducted by Cragun et al. (2012, 114) on discrimination toward the non-religious in the United States reveals that nearly 79% of religious nones "do not report experiencing discrimination as a result of their lack of a religious identification in the last five years." When this categorization is broadened from the general "non-religious" label to atheist and agnostic specifically, incidences of perceived discrimination jump to 41% and 44%, respectively. This suggests that the labels used to think about the non-religious continue to play a powerful role in people's perceptions, with many still holding a negative perception of those identified as atheist or agnostic – as if these identifiers are more permanent, intentional, and hostile to those with religious identities. In particular Cragun et al. (2012) show that perceived discrimination toward atheists and agnostics tends to occur among family members, co-workers, or those at school.

Though religious nones are not as prone to form or join specifically non-religious groups (Bullivant and Lee 2012), some of the ways that the secular community find solace and belonging among those similar to themselves is through face-to-face and online groups and organizations. Some participate in book clubs or political discussion groups, others provide children and youth camps and programing with a secular angle, and several proactively campaign against the strong public presence of religion in society and the often accompanying hostile oppression toward secular individuals and groups (see Pasquale 2007; Manning 2010; Niose 2012; LeDrew 2013; Williamson and Yancey 2013).

Third, in addition to reasons linked to apostasy that I deal with in chapter 5, religious nones are on the rise because of an adverse response to increased influence among the American Christian Right and religious fundamentalists in general since the 1980s. Hout and Fischer (2002, 168) initially advanced this argument: "The growing connection made in the press and in the Congress between Republicans and Christian evangelicals may have led Americans with moderate and liberal political views to express their distance from the Religious Right by saying they prefer no religion." This perspective has since been supported by Hunsberger and Altemeyer (2006, 15) in their research on apostasy, Clydesdale (2007, 196–7) in his study of American university students, Kinnaman and Lyons (2007) in their research on young non-Christian's perspectives on Christians, Baker and Smith (2009) in their study of American religious nones, Putnam and Campbell (2010, 499–501) who identify religious Americans as the most intolerant Americans, and Zuckerman (2012) in his study of American apostates. Hunsberger and Altemeyer (2006, 82–4) show that both American religious fundamentalists and atheists are highly prejudiced toward others not like themselves (especially toward each other). Canadian fundamentalists and atheists, however, are less prejudiced than their American counterparts. Together the cumulative research reveals that religious nones reject the intolerance, hypocrisy, and abrasive beliefs and practices common to religious fundamentalists, realities most evident when religious groups fight against legalizing gay marriage, abortion, euthanasia, or stem-cell research in the name of protecting "family values." Some might say that this is an American phenomenon and does not apply in the Canadian context. In part this is true, but given Canada's physical proximity to the United States, together with the strong influence of American media in Canada, the realities south of the border do have an impact on Canadians. Many I interviewed take their cues about religion from what they see and hear in the American media about televangelists, religious groups lobbying politicians, or religious intolerance toward homosexuals.

How do the research findings on religious nones to date compare with the many stories that I heard during thirty interviews with religious nones in Calgary? How does the Canadian cultural context help us to think about the attitudes, behaviours, and experiences of these religious nones? Our answers are initially found in the following three vignettes with Wendy Yandle, Christopher Rearden, and Nathan Jenson.

WENDY YANDLE

A few days before her fifty-sixth birthday, Wendy Yandle agreed to meet me at a local coffee shop to speak about religion. As with other religious nones that I interviewed, I had very little idea of how much exposure she had to religious belief or practice in the past and thus how much or little she would have to say in response to my questions. Some of my shortest interviews, around 25 minutes, took place with religious nones that were not raised with any religious background, had never given much thought to this subject, and were quite content with their life. Other interviews ranged over one hour with individuals sharing how and why they left their religion, why they would never consider turning to religion again, and why they thought religion was bad for society.

Wendy was a delightful woman, very willing to share her thoughts and experiences during our 50 minutes together. Wendy, who has been married for 30 years and has two daughters in their 20s, double majored in French and history in university. She has never worked in a job related to either degree, moving her way through various part-time jobs and currently is a bookkeeper for her husband's business.

Wendy is the middle child in her family. Her father owned his own construction business, her mom worked for her dad, and her grandmother lived with her family while she grew up. I ask her about her religious upbringing and she notes that her father comes from a Baptist background and her mother converted to Roman Catholicism during the war years. Wendy notes that the Catholic Church did not want her mom to marry her dad because he was not Catholic; Wendy's mother never attended church after that point. Wendy's parents did not take her to church nor really talk about religion much in the home aside from saying grace before some meals or praying before bedtime and reading the Bible at Christmas. She says, "I remember going to church with my grandfather a lot. I hated Sunday school. I couldn't stand it. I thought it was really belittling and stupid ... You'd arrive and then you're supposed to eat Rice Krispies with chopsticks, have a nap, and recite Bible verses that you were supposed to memorize that didn't make any sense to me. I couldn't see the point. I felt like I was being babysat." Her grandpa passed away when she was in grade five and that was the last time that she attended religious services. Wendy indicates that she does not miss attending church. She casually explored other religions while in university, but ultimately concluded that "religion's really all have the same beliefs, from what I could tell ... I didn't feel a real need for it, but was sort of reassured that religions across the world are the same. They all have the same fundamental beliefs and there were a lot of things about religion that bothered me and it's about the institution, not about the beliefs. Then they go off the rails ... Decided not to affiliate myself with any of them." Incidentally, despite her experience as a child, Wendy still got married in a Baptist church, mainly because of "tradition." Wendy and her husband also took pre-marital classes through the Baptist church with plans to learn how to raise their children with some religious exposure. As it turns out they never exposed their children to religion of any kind, nor have they returned to any church involvement individually or as a family.

I ask Wendy how she identifies herself today and she says "sometimes I say Christian; sometimes I say none." This is a response that a handful of religious nones provide and when pressed to explain further, they often disclose that Christian is "the closest thing to what I know," referring to how they were raised. For them the ascribed religious identity from their upbringing is difficult to completely shake off (see Day 2011). Yet as the interview progressed and I heard more of Wendy's story it became clear that she leans more toward the "religious none" label. In response to my question about how important her religious identification is, Wendy, like most other religious nones, says that it is "not important." In the context of Colin Campbell's (1971, 38–9) latent versus manifest distinction, religious none identification plays a latent role in most interviewee's lives. Identifying as a religious none does not figure prominently in how they think or behave or define themselves, or in how they want others to perceive them.

Similar to one-third of religious nones in this study, Wendy believes in God or some type of spiritual force, but does not think that the supernatural intervenes in human affairs. For this reason she does not pray, even citing a recent operation that a family member underwent and noting that "it never occurred to me to pray." She does not believe in the afterlife, like nearly two-thirds of religious nones that I interviewed who either do not believe in the afterlife or are unsure if there is life after death. Contrary to theists who maintain that non-religious folk lack meaning or purpose in life without religion, Wendy believes that she has meaning, purpose, and direction in her life, largely a result of her family, relationships, and job.

I summarize the responses above to ensure that I capture Wendy's views on religious belief and practice, but she stops me to discuss her concern over religious fundamentalism: "The one thing that I do really feel quite strongly about is the fundamentalism that I see developing around the world in our own culture and in other cultures, is absolutely terrifying." Elsewhere in the interview Wendy returns to this topic in the context of her children who became friends with others who belonged to the Christian organization "Young Life." Rather suddenly Wendy's daughters began attending Christian church services and this made Wendy and her husband uncomfortable for a host of reasons:

> Both my daughters went to Young Life and the younger one took it very seriously. So seriously that I was actually quite concerned and so started attending then. I was feeling probably the opposite of what I should be going to church for. I was feeling very protective ... I didn't like the church that she was going to ... It was totally foreign to the kind of church I had gone to. More modern, standing up ... It was different yeah, and it frightened me actually. It felt cult-like, and so that really scared me ... The blind worshipping was, to me ... you can believe whatever you want but always keep your mind open, asking questions. As soon as anybody says to you, don't ask, just obey, that to me is a huge warning sign just to back away from that. It seemed to me that it was a whole lot of just worship ... There was no critical thinking in it, no understanding of why this was a group of teenage kids who were, at that time, you know, they're trying to figure out who they are, what they are, and it seemed to take advantage of that in not a good way.

Wendy continues to unpack this experience, sharing her husband's hesitation toward their daughters' experience: "He was really offended when, during the Young Life thing somebody had said, 'you know, it's too bad your parents aren't Christian,' and he was really offended at that." Wendy's exposure to Young Life through her children tainted her view toward religious groups, views that would only intensify during our interview. Several religious nones express similar caution, and sometimes hatred, toward the deeply religious who religious nones believe are highly exclusive, intolerant, and "backward" in their thinking, sometimes using "cult" or "brainwashing" language to describe such groups. Incidentally Wendy and many other religious nones identify "open mindedness" as the greatest gain for being non-religious. They value not being tied to strict regimented beliefs handed down from a religious group that limit one's capacity to think openly and freely for themselves.

Thinking ahead Wendy does not envision a time when she might consider becoming more religious, joining a religious group, or attending religious services. She is fairly confident with her current view on religion and life in general and surrounds herself with those who think similarly about the world as she does.

CHRISTOPHER REARDEN

Christopher Rearden is in his early 40s and is married with two children. He holds a Bachelor of Fine Arts degree and has moved from job to job since finishing university. Asked if he feels settled in his current job, which he has held for five years, Christopher responds, "I've never felt settled." I probe to see if he is comfortable with this unsettledness: "It creates tension sometimes, but for the most part I think you get used to dealing with it."

Raised in a devout Mormon family, Christopher has four sisters. His father was a schoolteacher and his mom stayed at home to raise the children and look after the home. His family attended weekly religious services as well as mid-week church events, they prayed together in the home on a regular basis, and above all, they always sought to take care of each other. Family was the most important thing in the world. He recalls that he "had pretty strict morals growing up. You don't drink, you don't smoke ... all the typical ones that people recite." Such values did not bother him as a child, but as he developed awareness that there were other views in the world different than what his family taught, Christopher began to question his religion: "I went through a whole period of looking at a lot of different religions ... I just found that there was limitations, that there was a lot of conflict in the world between ... There was always arguing between religions. I'm just like, 'this makes no sense.'" He goes on to say that "my parents were pretty open to like, if I would say 'look, I'm interested in going to see what the Catholics do,' they're like, 'oh okay, so and so wants to take you' ... They were never like, 'absolutely not!' They were like, 'yeah sure! Go ahead, check it out,' which I appreciate cause I was like the person who was like, yeah if you wanna go challenge something, go do it. If you really believe that you're 'right' then you should be able to put it out there, challenge it, or test it." Amidst his exploration into different religions he notes different weddings or funerals that his family attended and his parents speaking condescendingly in those settings toward those who were not Mormon. This bothered Christopher because of the exclusivity attached to Mormonism (and later a value that he attached to many religions).

Christopher's quest to resolve his questions about religion continued when he started to spend his summers at art school in New York. The combination of space away from his family alongside new friends who encouraged open exploration into all sorts of belief systems helped to give Christopher the confidence to patiently examine his Mormon roots in greater detail. When reflecting on his new social environment he says: "I was like 'I'm going to go back and check out the religion I was raised in,' and they were kind of like, 'great. Go do it.' And then you'd come back and tell them what you thought and the whole time you think you're talking against some greater truth, they're really smart people. They're just like, 'well you're having your inner dialogue. You're discovering yourself,' and they always supported those kinds of things ... it was obviously for me, a great, unjudging environment to go through that. Kind of like a neutral, supportive place to sort out what I was going through."

On careful reflection of his experiences at the Mormon Church in New York Christopher comments on several aspects of the faith that did not add up for him:

> One summer I went and on my own accord I spend my Sundays going to the Mormon Church in New York. And then there just came a point when I was like, even when I'm left to my own devices I don't buy into this. I mean I think it's great that people get together and they worship but what are they worshipping? That's the problem for me, like what are you actually getting at? You seem really confident to tell me who this, or how this thing

works. I don't think you're any different than I am. You were born the same way I was. You were given some experiences and there's a lot of unknown that's never addressed. There's always an answer for things, there's never like, we don't know. No one ever says I don't know. They always have an answer. That's not the way like works in anything. I learn something new, I don't know. I go ask questions.

Christopher continues:

Another reason why I was not really interested in religion was cause it was like, you're making the wrong decision and in the next life you're gonna suffer for it. I'm like, you're gonna be out of your mind! What am I going to suffer for? I'm suffering for nothing. But that use of fear seems to be a common ... Whether it's identified by people in their own religions, fear is always a great motivator. It seems to be utilized a fair bit within religion. Inevitably you have to come to terms with how much you believe and if you're going to buy into the idea that there is something after this, and if you do ... It's so easy though cause when it's unknown ... There's this great unknown, something says, well you're gonna perish in like hellfire. That seems to be passé you know. In a lot of ways, we've made the devil into a character. What is it? I think people go into their own fear and then ... The fear of the unknown like you don't know. In some way I wish the focus was we don't know so let's go from that standpoint. We don't know as opposed to we do know.

This questioning process over a prolonged period of time, starting in his youth, culminated in Christopher making a conscious decision to no longer identify as Mormon or to attend Mormon services.

As with many others that I interviewed who left their religious upbringing, this decision created a level of separation between Christopher and his family: "Any parents who believe ... They still hold hope. 'I just hope that they can find the truth despite' ... there was always like an unspoken sorrow. But just like, 'hmm, wouldn't it be nice. I sure hope he's gonna do okay in the next life,' and that stuff, I just don't buy into it."

At present Christopher identifies himself as a religious none yet he resists this as a box that ought to define him. Rather, he thinks about his various exposures to and explorations of different religions over time that feeds into his current being. For instance, he believes there is some spiritual force beyond us on earth that binds all humans together, he occasionally prays to this spiritual force (but struggles to articulate the nature of such exchanges), and he believes there is an afterlife. He is unsure about what the next life might look like, though he emphasizes that focusing on this life is far more important. As for what is required to obtain the afterlife, Christopher replies, "I don't think there's something you have to do in this life to be in the next existence." I clarify, "Everyone carries on?" "Yeah" Christopher responds.

Christopher was married in a backyard without any religious or spiritual elements, though he describes "God's planet" as the "biggest spiritual building." He has no intentions for his funeral to have any religious or spiritual components. When it comes to raising his children Christopher proactively encourages his children to remain open-minded and to explore all kinds of religious and belief systems. For example, both sets of grandparents are of a different faith. Christopher is fine with his children learning about those faiths from their grandparents. His children also interact with friends at school from different religious backgrounds. Here too Christopher invites his children to learn about the different faith traditions. At the end of the day he wants his children to be well informed about the religious options available in order to make decisions for themselves as to whether or not they will be religious. He concludes, "they're exposed to it and they're encouraged to follow their hearts and souls." Like Wendy Yandle, Christopher values the freedom of open-mindedness that comes with not being tied to a religious group or a definitive all-encompassing religious belief system.

For Christopher the trade-off for not identifying with or participating in a religious group is the community that active affiliates tend to experience in their religious group. For some religious nones (and marginal affiliates) being part of a community is a genuine desire that they do not believe is currently fulfilled elsewhere in their life. Others acknowledge that this absence of community could be interpreted as a trade-off, but this does not trouble them as they experience community in other social settings. On this subject, and in a tongue-in-cheek manner, Christopher says, "I've learned some practical things like a support network, but I mean, we find those in friends. When you're part of a church you can use that guilt like, 'listen, I've got to get this job done, can you watch my kids tonight?' And they'll do it cause they don't wanna go to hell. Whereas my neighbour will be like, 'I can't man. I've gotta watch the baseball game.'" On the surface his point about religious community is evident, yet beneath this is an important point referenced by several religious nones in this study: they are free from all forms of guilt connected to irreligious thoughts or behaviours as defined by religious groups.

Christopher and I enter into a conversation about social influences on his religious beliefs and practices, from what he reads to those he hangs out with. He does not read anything that particularly shapes his religious world view nor does he really talk about these things with his friends, but he makes a point to express his thoughts on those who wish to tell him about their faith:

> There's not a ton of people who are actually willing to sit down and talk. Lots of people are willing to sit down and tell. They come to my doors all the time. Jehovah's Witnesses comes and are like, lemme tell you. I'm like, you know what? ... I let them come in all the time and I finally said, I don't wanna be your friend anymore and they're like, what? Like I just don't wanna be your friend. You always wanna tell me stuff. I don't wanna be told stuff. I'll go talk to my dad. At least I have some sort of obligation to let him tell me stuff ... I want you to hear what I have to say. If we're gonna have a conversation it should be shared. You don't wanna share. You wanna tell cause you're afraid. You're afraid that something's gonna happen. There's a greater truth that's gonna come down upon me. That's really just a way for you to stem off their anxiety. Well if I get out there and I get active and I ring their doorbell, I try to save his life. Well, I'm doing good and I can go to heaven, then I've done my part and I can ... It's very selfishly motivated. It's always like; I'm coming to help you. No you're not. If you were coming to help me, you wouldn't come at nine o' clock in the morning. You'd let me sleep in cause you'd know that I work hard.

Christopher's sentiments repeatedly emerged during my interviews with religious nones, marginal affiliates, and even active affiliates from non-evangelical religious traditions. Akin to a pervasive Canadian narrative, my interviewees do not support a religious style that is pushed or forced on individuals, particularly in one's own personal space, their home.

To summarize, Christopher Rearden is a religious none by definition, but he holds an array of spiritual beliefs that are important to him. He is not militantly opposed to those who are religious and is quite open to people freely exploring and adopting different beliefs and practices. However, he is vigorously opposed to religious groups that stifle an individual's ability to think carefully and critically for themselves, and worse, those groups that seek to impose their values on to others.

NATHAN JENSON

Nathan Jenson is your typical religious none in Canada – male, young, and politically left leaning. He is in his 30s and works as a software developer, building on his Bachelor of Arts in Computer Science. He is not married but would like to eventually marry, potentially in a church if his spouse desires a church wedding (not his lead desire). He is 50–50 on whether he wishes to eventually have children. If he does have children he will attempt to stay "objective with the kids" when it comes to religion, for them to "keep an open mind about things. They're free to choose their own path in the end." Since Nathan does not know much about other religions he does not plan to proactively expose his children to the various religious options available, preferring a "hands off" approach because "it's not fair to push my beliefs."

During our 28-minute interview I learned that both of his parents immigrated to Canada before Nathan was born – his mom from Germany and his dad from Norway. His mom bounced around a few jobs over her career and his dad, now retired, attained a PhD in chemistry and worked as a research scientist. Nathan was not raised in a religious home nor did his family really talk about religion, aside from the rare comment from his father who identifies as an atheist. Nathan says that his dad does not direct his comments to others in the family so much as "at maybe something we heard on the news that spurred ... a thought. And then he would ... give his opinion about something ... he wasn't ... forcing anything upon us." I ask Nathan more about his father's opinions and the most that I can draw out of him is that his dad is "very scientific ... he thinks of things very logically." His dad also watches video clips online from Richard Dawkins, which Nathan watches from time to time. He finds the videos interesting and informative at times, but he is not left persuaded either way on the matters that interest Dawkins. Nevertheless,

Nathan's exposure to and thoughts about religion growing up are summarized in this statement: "I never really had a moment where I was kind of thinking of whether I should join a religion or not. That never really crossed my mind ... I recognize the ... advantages of it ... it's a community, and it ... brings people together and it's ... peaceful in many ways. But it's just not really ... who I am ... I'm not a disbeliever, but I just ... don't like to believe in things that I ... have nothing to support."

Nathan claims that his identification as a religious none is not an important identifier to how he defines himself or how he wants others to see him. He acknowledges that this position "makes me a bit ... more free ... I'm not tied down to something ... And just having an open mind ... If you're agnostic, I think you probably tend to be a bit more open-minded toward other religions and other people. Maybe not so much if you're atheist." Incidentally most of Nathan's friends are similar to him, identifying as agnostics and taking a laid back approach to religious belief and practice.

I ask Nathan if he believes in God and he replies, "I wouldn't say I don't believe in God, but I wouldn't say I believe in a God either ... if you don't know what's in that box, then why guess what's in there." His agnostic position on God carries into his beliefs about the afterlife. He is unsure if there is life after death, though if forced to choose he would lean toward "no." Some active affiliates that I interviewed think that those who do not believe in the afterlife are likely troubled by this perspective. If this is the case, Nathan is not one of the troubled souls. He suggests that his uncertainty about life after death "almost encourages me to live to the fullest."

In response to my question of whether religious beliefs and practices are primarily up to the individual to develop and foster, or things that should happen in a group or a community context, Nathan leans toward the individualist orientation. He states, "I'd say better up to the individual cause otherwise, I think you can get persuaded ... You should kind of have the freedom of choice for a while." He carries on to express that people should be presented the options if they wish, and to decide for themselves as opposed to anything that is "pushy."

As for whether religion is a positive or negative force in society, Nathan takes the middle ground. He claims that the "negative aspect of it is people get very defensive about their religion and can, well, defend to the death sometimes. Positive ... it creates a nice community of people ... it gives people something to believe in and it gives people a purpose if they don't have their own. It can get people out of a tough situation if they're having a hard time."

As Nathan acknowledges the potential benefits to religious belief and practice he is unlikely to entertain greater involvement in any religious group and he is opposed to dating someone who is actively religious because "you can get close to somebody more if they're more like you." I inquire about Nathan's overall level of confidence in his approach to religion. He states that he's "not super confident, but ... I'm confident enough not to be persuaded easily."

OPEN-MINDED AND FREE

Religious nones are straightforward and nearly unanimous in the few benefits and drawbacks that they associate with their identification and world view as religious nones. They overwhelmingly believe that by not being overly religious they are open-minded, liberated, and free, qualities they do not associate with active or marginal affiliates. Bob Kail, who is 55 years old, says, "I think it frees you up and liberates you to think about things in purely intellectual ways. It allows you to question things that you might not allow yourself to question if you were genuinely religious." James Munns grew up a practising Anglican and states, "I think I have a lot of freedom in terms of what I think and when I think ... if there's something new to think about, I am not ... confined by a certain belief structure." Laurie Stickle grew up in a Roman Catholic context and now identifies as a religious none. She reflects, "I think I'm more open to different beliefs and stuff ... since I'm not one religion, I'm open to other beliefs and stuff that way." Interview after interview I heard statements to this effect where religious nones demarcated a clear line between their open-minded approach to the world as a good thing and the closed-minded world view associated with religious individuals as bad (see Williamson and Yancey 2013). For those raised in a religious tradition who now identify as religious nones, many of their stories resonate with the positive and freeing "irreligious experience" that Stephen Bullivant (2008) characterizes is common for converts toward irreligion (as opposed to away from religion). They are filled with joy, freedom, and euphoria at the prospect of there being no God or religion, a similar joy found among religious people who believe that God does exist (also see Altemeyer and Hunsberger 1997; Wright et al. 2011; LeDrew 2012; Zuckerman 2012, 133–8).

I imagine that religious nones would struggle to agree with the strictness thesis in rational choice theory, for strictness is a notable barrier for religious nones to identify with or participate in a religion in Canada where inclusivity, tolerance, and diversity are regarded with high esteem.

The only other reward that a handful of religious nones acknowledged is time. As people attend church on a weekly basis or invest time to volunteer for their religious organization, religious nones are enjoying their extra sleep, television viewing, or time with family. In response to my question "do you gain anything by not being particularly religious," the following statements are each followed by laughter: "a couple extra hours of sleep on Sunday"; "you don't have to go to church ...You can watch football easier on Sundays"; "My Sunday's are free. Although I tell the kids ... they shouldn't shop on Sunday's because it's not fair to the people who want to go to church"; "Time. Because of my views, I think I view those hours that would be spent doing that as a waste of time. I can spend it doing something – I'm sorry – productive."

With respect to costs, two-thirds of religious nones continue to reinforce the dominant finding in earlier chapters that individuals do not associate any costs with being a religious none. The remaining interviewees, similar to Christopher Rearden, point to the community that religious adherents experience with fellow believers at church. Sonita Johnson, in her mid-30s and currently on maternity leave, states, "You can develop great friendships and a great community by attending a church. Like if you find somewhere that you really fit in with, I believe you can really find a good community ... you belong then to a group." Interviewees talk about religious communities providing a space to meet a potential spouse, for children to make friends, or to have a network of individuals who can help each other in a time of need. Rita Alexander had no religious upbringing and says, "When I hear of stories about, say how a church has gotten together and raised money to do this for this person, or this person's house ... burnt down, and so the church has taken up a cause, and ... they're helping rebuild her house or, and I think that my family and I do miss out on that community." Unlike most others that I interviewed Rita does not feel that she has this type of community in her life and believes that if she belonged to a religious group, she would have other families to hang out with. Research on apostates identifies this lost community as a drawback to their apostasy, sometimes to the point of longing for that community again (Altemeyer and Hunsberger 1997; Wright et al. 2011; Zuckerman 2012, 129–33). Some who are not particularly religious also single out community among regular attenders as a drawback of not being more religious (Madge et al. 2014, 108).

Others, representing the majority of those who discussed community as a trade-off, claim that while they do not have a religious group to provide them with community, they do experience community elsewhere or they say that the time investment in a religious group is too great for their preferences in order to receive community in return. Edwin Booth, in his mid-20s, says, "There's definitely a strong social aspect ... but I do a lot of other social things that make up for it ... I just do different things instead of church." For instance, people experience community on a sports team, through volunteer initiatives, with co-workers, or in a book club.

Finally, some religious nones who were once actively involved in a religious group, referenced that their religious friends stopped being their friends when they abandoned their religious group and faith (see Altemeyer and Hunsberger 1997, 215; Hunsberger and Altemeyer 2006; Zuckerman 2012, 70–1). Here is an exchange that I had with Martha Miles, a university student:

MARTHA: 'Cause usually what happens is the ones that are super religious don't want to be friends with me, because I'm not religious, so they kind of just cut themselves out.
JOEL: Does that bother you at all?
MARTHA: Big time, big time.
JOEL: Do you have conversations with them about that?
MARTHA: Not anymore, no.
JOEL: You just go your separate ways and stuff?
MARTHA: Yeah.
JOEL: How do they react when you voice those concerns ... that they essentially don't want to be friends with you anymore because you're not religious and they're hyper religious?
MARTHA: I can't voice my concerns because they're ... not open ... I'm not religious, so we can't be friends anymore kind of thing.
JOEL: Does that deter you in any way from ever wanting to be religious?
MARTHA: Big time, yeah, big time. It's super frustrating, because it's just like, you're a good person, I'm a good person, we have like

similar morals and similar guidelines of what we want to be. You live your life the exact same way I live my life, you know. You want to be good, be happy, whatever, but because I don't believe that there's a spaghetti monster in the sky that you know sent his firstborn son to do this and says this and everything else, I'm not allowed to be friends? Yeah it's super frustrating.

Melinda Stamkos, a mother of two in her late 20s, had no religious upbringing. She recalls, "My brother-in-law almost lost a friend, because when he first met him when they were young kids, he asked my brother-in-law if he was Christian, and when he said 'I don't think so,' he said 'I don't think we can play together anymore.'" In Christopher Rearden's vignette similar sentiments emerge from his Mormon upbringing, reinforcing that religious people who abandon social ties with relatively irreligious individuals does not sit well with religious nones and only adds fuel to their negative perceptions toward religious individuals and organizations.

THE SUPERNATURAL

What do religious nones believe about the existence of a supernatural being or force beyond the natural world? Twelve interviewees believe in some type of deity or supernatural force though few could characterize this entity or power other than to clearly distinguish it from the Christian God and to label "it" as a spiritual force or higher power. Martha Miles states, "I kind of think that he's not Christian, he's not Jewish, he's not Muslim, he's nothing ... I don't know kind of what I picture ... what it is ... at all, to be honest ... I think that we just couldn't have come out of nothing. I think that there's too many things that have happened, especially in my life and my friend's life and everything else that, you know, have happened for a reason, and you've been guided that way and...to believe that everything is just chance and coincidence." Jasper Goltz is in his early 30s, regularly attended a Catholic church growing up, and states, "I believe that something created us ... [but] in the religious form as like their God and what they picture Him as, or like it's been written to be, I don't believe in any of that." Patricia Capps, in her 60s, says, "I believe in a higher force ... I wouldn't call it God in the way that most people would define God ... I just feel like there has to be something outside of what happens on Earth. I do feel that we have a life force within us and when we die, that life force is released, and that it may or may not come back in another form." Reflecting on her exposure to the popular 2007 book *The Shack*, Carol Ward, a schoolteacher, says, "I hope it's a big black woman in the sky because that would be awesome." Carol values that a deity could possess masculine and feminine traits, very different than the conventional Christian, masculine, white God up in heaven. Yet even her phrase "I hope" suggests that she does not hold a concrete sense of who or what this divine being is. Eleanor Robbins grew up in the Anglican denomination and echoes Carol's ideas on gender: "I believe in a spiritual being. I struggle with the concept ... as it's presented by the church ... I never much understood why God had to be male or male-based."

One-third of religious nones in this study are agnostic, and they too are not that clear of what their agnosticism entails. Many are not able to self-identify as an agnostic because of their uncertainties surrounding a higher power (e.g., I asked one individual if she believed in God and she responded, "I'm not sure. I'm going to tell you the story and then you can tell me"). As we saw earlier with Nathan Jenson, "I wouldn't say I don't believe in God, but I wouldn't say I believe in a God either. So I guess ... There's nothing really specific that I've adopted ... It makes the most sense to me ... if you don't know what's in that box, then why guess what's in there." When I ask Penny Beckford, who works for an oil company, if she believes in God or a supernatural entity, she replies, "That's a hard question for me. I think ... I'm kind of on the fence. Like, I don't not believe, but it's not something that I think about regularly, and I don't ever, like, pray to God or anything like that. So I don't really think I have a yes or no answer for that."

Seven religious nones identify as atheist and they are clear about what this means to them. Christine Graham is in her mid-50s and works in health care. She validates current research on why people do not believe in God (see Hunsberger and Altemeyer 2006, 37–40; LeDrew 2013; Williamson and Yancey 2013) when she states, "I guess I'm an atheist ... I believe in science and I believe in nature ... I don't believe there's anything more than science and nature." Darryl Lawson agrees: "If someone came to me with some evidence, I'd be happy to ... to look at it. But unless and until there's that evidence, there ... I believe that there is probably not a God." Bob Kail goes into great detail to explain his atheist position: "God has many different names and different manifestations. First point is Allah,

Muhammad, God ... Everybody's got a different one in the world today, and they're killing each other because ... theirs is the right God. So from that ... philosophically ... I can't agree with it ... I'm not gonna say I believe in something and somebody's gonna disagree with me and we have to kill each other over it. That's just not the way it's gonna work." As atheists spoke with me I never once got the impression that they felt convicted or compelled to convince others to also identify as atheists. These atheists do not resemble the fundamentalist kind that some have in mind when they hear the word "atheist," and some in this study went as far as to qualify their alignment with atheism by saying that they are not like the "fundamentalist atheists like Dawkins or anything."

For religious nones who believe in the existence of something or someone beyond the material world or at least do not rule out the possibility, do they perceive the supernatural or force to be dependable or responsive, like many active affiliates claim, or are they less inclined to have a favourable response, similar to marginal affiliates? How do their personal experiences and interactions with the supernatural inform their response? On the whole religious nones do not believe that the supernatural is actively involved in the natural world. Events on earth occur because of human decisions and activities or acts of nature beyond any deity's or human's control. Keenan Bush had a Roman Catholic upbringing, but now as a religious none reflects that *if* there is a God, "I think He's given us the tools to do it ourselves." Madeline Vargas is in her late 20s and agrees: "He isn't gonna change anything. So no, I can't depend on Him." I ask her if she thinks God has an active role in the world and she responds, "no." Jasper Goltz goes into more detail saying, "I don't think He controls my daily life ... if I get cancer tomorrow, I'm not going to go and blame God ... like He didn't give me cancer ... I think it's an oddity and then it's like, something that could happen to all of us ... And then it's like, at the same time as people believe in God, they go and they're ready to blame Him on everything ... You know, it's like oh, I hurt myself, that's God's fault and, you know God doesn't have an input in it ... Just as he doesn't have input in the curing of it ...What's meant to happen will happen." Wendy Yandle says, "I certainly don't believe in God as somebody that is going to look down and ... What's the old example of ... both football players are on either side of the play and I don't think He cares ... If there is a God, I give him more credit than that." Recalling from her vignette, Wendy carries on saying, "My dad just went through heart surgery and it never occurred to me to pray." Patricia Capps concludes, "I don't feel like there's ... someone or something out there directing what happens in the world."

Religious nones and marginal affiliates are similar in their view that the supernatural is by and large not dependable or responsive, with religious nones more strongly holding this position. Their reasons for arriving at such conclusions are different. Marginal affiliates adopt a humanist world view that negates the role of the supernatural in the world or they had negative personal experiences with God that led them to conclude that God is not dependable or responsive. In contrast, religious nones do not speak about the supernatural letting them down in any way that would lead them to denounce the supernatural as dependable or responsive. Instead religious nones subscribe to a humanist orientation rooted in how they were socialized, who they interact with, what they read, and personal experiences.

THIS IS IT! LIVING MEANINGFUL LIVES ON EARTH

As is the case with active affiliates, an important function of religion is to provide people with meaning and purpose in life. Related, people turn to religion to process questions about death and the afterlife, though my findings from active affiliates and marginal affiliates are that the afterlife does not figure as prominently to individual's religious decision-making processes as Rodney Stark, Roger Finke, and Reginald Bibby might have us believe. How do religious nones approach these subjects? Do they experience meaning and purpose in life, and if so, what is the source of these things? Do they believe that there is another life beyond this one on earth, and if so, do they desire that next life? What do they think is required to obtain the afterlife?

I did not ask active affiliates to comment on religious nones other than to hypothesize at a general level why people do not attend church on a regular basis. Some, however, meandered to share their belief that the irreligious (some equated irreligion with not attending church regularly) lack meaning, purpose, and direction in life and non-religious people need to fill their "god-shaped hole." I ask religious nones if they believe that they have meaning and purpose in life and they, like Wendy Yandle, overwhelmingly tell me that they do, and the source of this is their family and friends, their job, their recreational activities, and their volunteer initiatives. They also reveal that they are not troubled by life's big questions such as what happens after we die, a finding that Phil Zuckerman (2012, 125–7) came across in his interviews too. Here is a sampling of the quotations that I received: "Well I think with my kids it's really easy. That's inherent. I love my kids. I can always look at them and I'm like, I have meaning"; "I guess maybe before I had kids I wouldn't have known what my purpose was! … Because it was kind of like, all I did was work and live … Now that I have my kids, they are my purpose in life"; "Probably family and I like the work I do"; "Meaning is how, I guess, how to contribute to the world, so I'd say yes cause my job affects other people. So I'd say I have meaning"; "It's meaning in a personal way. I mean, my life means something to me, and it means something to the people that I know, and the people who I come into contact with, and the people whose lives my behaviour affects. But I don't really believe that my life has much significance beyond the people who I have direct dealings with"; "I do on any given day. I mean, right now, I have meaning and purpose to my wife, my family, my children." As Bibby (2011) also discovers, religion is an important source of meaning and purpose for many people, but religion is only *one* of many sources of meaning and purpose. I agree with Stark, Finke, and Bibby that religion will always be with us and will not altogether disappear, however individuals are experiencing meaning and purpose in life apart from religion and they appear quite content with the alternatives. Rational choice scholars should cease to naively equate and confuse the pursuit of meaning and purpose with an unending and widespread demand for religion.

What about beliefs regarding the afterlife? Two-thirds of religious nones either do not believe in the afterlife or are unsure about what happens after they die. Gavin Gerard is in his mid-30s and works in the information technology sector. He says, "When you're dead, you're dead." James Munns proclaims, "When you're dead, you're done. Your everlasting life, which is a real thing, is the legacy that you leave to other people and to how they remember you and your good works are the things that are remembered." Bob Kail surmises, "It's something that people wanna believe because they find the prospect of death so intimidating otherwise. The idea of an afterlife sort of makes the prospect of death seem a little less traumatic. But like most of my views about religion … if I haven't seen any sort of objective evidence that there is an afterlife, I have no reason to believe that there is one." Jasper Goltz outlines a series of troubling angles to the afterlife question:

I don't believe in paradise, per se ... if all of us were to go to paradise ... there's a paradise for every one of us and then you think of billions of generations of people, well paradise will be infinity amount of people ... it doesn't make sense ... It's not functional ... And it doesn't like, if all or like, only a selected few, some religions, again religion is like, "oh, only twenty thousand of you will get to go" ... you have to fight for your way and then it's like, how come it's so limited, how come, and it's like, with twenty thousand your odds are, you're fighting trillions of billions of people, you know, but it doesn't make sense that it's so limited ... Or reincarnation, I don't know ... I think your dog and everything, like, the way the magic of like, creation, something we can't control, something that's fascinating, but that life renews itself all the time.

Then there are those who say that they are unsure about the existence of the afterlife, using phrases such as "I don't know," "I'm on the fence," "it's a mystery," or "there may be, there may not be."

One-third of religious nones believe in the afterlife or in reincarnation and they desire to "be there" when they die, wherever "there" is. Rita Alexander stresses the absence of suffering and the presence of all things good in her conception of the afterlife: "I like to think that we go to a happy place ... I don't believe in reincarnation ... But I do believe that we do go somewhere, or our spirit does anyway. And I'd like to think that it's all roses and butterflies and happy ... sometimes I kind of picture just everybody bouncing around on clouds having a good time ... And then sometimes I picture like, an identical universe to what we're living in right now, without all the bad stuff." Martha Miles reinforces some of Rita's reflections when she says, "I think heaven is just like your own personal heaven. It's just like all the people that you love are around you and they're all happy ... I kind of think that when we die, you go to that happy place, you go to the place before all the bad stuff happened, and you're surrounded by people that were good." Melinda Stamkos speaks about reincarnation: "I do believe that you do get reincarnated. I don't know if it's a choice to get reincarnated or not, but I also think that you put yourself where you think you need to go. So if, when you pass away, you think that you're going to go to heaven, you're going to go to your ideal place of heaven ... If you believe that you're going to go to hell when you die, you're going to go to your own personal hell ... I don't think that there's somebody deciding for us. I think that people judge themselves far more harshly than anybody else could every judge them ... And you're going to put your punishment the way that you see fit or your praise the way that you see fit." I ask Melinda if all people are reincarnated and she responds, "I don't know. I really don't. Personally for me, I think that I will get reincarnated, because that's what I believe ... If you don't believe in reincarnation, I don't think you'll necessarily be reincarnated ... I also think that your spiritual self is the one that decides how you're going to be reincarnated based on what they want to learn ... so if you want to learn more about the suffering of people, then you would put yourself in a harder situation. Say, for example, in our time out in ... the Middle East, or ... a starving country, or even in an abusive home or something ... You can learn about suffering that way, and when you're done learning the lesson you'll go where the next lesson that you want to learn."

What is required to obtain the afterlife? Religious nones who believe in a possible next life are similar to marginal affiliates: either people need to live good moral lives or this is an irrelevant question because all people carry on to the next life regardless of how they live their life on earth. Carol Ward frames her response against the backdrop of church attendance: "I think that if you're a good person and you treat people well, and you, like, are accepting of others beliefs and opinions and lifestyles, then I think you should get a chance to have the afterlife. Like, even if you don't go to say set church or set religion ... I don't think that necessarily everybody that goes to church is necessarily an amazing great person either ... just because you go to church doesn't mean that you're like ... I think that the way you act and treat, you behave is like more important than what you do on Sunday or Saturday." Others like Madeline Vargas believe that "bad" people will not go on to the next life – "You can't be, like, a murderer" – and as long as people avoid doing really bad things, they will obtain the afterlife. Jude Davis is in his mid-30s and works in construction and echoes Madeline when he says, "I've never done anything to break the law or criminal, never ended up in jail ... I've had ... my share of alcohol and drugs and whatnot. Never anything bad ... I don't think I've ever done anything wrong to not go there." Rita Alexander partially disagrees, saying that everyone goes on to the next life with a clean slate: "I don't really believe in a bad place, like I don't believe in sort of a hell per se ... like the molesters, and all, you know murderers and all these terrible people, I've never really thought ... I guess I would like to believe maybe that when you go, everything's erased and no one knows who you are or what you did and you get a fresh start."

Capturing the conclusions from the previous two chapters, belief in, desire for, and demand for the afterlife is not central to the religious none world view, but if people do believe in and desire life after death, being a good person is sufficient to secure the afterlife ticket. Perhaps more telling in the responses that I received from active affiliates, marginal affiliates, and religious nones is that very few have a clear conception of the afterlife. These findings verify Bibby's (2011, 170–4) recent observations about Canadian views regarding the afterlife. It remains surprising then how and why Bibby and rational choice theorists continue to essentially guarantee a place for religious belief and practice moving forward because of the supposed unending desire for the reward of life after death found in religion.

MORALITY IS COMMON SENSE

In contrast to active affiliates who largely hold a positive perspective of religion's role in society, I expected religious nones to adopt a negative view. I was surprised to discover that many religious nones are similar to marginal affiliates in their acknowledgement that religion is both a positive and a negative force in society, often referencing many of the same examples that marginal affiliates did – religion contributes in meaningful and harmless ways to individuals and communities, while it is also the source of immense strife, destruction, and pain in the world (see Madge et al. 2014). In a similar vein, religious nones mirror marginal affiliates on whether people need religion in order to be moral or ethical. Two-thirds of religious nones categorically respond "no" to this question, while the remaining third do not feel that religion is necessary yet they appreciate how and why some benefit from religious guidelines to shape their morality.

The religious none standpoint on what motivates individuals to be moral is the most instructive insight to emerge from my interviews. Religious nones are similar to active affiliates and marginal affiliates in that they believe in a moral code that ought to guide people's attitudes and behaviours, largely defined by treating people kindly and with respect and not stealing, lying, or murdering. Religious nones differ in the motivations behind their moral convictions, a point that Phil Zuckerman (2012, 123) aptly captures: "religious believers ...

felt it was wrong to steal or lie because it was bad in the eyes of God. As secular non-believers, they see stealing and lying as wrong because it causes others pain or loss, and it helps foster a world lacking in trust or concern for the well-being of others." Certainly religious people would agree with religious nones on the latter points, but it is not the lead motivation that they cite when discussing morality. This is an important distinction that religious nones make, as referenced in Christopher Rearden's narrative.

DON'T BOTHER ME AND I WON'T BOTHER YOU

I asked religious nones a series of questions about their views on and approach to the "social" side of religion, and in turn their level of confidence in their pervading world view on religion. Do they think that people should develop their religious beliefs and practices mainly on an individual level or in the context of a group? To what extent should religious groups shape people's beliefs and practices both in and outside their group? Of their closest friends, how many of them also identify as religious nones, or have relatively low levels of religiosity, and how many are nominally or actively religious? Last, I asked them about their level of confidence in the things that they believe to be true relative to religion.

Religious nones mirror marginal affiliates in their belief that people's religious beliefs and practices should develop on an individual basis rather that in the context of a group or community. They believe that people should pursue religious belief and practice on their own or if they do so in a group, which religious nones are not wholeheartedly against, then do so without harming others and, most importantly, without trying to force their religion on to others. I intended for this question to deal with the merits of individuals believing and behaving in the context of a religious group, yet religious nones immediately steered conversation toward the subject of "pushing religion on outsiders." Martha Miles states, "I think as long as it's shared in an appropriate way, there's nothing wrong with it. If it helps people deal with things, go for it, you know that's fine. Like if it's doing good, then sure, but I think that sometimes it's pushed a little bit, and that's when it's ... not good anymore." Carol Ward agrees: "I think that once that person decides they want to be part of that religious group, then that's fine, but I don't believe in soliciting religion, I don't believe in, like, propaganda around religion ... I think it should be more individual. To be honest, I really don't like when people push religion onto others. I have a really big issue with that." Rita Alexander states, "I don't believe in pursuing someone who doesn't want to be pursued ... I don't necessarily believe in ... standing on a street corner preaching to anyone who walks by ... I believe if this is something that I want, I would go to that person ... to that group." Jasper Goltz adamantly communicates, "I guess like, what bothers me with religion the most is like, why can't you believe quietly? How come it has to be so pushy, how come you have to convert everybody? ... How can you be so aggressive?"

Religious nones do not like it when others force their faith on to others, and they do not have a desire to spread their world view to others either. Hunsberger and Altemeyer (2006, 69–71) show that Canadian atheists, though not synonymous with religious nones, do not feel the need to share their world view with others – a stark contrast from their atheist counterparts in the United States. This observation of a latent religious none identity is not surprising when considering the pervading Canadian emphasis on individualism, pluralism, diversity, and tolerance. Canadians strongly support an individual's right to believe and behave as they want so long as they do not harm others and they do not impose their values on to others. The irony of this position is that Canadians (including the law, media, and political governance system) impose this view on others who are not as tolerant, breeding a level of intolerance toward intolerance in the process.

What about their close friends? Who do religious nones associate with? With the exception of a few interviewees, nearly all religious nones exclusively associate with others who are not at all religious. Religious nones are quick to point out that they do not actively seek out friendships with people who are not religious or avoid those who are religious. It is just by chance that they are close friends with those who also are not that religious. Further to this fact several say that they do not talk about religion with their peers and thus they assume that their friends are not religious. Laurie Steckles says, "The people that I am friends with ... we don't talk about religion." Patricia Capps states, "I don't think any of them have much of an affiliation. We've never really talked about it, so to me, that just shows that it's not big ... in their life." Jude Davis struggles to answer: "I honestly couldn't answer that because I've never asked them what their religions are. Don't really know a lot about their religious backgrounds."

Religious nones tend to associate with other religious nones, yet they favour an individualist approach to matters of faith and none are part of a "secular church" (e.g., The Sunday Assembly, which launched in London, England, in 2013, has spawned dozens of secular church "plants" around the world including Canada) nor do they desire to be. Still, religious none views on religion are situated in a deeply social context: they are in social settings with people who are not particularly religious and several casually read literature that encourages secular world views, which inform their perspectives on religion. With respect to their social ties religious nones do not debate or discuss their views on religion with others, but the absence of conversation about religion seems to reinforce the dominant view that religion is not important to them, others, or society. Though we did not talk about this directly in our interviews I suspect that religious nones' approach to religion is strongly reinforced and strengthened from public discourse throughout Canadian society, including in the news, movies, books, music, politics, or education that they consume. That is to say, the pervading Canadian cultural ideal toward individualism, tolerance, pluralism, and diversity is so steeped in Canadian consciousness and institutional life that religious nones do not need to regularly gather with other like-minded religious nones because these growing Canadian values are taking a hold of Canadians in all kinds of cultural contexts. For example, attempts to ban religious symbols in public (e.g., in Quebec) or to limit public religious expressions in the school system or in the media reflect the Canadian effort to remain inclusive of all religious beliefs. Yet make no mistake, such efforts equally communicate and endorse (perhaps unintentionally) a secular preference and orientation among the Canadian public. Returning to Berger and Bruce's ideas on secularization, none of these developments are surprising when one considers the logical implications of societal secularization, and social and structural differentiation in particular that set the wheels in motion for privatized religion as a cherished social and cultural value.

If it is true that religious nones are situated in a social context that affirms and enhances their perspective on religion, then in line with Stark and Finke's assumptions regarding confidence in the religious explanations that one holds to be true, I expect religious nones to be confident in their approach to religion. Not as many religious nones show as high a level of confidence as active affiliates do (28 active affiliates are highly confident), but most religious nones are very confident in their views on religion – more so than marginal affiliates. Interviewees say, "How confident does a person have to be? I don't think ... I could be more confident"; "About as confident as I can be." As confident as religious nones are, they are not closed to the possibility that their views could change with time, mainly if new evidence emerges to show them something different about religion. Laurie Steckles says, "I'd say with my knowledge base, I'd say very confident. I'm willing to change if I ... learn different things or whatever. But I think I'm pretty confident in them." Bob Kail declares, "Extremely confident ... But I'm always open ... I'm not so set in my ways that I won't, at some point, examine anything I believe in light of the evidence. But without the evidence, I'm convinced." Similarly, Martha Miles says, "Super confident ... I'm really open into listening to other viewpoints and things like that, but I think that for myself I'm very strong because I have always been so open to it." Akin to Hunsberger and Altemeyer's (2006, 62–3, 92) observations that Canadian atheists are not as dogmatic as American atheists or Canadian or American fundamentalists, Wendy Yandle reflects that she is very confident, but "I always have questions. I'm always willing to talk about it. It's a topic I'm interested in discussing, obviously, I'm here. So no, I'm not dogmatic."

Indicative of their individualist approach to this subject religious nones are swift to note that their confidence is based strictly on their approach to religion, not a belief that their approach is necessarily the right one for all people in all times and places. James Munns states, "I'm very confident about it ... [but] I don't think I'm ... better or ... that I'm right and they're wrong. I'm just saying that this is what I believe." Angela Balmer agrees: "They're right for me. But that doesn't necessarily mean they're right for everybody, like there are, obviously many people that find comfort in faith and things like that and that's right for them, it's just not right for me. So, I don't really think there's one answer."

MY AIRPLANE BUDDY, MIKE

Last year I was on a flight in Canada, finalizing material on religious nones for a conference presentation the following morning. As the plane descended and I put away my computer the male in his early 30s beside me, who I will call "Mike," leans over and comments that it looks like I am giving a presentation on religion. I affirm his observation, intending to keep to myself for the remaining minutes of the flight. Mike proceeds to ask if I am aware that religion is a very controversial topic, one that should not be part of public conversation. Again I acknowledge his remarks. Then he proceeds, unsolicited, to share his views on religion. Mike does not consider himself a religious person. He expresses that his wife is moderately religious and when they visit his in-laws, who are fairly religious, the expectation is to say grace prior to eating. This religious ritual is not Mike's preferred course of action, but he understands that this is not his home and thus he respects their religious beliefs. Mike then shares that when his in-laws visit his home they expect to say grace before meals. This bothers Mike because he believes that they ought to respect his approach to religion when in his private home, which he justifies as the "Canadian thing to do." Instead his in-laws impose their religion on Mike and his family, which irks Mike and partially contributes to why he has no intention of becoming religious in the future.

In my brief conversation with Mike I quickly recognize a mirror reflection of the core values that religious nones in my sample hold, as diverse as their religious/secular beliefs and practices are. They believe that they are more open-minded and freethinking than active and marginal affiliates. Those like Wendy Yandle, Christopher Rearden, and Nathan Jenson oppose exclusive religious beliefs and practices on grounds of narrow-mindedness and intolerance that they believe contravene fundamental Canadian (and human) values and rights. At the same time, religious nones respect an individual's right to believe and behave as they wish so long as they do not impose their way of life on to others. In other words, religion is a private matter. Religious nones are not passionate about their identity, to convince others to become religious nones, or to gather with others who share a similar world view in order to reinforce that perspective. Herein lay one of the major differences between religious nones in Canada versus the United States. Religious nones in this study do not perceive or experience intolerance toward them; it is okay to not be religious in Canada, and it is even preferable. This is not the reason why religious none interviewees do not participate in formal "secular" communities akin to religious groups, but not seeing themselves as a cultural minority in Canada certainly alleviates the felt need to organize and lobby against other Canadians for greater social respect and acceptance. As religious nones feel free from religion, they also respect others who wish to remain free from their point of view.

5

Dwindling Demand: Stop Blaming Churches

I am regularly invited to speak with church leaders across Canada about active affiliates, marginal affiliates, and religious nones. Groups are generally interested in how Canadian society is changing or remaining the same and the dialectical relationship between culture and religious belief and practice in the twenty-first century. A particular interest for groups is why people are leaving the church and what it will take to bring them back. What can they do to improve their supply of religion? I can immediately tell that many of their inquiries are informed by rational choice assumptions of an unending demand for things that religion offers (e.g., meaning and purpose in life, life after death), a supposed "God shaped hole" that exists in everyone, and that if religious groups can simply figure out the five steps to bringing people back to church, then a religious renaissance of sorts is likely on the horizon.

Many of these questions, assumptions, and interests intrigue sociologists of religion too. I am interested in the meanings and processes at work among the 80% of marginal affiliates and religious nones in this sample who once identified with and were actively involved in a religious group. What contributed to diminished religious involvement and in the case of religious nones, completely abandoning religious identification? Building on rational choice theory, did they leave primarily because of faulty "supply" or lack of "demand"? What is the likelihood that marginal affiliates or religious nones might pursue greater involvement in a religious group in the future, and if there is openness to doing so, what would make greater involvement worthwhile? Here too I give attention to whether "supply" or "demand" variables are predominantly at work. Also, how do marginal affiliates and religious nones approach (or plan to approach) religious socialization with their children, and what might their responses reveal regarding the possible trajectory for religious belief and practice among those not actively involved in a religious group?

WHY THE DEPARTURE?

Setting the Context

Why do people turn away from their religious identification, involvement, or both, or as Stephen Bullivant (2008, 12) frames it positively, turn toward something else? Countless explanations are given in the literature that range from resisting religious strictness and exclusiveness to intellectual disagreements with religious doctrine to hypocrisy in religious settings to tension with others in a religious group to changing social ties to negative experiences with God. Rarely is any single factor at work nor is diminished religious involvement or identification typically a sudden occurrence (see Jamieson 2002; Bullivant 2008). Among the nearly twenty reasons given during my interviews I focus on the eight most cited and sometimes overlapping explanations to arise among the 48 marginal affiliates and religious nones who reduced or abandoned involvement in a religious group, and in many cases, to set aside religious affiliation altogether. These include the belief that religion is too exclusive, a life transition, parents who give the choice to attend, people are too busy, religious scandals and hypocrisy, intellectual disagreements, bad personal experiences with others in a religious group, and social influences that discourage or detract from religious involvement. In turn these explanations also inhibit increased involvement in a religious group in the future (see Bibby 2012, 97–8).

Apostasy refers to a defection or disaffiliation from a religious group or set of religious beliefs (Zuckerman 2012, 4–5). Marginal affiliates are not technically apostates, though Phil Zuckerman's (2012, 5–7) apostasy typology, distinguishing between the timing, depth, and severity of one's apostasy, is useful for exploring and interpreting what surrounds diminished religious involvement. Zuckerman begins by comparing early and late apostasy. Early apostasy refers to those raised in a religious home but who abandon their faith as soon as they are given the freedom to do so as a teenager or young adult. Late apostasy denotes those who consciously take up a religious faith in their adult life and later turn their back on that faith. Zuckerman also differentiates between shallow and deep apostasy. Shallow apostasy includes those who reject their faith but who still hold on to fragments of their spiritual and religious life, not altogether committing to secularity. Deep apostasy involves those who completely abandon all forms and expressions of religious life, totally adopting a secular orientation to the world. Finally, Zuckerman separates mild from transformative apostasy. Mild apostasy entails that apostates were not overly religious in the first place, while transformative apostasy means that apostates were deeply religious prior to leaving their faith behind.

Early, shallow, and mild apostasy is the most common among 22 of my interviewees (13 marginal affiliates and 9 religious nones). This is followed by late, shallow, and transformative apostasy, evident in thirteen interviewees (12 marginal affiliates and 1 religious none), and early, deep, and transforming apostasy among 6 religious nones. A handful of individuals experienced early, deep, and mild apostasy (3 religious nones), early, shallow, and transforming apostasy (2 marginal affiliates and 1 religious none), or late, shallow, and mild apostasy (1 marginal affiliate).

Three initial observations materialize from these data. First, the majority who left most of their religion behind at the soonest possible opportunity (i.e., early apostasy) is not surprising given that they did not see themselves as overly religious to begin with (i.e., mild apostasy). This is largely attributed to minimal religious socialization and reinforcement in the home. Sometimes parents do not attend religious services with their children, parents do not believe or practice themselves, or they give their children the option to attend religious services on reaching their teenage years. These variables set the conditions for religion to matter little to individuals and ultimately to set aside their regular involvement or identification with a religious group. Second, I would expect to find deep apostasy concentrated among Canadians raised in conservative religious homes, against the backdrop of a liberal and tolerant Canadian society. The reaction against religion in these circumstances is a reflection of newly acquired values and beliefs (e.g., science, belief in individualism and pluralism) that individuals believe stand in stark contrast with attitudes and behaviours that they were raised with in their religious tradition. Third, those who set aside their religion later in life understandably had a deeper commitment to their faith, thus apostasy was a far more transformative experience compared to early, shallow, and mild apostates. In these circumstances people's negative reactions and experiences with religious doctrine, behaviours, and other religious people contribute to a visceral reaction away from religious involvement or identification.

Reject Exclusivity

In line with the guiding thesis of this book, the leading reason for why interviewees set aside religious involvement or affiliation altogether is because they believe religious groups adopt attitudes and behaviours that are too exclusive and that separate "us" from "them" (see, e.g., Dudley 1978; Rauff 1979; Perry et al. 1980, 395; Altemeyer and Hunsberger 1997; Roof 1999, 231–2; Dillon and Wink 2007, 34; Putnam and Campbell 2010; Zuckerman 2012, 25; Bengtson et al. 2013). Exclusivity is a factor for nineteen interviewees (12 marginal affiliates and 7 religious nones) such as Rose Eskin in chapter 3 and Wendy Yandle and Christopher Rearden in chapter 4. Many of those I interviewed hold this position because they were raised in staunchly conservative religious homes and eventually rebelled against their strict religious heritage, or because they find themselves as adults with a greater appreciation for Canadian values of inclusiveness and tolerance that they do not see a place for religious exclusivity in society. These views extend beyond Christianity too. Beyer (2013a) shows that some Muslims in Canada who emigrated from totalitarian nations such as Iran similarly left their faith, in response to religious strictness, extremism, and exclusivity.

Heightened support for societal-wide inclusiveness over and against religious exclusivity aligns with what Peter Berger and Steve Bruce anticipated with structural and societal differentiation and social and religious pluralism. The multiculturalism policy and ethos that undergirds a highly modern, urban, and educated Canadian society entails that ordinary Canadians constantly confront people and ideas and behaviours that are different from their own. Interviewees talked about how their views on various issues had been challenged based on interactions in their neighbourhood, workplace, school, or business dealings with people of a different socioeconomic status, educational rank, race and ethnicity, religion, or political viewpoint (also see Putnam and Campbell 2010). Marginal affiliates and religious nones express how education opened their eyes to other ways to view and experience the world, magnified in a globalized era where technology and media continuously bombard the senses with knowledge and insight into all kinds of perspectives. Nancy Nason-Clark and Cathy Holtman (2013, 163) similarly document how Hindu women in Canada point to high school and university courses opening their eyes to world religions, in many cases "eroding their Hindu identities." Kathryn Carrière (2013) offers an excellent exposition into Muslim, Hindu, and Buddhist lived realities in Toronto, Canada's most religiously and socially diverse city. She provides countless examples of how and where individuals inevitably and constantly rub shoulders with people who think differently about the world that in turn changes how Canadian Muslims, Hindus, and Buddhists view and experience the world. Some marginal affiliates and religious nones cannot reconcile how and why exclusive religious beliefs and practices should persist in a cultural milieu dominated by religious, ethnic, gender, age, socioeconomic, and sexual orientation diversity. For these individuals religion functions as a divisive rather than unifying force in society.

To this end several speak about Roman Catholics, evangelical Protestants, Mormons, Jehovah's Witnesses, and Muslims, and their strict views on salvation, freedom of thought, or sexuality (e.g., when someone is allowed to have sex, with whom they can have sex, birth control use, as well as constricting views on homosexuality). These are identified as push factors away from one's religion and hurdles if interviewee's are to ever consider pursuing affiliation or involvement in a religious group again (see Altemeyer and Hunsberger 1997; Kosmin and Keysar 2006, 60–1; Kosmin and Keysar 2007, 21; Zuckerman 2012, 56–87). Zuckerman (2012, 79, 83) captures apostates' thoughts on sexuality in the following way:

> While they were religious, they saw their own sexual desires as unclean, unnatural, immoral. They had been raised to feel shame about having sexual fantasies and to feel guilty about masturbating. And they were socialized to repress their sexual urges until marriage. Premarital sex was a despicable affront to God that could adversely affect the state of one's eternal soul. It was intrinsically sinful and to be avoided – at all costs ... And it is just this narrow and essentially unrealistic conception of human sexuality that many apostates simply cannot abide. For them,

sex prior to or outside of heterosexual marriage is not only inevitable but something to be celebrated. And they harbor varying degrees of resentment toward those, be they parents or preachers, who taught them otherwise. Their rejection of religion was intimately linked to the pain they experienced during their prolonged attempts to suppress their natural sexual urges.

Perceptions of restrictiveness extend into areas of drinking alcohol, dancing, how one dresses, and who one can and cannot be friends with. Interviewees are also disgusted with exclusive views about women in church leadership, women's roles in the home, and abortion. Michael Conrad, in his early 70s, who is marginally affiliated with the Roman Catholic Church repeatedly discusses strict views toward women in religious groups: "Women make up over fifty percent of the world and still they have no say? … And so why would you exclude them … in the Catholic Church and a lot of other – like, you take the Mormons and all that – they're still … in a way, they still can't vote in the church, so they're non-entities … and then you go back to the Muslims. Well, they're totally shut down, there. The women. And I think … to make the world run, we need them both."

Others that I spoke with are upset with self-righteous attitudes among Christians. They disagree with groups that claim to have an exclusive hold on truth, that their way of thinking about God, humanity, or the afterlife is the only acceptable perspective. Emily Foster laments, "I think that some religions – and, I would say, especially Catholicism – you're either in the box or you're out." Jasper Goltz adamantly argues, "that's another one … if you're a Muslim you can't marry … like what the hell not, like what makes me not good enough anymore? Just because I'm not in the same religion." Several cite wars over the course of history as evidence of oppressiveness among strict religious groups, most recently evidenced in the Christian Right in the United States and Islamic extremism worldwide. Combined, these examples of strictness are enough to push and keep marginal affiliates and religious nones away from organized religion, particularly when some believe that they can experience and contact God outside the churches without trained specialists holding their hands along the way. At the same time, maybe ironically, marginal affiliates want trained religious leaders to be available and offer guidance for important religious holidays and rites of passage (see Roof 1999, 234).

Life Transition

The second main reason people fall away from their faith (fifteen marginal affiliates and four religious nones) is because of some transition in their life, including their family moving locations for work, a divorce in the family, leaving home for university, or the death of a parent (see Hadaway and Roof 1979, 199; Rauff 1979; Roozen 1980, 430; Wilson and Sherkat 1994; Sherkat and Wilson 1995, 1004; Stolzenberg et al. 1995; Dillon and Wink 2007; Wuthnow 2007; Smith and Snell 2009; Penner et al. 2011; Bengtson et al. 2013). Some speak about their families moving locations during their childhood years and not finding the "right" church in the new city, not knowing other people to attend church with, or not finding a church in their neighbourhood. Martha Bergen, a Roman Catholic marginal affiliate in her 50s, recalls: "my husband and I moved to a different area of town, so we went to the one that was closer to us. And it just happened to be a different sort of set up. It was still a Catholic church but much more … modern … as far as worship goes. The songs were more upbeat, not traditional church songs." I ask her if she enjoyed the different music and she replies, "Yeah. I did, for awhile … I thought it was nice to see that people could be that open. I see it a little bit differently now because after I stopped going, I went back a few times, and I'd think, 'Ooh, strange.'"

Others share about leaving their church attendance behind when they moved out of their parents place, often for university. Mary Ensworth, a Roman Catholic marginal affiliate, says, "I didn't even think about going to church … never even crossed my mind." Janet Shields, a religious none, reflects, "I went to university away from home … I was into my own life. Weekends became more about studying and working and I think, probably, if I had gone to church … I'm just thinking of the people I was living with … it would have been seen as the anomaly, and of course, you don't really want to stand out and really want to be accepted, like I did, as part of the group … but I don't think it ever occurred to me to go." Vicky Lewis, in her mid-20s, and a conservative Protestant marginal affiliate, says, "When I moved … to do college … I didn't really know anybody … I think it's different. Like, in Victoria, it was, like, my group of friends, and we would go, and it was sort of … not necessarily a social thing, but … to go by yourself is … less appealing … just went less and less frequently … and my friends didn't seem to have any interest in it. I no longer lived at home, so the rule was with my mother that if you lived at home, you went to church. And so, when I left home, there was no longer any compelling force." Diana McEwan, in her late 50s and tied to the United Church of Canada, recalls, "as a young person leaving home, you sort of break out on your own ... different lifestyle as a young person ... a small town girl in a big city ... we lived downtown and the United church was the closest church but, it wasn't that easy to get to because we didn't drive and didn't have a car." Donna Wick states, "I think my real ... breakaway from that was when I did move down to the US because I was able to choose what I was doing on my Sundays ... It was now my life, I'm living on my own in another country where I don't have my mother's guilt trip kind of on my shoulders so I would go every once and awhile but I'd say, like, maybe two times in a year, kind of thing. I never found a church where I went to university that I felt comfortable at. None of my teammates or friends went and so you just feel like you're sitting in the back of a church by yourself and not really connecting."

For some, their parent or grandparent died, the one mainly responsible for taking those I interviewed to church during their childhood years, and this facilitated diminished levels of involvement afterwards. Roger Steinberg, a religious none in his 40s shares that when his father passed away when Roger was in his early teens, his mom was left to care for six children on her own. Beyond the sheer busyness associated with living in a single parent home, Roger states, "When my dad was alive we attended a lot more. It was kind of mandatory in our family to go to church. After he passed away, by that time it was really up to us if we went or not." For others the loss of a family member facilitated questioning and skepticism toward God and religion that resulted in diminished church involvement or religious affiliation altogether. Rosemary Fleury, a widow in her 70s, is a marginal affiliate connected to the United Church of Canada. In response to my question of whether she currently attends religious services, she says, "I haven't for a very long time. No. I had a very difficult time after my husband ... died in an accident ... I just had a very difficult time ... for a while I thought I was angry at God." I ask Rosemary if she thinks God was responsible for her husband's passing. She replies, "I think that's what I felt at first, but ... you can't blame everything on God ... I think it just hit me ... really difficult because my father had died three weeks before and my husband died and it was just like ... wow. Why did this happen?" The combination of grief and anger along with no longer having a close family member to attend church with contributed to Rosemary reducing her church involvement. Rosemary's experience is akin to various misfortunes (e.g., death, divorce, job loss) that at times contributes to people leaving behind their faith (see, e.g., Jamieson 2002; Kinnaman 2011; Wright et al. 2011; Zuckerman 2012, 40–55). Yet as noted in chapter 2, active affiliates also experience these misfortunes but their sacred canopy appears to be more solidly in place, grounded in a social narrative (e.g., church leader's sermons, biblical readings, extracurricular religious readings) that explains and justifies such misfortunes in a way that they do not question God, their faith, or those in their religious group to the degree that former active affiliates do.

Teenage Choice

Third, religious decline occurs because parents give their teenage children the option to attend church. Bengtson et al. (2013) recently documented this reality, and Roozen (1980, 434–7) suggests choice is a leading explanation for why so many people leave their faith at the first opportunity. Seventeen interviewees (6 marginal affiliates and 11 religious nones) reveal that their parents gave them the option to stop attending when they reached teenage years or they gave their own children the option to attend, which led to diminished religious involvement or affiliation. Tim Davis, who is 51 years old, recalls that "as we got into our mid to late teens, we were sort of just let loose to decide what we wanted to do … keep going if you want. Nobody's forcing you to be there. Go find another religion if that's what you want to do." Peter Johnston, who is 48 years old, says that he first stopped attending because of the absence of "the driving force of … my mother trying to get us to go. And once … we hit teenage years, I think she pretty much left it up to us to decide … we weren't forced, like, 'You have to go to church every Sunday' … she left the decision up to us. And I guess I just didn't find it relevant enough." Similarly, some participants who are parents themselves stopped attending when their own children complained about going to church. Greg Rocket says, "We got tired of fighting the kids to go to church. That's not an excuse, I guess, but it's a fact." Abby Olson speaks about her children: "For about three months before I stopped going, they would just sit there not even looking up. They'd just kind of sit there … like they were bored out of their skulls. And I thought, 'Well, I could go by myself, or I could just not go.' It just kind of fell apart after that."

Regardless of faith background, evidence overwhelmingly supports that religious socialization in the home is the greatest predictor of whether children will be religious as adults, and the degree to which this is the case (see, e.g., Sandomirsky and Wilson 1990; Sherkat and Wilson 1995, 1005; Myers 1996, 864–5; Altemeyer and Hunsberger 1997; Dudley 1999, 118–19; Jamieson 2002, 12–13; Sherkat 2003; Dillon and Wink 2007; Wuthnow 2007; Kosmin and Keysar 2008; Beyer and Martin 2010; Voas 2010; Warner and Williams 2010; Penner et al. 2011; Bengtson et al. 2013). When parents share the same faith, they are more likely to pass on their faith to their children than those who do not share the same faith background, and children are more likely to be religious themselves in turn. Young people are prone to maintain the faith when their parents are actively involved in their religious group, when parents bring their children to religious services, when young people are actively involved in their religious group and maintain personal religious practices, when they have good relationships with older mentors who are religious, and when they are given responsibilities in their religious group.

Nearly all individuals over the age of 55 that I interviewed, including active affiliates, marginal affiliates, and religious nones, recall never being given the option to attend religious services when growing up; attending church as a family was non-negotiable. Times have changed over the last half-century with less religious socialization occurring within the home (Hunsberger and Altemeyer 2006, 16; Voas 2010). Bibby (2011, 13) shows, for example, that in 2005 19% of Canadian school-aged children attended Sunday school or religious instruction classes, in contrast to 36% in 1975. Conversely, 51% of children never attended, up from 23% in 1975. This optional approach to faith is magnified in mixed faith families. In Arweck and Nesbitt's (2010) study on the growth of mixed-faith families in the United Kingdom, evidence is clear that parents in these settings are most likely to encourage their children to examine religious options for themselves and to decide on their own if or how religious they might be (also see Saha and Beyer [2013]). Lack of religious transmission in the home is an important contributor to declining levels of religiosity across cohorts in many nations throughout modern Western nations, including Canada (see, e.g., Crockett and Voas

2006; Bibby et al. 2009, 162–87; Burkimsher 2009; King-Hele 2009; Voas 2009; Pew Forum on Religion and Public Life 2010; Wilkins-Laflamme 2014).

Why the shift away from religious socialization in the home? Voas (2010) shows changing parenting values that deemphasize strict obedience and loyalty to church involvement, in turn emphasizing independence, choice, and tolerance (also see Hervieu-Léger 2006). Characteristic of broad social values of choice and individualism (see Bellah et al. 1985; Roof and McKinney 1987; Bibby 2006), parents today pride themselves on providing their children with several options to choose from and for children to identify which option(s) most appeals to them. This is best captured in the volume of extracurricular activities that children today are exposed to from ballet to hockey to swimming to art classes. Religion is not exempt from the world of childhood choice. My interview data show that parents might expose their children to religion during the child's early years, and then give their teenagers the "right" to make religious decisions for themselves rather than imposing parental or religious authority to force their children to observe certain religious practices, such as church attendance. Symptomatic of the traits that Berger and Bruce theorized are associated with societies with multiple and competing world views, parents who give teenagers choice about religious belief and practice is particularly cherished and celebrated in a diverse, pluralist, and relativist Canadian culture that is generally at odds with exclusive or absolute values and beliefs, above all religion. However, this approach is likely to contribute to failed religious transmission from one generation to the next, reinforcing past, present, and anticipated future generation over generation declines in religiosity levels.

The one caveat is that in today's pluralist and relativist social context some parents hesitate to impose religion on to their children, fearful of the unintended consequence that their children will rebel against an exclusive way of believing or behaving. This outcome is always a possibility, evident in the lead reason for marginal affiliates and religious nones to reduce their involvement or affiliation. In his discussion on the impact that rigid family backgrounds have on long term religious commitment, Wade Clark Roof (1999, 231–2) highlights that while exposure to strict parenting styles help some children to maintain their childhood conservative religious values and behaviours into their adult years, authoritative parenting can also lead to "heavy baggage resulting in resistance, if not outright rejection" of those religious values (also see Rauff 1979; Bengtson et al. 2013, 142–3). Yet Penner et al. (2011) suggest that parent-child relationships which are grounded in dialogue about religious matters rather than top-down authoritative parent-child ties are essential to buffer against the possibility that teens and young adults will rebel against their parents' faith. Others (e.g., Wilson and Sherkat 1994; Sherkat and Wilson 1995, 1005; Bengtson et al. 2013) suggest that when parents and children have a good relationship, rooted in warm and affirming parents, children are more likely to maintain strong religious belief and practice throughout their life. This finding is verified in my study: many of those who left behind their religious affiliation or diminished their religious involvement had weaker ties with their parents compared to active affiliates. Rubina Ramji (2013) shows comparable findings among Muslim apostates in Canada too.

Expressed succinctly, both choice and coercion for lack of a better term can be beneficial and/or problematic for a child's faith development. Still, if children are not exposed to faith that is modeled, practiced, and dialogued about in a loving and nurturing home, it is uncommon for people to take on religious faith later in life. As Peter Beyer (2013a, 85) expresses relative to Muslim immigrants in Canada, "religious socialization may be a necessary but not sufficient condition for religious offspring." Put simply, while coercion may contribute to people leaving the faith, religious groups will benefit far more by families who regularly expose their children to faith in the home than children who are given limited to no religious instruction and are unlikely to take up faith later in life.

Too Busy

Twelve marginal affiliates and three religious nones limited their religious involvement as they became busy with other things, a common response by many young families in today's fast-paced society with many options vying for people's attention (see Rauff 1979; Dillon and Wink 2007; Wuthnow 2007, 215; Smith and Snell 2009). Interviewees share that juggling work demands, transporting kids to different events, and tending to basic necessities on the home front such as grocery shopping or laundry squeezed out church attendance.

Extracurricular activities are a common theme to arise during my interviews. Erin Pitt, a marginal affiliate in the Lutheran church, recalls that her family attended less as her brother's hockey picked up. She says, "Hockey took precedence on the weekends ... my dad was coaching his team for a long, long time. And that was Saturdays and Sundays. It was all the time after a while ... and I played competitive soccer. We skied all the time on the weekends ... all winter, we would start skiing, and ... that took precedence. But we would always go back at Christmas and Easter and stuff ... it just didn't seem as important anymore after ... we kinda got really into activities and stuff. And then we would do family activities, and then my mom would always wanna go, but then ... she'd say, 'Well you know, we're all as a family anyway. So it's ok we're not going to church, we're all going skiing on Saturday and Sunday.' And we would just have so much fun." Similarly, Martina Connors, a Lutheran marginal affiliate in her 20s, says, "We went to church quite a bit when we were younger ... every Sunday type of thing. I think, as we got older it became more difficult for my parents to manage between sports and things like that. My sisters and I, so the three of us girls all danced competitively for years, and my brother played competitive hockey. So, we always went at Christmas, always went at Easter."

Beyond extracurricular activities, university students speak about trying to balance school, work, and personal life, and single parents share the challenges to work and care for children that it is not feasible to still attend church regularly. Even if interviewees do have spare time on Sunday, they long for a day of rest where they do not need to get dressed and leave the house yet again, or they can watch football or read a book or spend uninterrupted time with family. Without attaching any normative evaluation to such decisions, it is clear that these marginal affiliates and religious nones – and I suspect a growing segment of the Canadian population – now gives less priority to religious involvement compared with other things vying for their time. Moreover, returning to Zuckerman's apostasy typology, it seems that for these individuals, religious involvement was not too deeply important to them prior to them leaving behind their religious involvement or affiliation.

Scandals and Hypocrisy

Eight marginal affiliates and four religious nones, like Rose Eskin, Wendy Yandle, and Christopher Rearden left their religion as they witnessed and experienced scandals, hypocrisy, and inconsistencies between the teachings, words, and actions among their parents, once local congregants or religious leaders, or the church at large (see Mauss 1969; Rauff 1979; Altemeyer and Hunsberger 1997; Jamieson 2002, 29; Hunsberger and Altemeyer 2006, 54; Kinnaman 2011; Penner et al. 2011; Wright et al. 2011; Zuckerman 2012, 26, 90–4; Bengtson et al. 2013). Interviewees frequently mention religious scandals, whether priests abusing children, televangelists swindling people's money, or false claims by religious leaders to performing miracles. Some interviewees chastise religious groups for being selfish and inward looking, others point to violence and wars in the name of religion, a few critique churches for always asking for money, and several single out hypocrisy.

Jacob Hewson is in his 40s and identifies with a conservative Protestant religious group. Prior to diminishing his involvement he recollects a woman in his church who would "tell everybody about her faith, but she smokes, she swears, she doesn't drink, but ... they wouldn't let her be a church board member because she smoked ... but she's probably led more people to God than anybody else in the town." Jasmyne Court, a religious none in her 60s, recalls her younger years in Sunday school: "one of the leaders was talking about loving your fellow man. And it just irritated me. And I said, 'None of you do that here. You're all just ... selfish and we have one alcoholic who comes to church on Sunday nights. None of you sit with him. Our family goes, pays attention to him. And none of you do. And I don't understand it. And I'm leaving.' And I left." Later in the interview Jasmyne continues with her frustration with Christians: "I think a fundamentalist and evangelical, they do no questioning whatsoever, and in that way they come off, again, as superior. And I'm sorry to use that a lot ... to me, it's egotistical, superior attitude. I have someone very close to me who is ... a born again Christian ... we were just sorta chatting and I said to her, 'What is it you want out of life?' And she said, 'I want to be more Christlike.' And I said, 'And what does that mean?' And she couldn't answer. She said, 'Well, I don't really know, but I know that's what I wanna do.' And I said, 'Don't you think it's important that you know?' And I just said, 'I don't get it.' So it's platitudes and ... so often, people don't even know what the platitudes mean. It's just words. Never think it out."

When I ask Victor Chancel, a marginal affiliate in his 20s with ties to conservative Protestantism, why he diminished his involvement he quickly replies: "A lot of gossip. That's why I stopped going. A lot of people were really gossipy. Really like back-stabbing. They'd be nice to your face and then say a bunch of stuff when you weren't around." He carries on later in the interview:

> I see a lot of hypocrisy in some churches ... they have tax exempt status but there is just this extravagance. There was this 30-foot glass waterfall thing which, I did glass work, I know that didn't come cheap. It's like, there's kids starving all over the world. Couldn't that money have gone to making the world a better place instead of making a flashy church? ... It's got stores and stuff in it and that really irks me because there's the story of Jesus going into the temple and throwing out all the vendors. I don't know. I kinda find it weird that they're selling stuff inside the church. It's right there in the book of Matthew. It didn't go over so well ... It's just there's so much money going into and I think that as a church, you should be going into helping the community and helping make the world a better place. Not making a flashy temple right? I don't know how they can justify spending that much on something that really has no functional purpose and doesn't make the world a better place.

Nicholas Wallen, a religious none in his early 40s, ties religion to evil in the world: "I've read books about ... the Crusades and you see what happens in the Middle East over and over again. World War One, World War Two, it seems like all the big fights are religiously based; one religious group against another religious group or a religious against another religious group. It seems like ... it just creates tension, violence, murder, rape ... all the time ... you just see it over and over again ... and the hate that they seem to inspire, especially between the groups. Yeah, we could do without that. I really think we could."

Scandals and hypocrisy are not new, as those I interviewed attest to in their quotations. But people's awareness of the magnitude and scope of religious scandals and hypocrisy that are part of many religious groups are changing. Access to and consumption of news media, social media like twitter and facebook, and other technological mediums that bind people worldwide means that now more than ever individuals are more aware of what is taking place in the world. Individuals in Calgary know about priest abuse scandals in Italy and the United States and about religious leaders from different religions living lavishly from member donations. As these stories continue to make waves in the news, perceptions of religious groups are forever coloured, like a bad experience with a hotel or car rental company. It is and will be difficult for religious groups to shake these images, even if they make substantial changes to operate more transparently, in large part because there will always be local and international examples of religious scandals and hypocrisy scrolling across the television, appearing in the news, and popping up on facebook or twitter. This is but one implication of globalization for religious groups today.

Intellectual Disagreement

Intellectual disagreement with a religious group's beliefs and practices is another catalyst for reduced involvement and disaffiliation among 4 marginal affiliates and 8 religious nones (see Mauss 1969; Rauff 1979; Altemeyer and Hunsberger 1997; Hunsberger and Altemeyer 2006, 42; Bullivant 2008, 9; Wright et al. 2011; Zuckerman 2012, 25, 33–9). Interviewees privilege science over religion, highlight multiple and competing religious views in society, reference personal tragedies that leave some to question God's existence, and grapple to form their own understanding of religion. The result for many is "deep" apostasy in the sense that Zuckerman speaks about.

William Bird grew up in the Roman Catholic Church. Now in his early 30s he no longer identifies with any religion, in part because of tensions between religion and science: "Well the advance of science kind of ... put in question ... basically ... you need to believe in what I say and you can't question the approach of the church, and then ... the big bang theory ... what's the science behind it? And then religion tells you, don't worry about the science, just believe blindly, like you need to believe ... but explain to me the science, and it's like, don't believe in the science ... Focus on just believing, and like, do what I say ... just go with blind faith ... and then you know your questions goes unanswered ... and then ... every time the community gets dumbfounded question, it's like, have faith, and then that's the answer." William continues to discuss the challenges that religious groups have with evolution, and then succinctly concludes, "Science versus the religion ... science ... it's more mathematical ... than religion where like, you don't have proof other than the Bible, which was written how many years ago by people you don't even trust."

Jack McEwan is in his late 50s. He grew up in an Anglican church, but no longer identifies with this faith. Like William Bird, Jack struggles with the discontinuities between science and religion and he additionally points to religious diversity to explain his graduate shift away from religion. He says, "As the older you get, the more experience you have. The more people you meet, the more experiences you see. And it was just through that whole process that I really started to not see the point of identifying with any one religious group because ... there's so many of them ... So I started to say, 'Well ... there's so many ... they can all be right. They can all be wrong' ... I just can't believe that there is one, omnipotent entity that is running the show." As Peter Berger (1967) and Steve Bruce (2002) predicted in line with advances in modern Western society (see also Dudley 1979, 18–32), religious and social pluralism make it difficult for people to accept any particular set of religious beliefs as true (see Altemeyer and Hunsberger 1997; Jamieson 2002; Kinnaman 2011; Wright et al. 2011). Zuckerman (2012, 94–5) validates this in his empirical research on apostates when he says, "Just meeting, getting to know, or learning about other people who have other religious beliefs, or secular world views, can have a corrosive effect on a person's own religious convictions." This occurs because individuals begin to ask questions about why they believe what they do, they recognize that there is good to be found outside their religious tradition, and most importantly, with an awareness that world views beyond their own exist, they realize that their religious world view can no longer be taken for granted.

Personal tragedies, suffering in the world, or God's vindictiveness in Scripture over and against His apparent loving and compassionate qualities leave some to question God's existence or role in the world, and for some their need for the church at all. Norman Patterson, a Roman Catholic marginal affiliate, recounts his brother's death in a car accident at the age of 24: "When you get a phone call so early in the morning ... saying that something happened ... you do go to church after that. But then, after a while, you start questioning it: 'Why did this happen?' and 'Was there a reason for it all?' And, you know, there's no answers because ... you don't normally get answers, right? ... I kind of tapered off."

When individuals reach their teen and young adult years they also begin to formulate their own views about religion and the world and some leave their faith behind in the process. For Darren Brazzeau, a religious none in his 20s who was raised in a highly religious family in a conservative Protestant denomination, this process began in his late teen years: "I started to really have some doubts. And at first ... I wasn't too keen on asking anybody any questions. I tried to work it out for myself ... because I knew, growing up, my parents were very open about ... our questions and everything. So I knew that doubts were something that you should go through. I just felt like I could, sorta deal with them myself ... then I started to ask questions ... the more I asked ... the more doubts I started to have. I didn't really find any answers that were satisfying ... it was kind of a snowball effect, where ... I ask one question, and then ... the next night I would ask another question, and then another few questions. And my parents, I guess, probably kinda scared them because ... I was coming out with all these questions at once that I had internalized for my last few years. They might not have had any idea that I was thinking about it even." I proceed to ask Darren about the kinds of questions he was asking: "The biggest one that I had was I wanted to know what genuine religious experience felt like or ... a conversation with God or something like that cause to the best of my knowledge, I had never had one and I wanted to know why ... I wanted to know what it was like. I wanted to know ... if it was something that I could just sort of write off as ... your own subconscious playing tricks on you, or whether it was something that ... definitely couldn't be that cause it was way too real ... then after that, I started to ask questions about ... the characteristics of God and ... with that, prayer because I ... and I still have problems understanding kinda how God can be ... all-powerful and omnipotent, but still give us the opportunity to change things with prayer ... or for praying even having an effect ... those were, I guess, the two big ones." What is relatively uncommon about Darren's experience compared with many young Canadians is he dialogued about some of these questions and doubts with his parents. Most young people do not believe that they can raise their doubts and questions with their parents who are devoutly religious or in their church that they believe frowns on such activities (see Jamieson 2002, 29; Kinnaman 2011; Penner et al. 2011).

Interpersonal Tension

One-third of marginal affiliates share tensions they experienced with others in their religious group as a contributor to reduced involvement in their religious organization (see Rauff 1979; Jamieson 2002, 44). Following Zuckerman's typology, these marginal affiliates diminished their church involvement later in life and continued to maintain some semblance of religious belief and practice, but their transition was fairly transformative, having once been quite religious as adults. The tensions that marginal affiliates confronted included others in their church who offended them, church conflict along with how leaders handled (or did not handle) conflict, attempts to get involved with a church but not receiving any response from the church, and churches that did not have a welcoming atmosphere (single females like Rose Eskin in chapter 3 especially note this in religious groups led primarily by males and filled with married couples and families with children).

When people believe that their congregation is not dependable or responsive they are less likely to maintain active involvement in that group. Rose Eskin's vignette in chapter 3 reveals that she left behind her church involvement in part because her priest made several errors in her grandmother's funeral such as using wrong names, dates, and marital information among family members throughout the funeral. In chapter 3 Opal Lackey's experience of missing a few church services and being chastised by fellow church attenders for doing so, and Ronald Darling's surprising confrontation with his pastor who critiqued Ronald for not being religiously strong enough in the face of several challenging circumstances in his life reinforce how people's negative experiences with others in their church can lead to diminished involvement.

Others left because they tried to connect with a congregation after moving cities, but the church never responded to their inquiry to get involved or interviewees did not find a sense of community among local congregants. Valerie Thomas is in her 20s and identifies herself as Lutheran, but when she reached out to a local congregation after she moved away for university she says, "They never communicated back. They kind of said that they would get back to me and then nobody ever did." Similarly Abigail Locke, who is in her 30s and identifies herself with a conservative Protestant tradition, has moved around a fair bit in her adult life for school, travel, and employment. She says that in the last few years "I went from church to church to church, and just didn't feel like I connected anywhere. And tried ... at some places to go multiple times ... about ten weeks in a row, and really try to meet people. And I tried to do all the things that you're supposed to do. Fill out contact cards, and join small groups ... nothing worked. I'd fill out a contact card, and nobody would call. I'd call the church and leave a message, and nobody would call me back ... it was kind of like all the cards were stacked against me ... I just got to the point where I kinda gave up ... I felt like I was pushing, pushing, pushing, trying to find a place. And it wasn't happening, so then I just stopped trying." Soon I explore the chances that marginal affiliates and religious nones might pursue greater involvement in a religious group in the future, but from Valerie and Abigail's narratives it is clear that some are trying to get more involved and churches are letting individuals down in this quest.

Social Ties

Finally, social ties play an important role for 5 marginal affiliates and 3 religious nones. Some left their churches or religion because their friends and family grappled with religious doubts that reinforced doubts that interviewee's held, or their friends and family believed that the interviewee's involvement in a religious group was problematic (see Mauss 1969; Dudley 1979, 77; Rauff 1979; Hunsberger and Altemeyer 2006; Zuckerman 2012, 28; Bengtson et al. 2013). Ronald Darling shares, "My social group ... doesn't really allow for ... me to continue on. I'd almost have to abandon family. So you have to have a really strong belief, be it them or anybody else, any other religion ... if I wanted to be [more involved], I believe I'd have to cut ties with my family. I'd have to change my whole lifestyle, my whole life, who I am, what I am, where I come from ... I think that the group ... the life that I have, I'd have to abandon it in order to partake ... in the other thing."

Friends moving away, leaving an interviewee in a congregation without knowing other attenders is another contributor to diminished involvement. Carmen Cooley is in her 30s and says, "I don't really just want to go by myself ... when it was convenient ... and I had friends going, I would go to church." This finding resonates with the observation in chapter 2 that community and belonging with others is among the most common rewards that active affiliates associate with their church involvement. For some marginal affiliates and religious nones, losing this important reward is a serious impediment to their continued involvement in a religious group.

Other interviewees were influenced by the "wrong crowd" (their words) such that they interacted in social settings that had little value, or even antagonistic feelings, for religion. Nelson Spencer, a religious none in his 50s, recalls his later teen years the following way: "When it started to change ... I was in high school ... we would go for

Christmas service all the time ... traditionally, I would always go to my best friend's place. His mom was there. His sister was there, and all my friends were there ... none of them went to church, and they were all having beers and staying up late. And I always was the only in a suit ... I was the guy who had to leave at ten-thirty to ... go to church. And so it's one of the first times I was sort of gone like, 'What's all this about? ... Why am I doing this?'" He continues to say that eventually this led to hanging out with friends on Saturday nights, drinking beer, and not wanting to get out of bed Sunday mornings.

Religious Supply or Demand?

How do these reasons align with the theoretical debate over religious supply and demand? Are rational choice theorists and Reginald Bibby correct to assert that religious supply is the driving variable to explain levels of religious affiliation and involvement? From my data and observations I contend that supply and demand are both at work, but religious demand or the lack thereof is a more compelling explanation to account for why fewer attend religious services regularly or identify with a religious group (also see Smith 2003; Norris and Inglehart 2011).

Of the eight leading reasons offered, only two are primarily supply-side issues – religious scandals and hypocrisy, and negative experiences with others in the church. On these matters religious groups have great control to ensure that their beliefs align with their actions and that they treat people well. Religious groups that wish to improve their public image ought to give attention to these areas. At the same time congregations and denominations cannot control individual actors within the group from behaving in the aforementioned and problematic ways, let alone the global dissemination via social media and the news when groups behave poorly.

A case could be made that three of the justifications (exclusivity, intellectual disagreements, and life transitions) are both supply and demand problems, though in my estimation they are primarily demand-side matters. Religions that are perceived as highly exclusive could be interpreted as a supply problem. If groups only change their views on sexuality, gender, or the afterlife, then they would be more palatable to the masses. Perhaps this is true, though one should wonder how much of a difference this would really make on religious affiliation and involvement numbers when considering the United Church of Canada as an example. This group is positioned as one of the most liberal streams of Christianity in Canada and yet confronts a continued downward spiral in religious affiliation and involvement figures (Stirk 2010). If exclusivity was mainly a supply-side issue, stronger signs of life in the United Church of Canada should be evident.

Where some may have a case to make is in how religious groups present themselves on matters of exclusivity, namely on same-sex relationships. The persistent assault on homosexuals in some religious sectors does not help religious groups that seek to connect with current and potential adherents, and many that I interviewed are put off of religion because of this. In spite of these things the real source of tension is between Canadian cultural values of pluralism, tolerance, and inclusivity and groups that hold exclusive beliefs. Recalling from near the end of Rose Eskin's vignette in chapter 3, she pursued greater involvement in different congregations and listed several reasons for why none of them stuck for her, but chief among her reasons is that church theology is not modern and inclusive enough. Canadians are accustomed to inclusivity as a value that it frames their relationship with social organizations that are perceived as too exclusive. In this case conservative religious organizations are at a loss to no fault of their own. In a similar vein, without changing their core religious beliefs and convictions, religious groups cannot be held responsible for people leaving due to intellectual disagreements that they have with their religion, save for the inability or unwillingness to entertain and dialogue with people about their doubts and questions.

When it comes to life transitions religious organizations could be criticized for not doing a better job of caring for their own who go through a divorce or who lose a family member, or for reaching out and responding to those who move into their neighbourhood for university or a new job. At the same time, transitions are difficult for individuals. Religious groups cannot solely be blamed for individuals diminishing their religious involvement because of the natural ebb and flow to processing the death of a loved one or working through the logistics of a divorce and new living arrangements or settling into a new city. At some point individuals are also held responsible for making decisions and as is evident in the next section, many that I interviewed admit that they did not try that hard to remain connected in their religious group or to pursue involvement in a religious group in their new city. As Roozen (1980, 438) reveals in his account for reduced religious involvement, "Twice as many [reasons] fall into the personal contextual category than any other category. This would suggest that events disrupting normal life routines are more likely to be sufficient causes of disengagement than any of our other general factors." Expressed differently, factors beyond what religious groups control significantly account for diminished religious involvement and affiliation.

The final three explanations for reduced involvement or affiliation (too busy, parents giving the option to attend, and social influences) are primarily demand oriented. It is difficult to fault religious groups for people being too busy and not attending church, though some might assert that religious groups have a responsibility to convince people that attending church is more worthwhile than the other things they fill their time with. Nevertheless, people are not leaving behind their religious involvement or affiliation because religious groups did something to make them leave. While religious groups can encourage parents to bring their children to church, ultimately parents are in the driver seat as to how they raise their children with religion. Again, religious groups have not done something that facilitated people's departure. When it comes to social influences, people's friends and family beyond their religious organization seem to have more influence than those within one's religious group. Religious groups might respond by seeking ways to increase their stock and influence with those in and outside their religious fellowship, yet once more, religious groups have not done something here to cause people to leave their religious group.

Further clues into the supply and demand discussion emerge in questions to marginal affiliates and religious nones about the likelihood of pursuing greater involvement in a religious group, and if so, what would make greater involvement worthwhile. What follows strengthens my argument that demand-side explanations of religious attitudes and behaviours deserve far more attention than is currently given in supply-side rational choice theory.

EXPECTING A POSSIBLE RETURN?

In *Restless Gods* (2002, 220) and *Restless Churches* (2004), Reginald Bibby advances that we can potentially expect a renaissance of religious life in Canada because, in part, 55% of those who attend religious services less than monthly (75% of the Canadian population attends less than monthly) supposedly desire greater involvement, if certain ministry, organizational, and personal factors are addressed. These figures increased to 62% (40% of the Canadian population) in his 2005 survey (Bibby 2012, 97–8). For example, if religious groups have more relevant preaching, livelier music, more and improved programs, and focus on helping individuals to live their lives and to feel loved and cared for in a community, then some Canadians would consider greater involvement. Bibby (2011, 212) also demonstrates that 38% of Canadian teens who attend religious services less than monthly are open to greater involvement if they found it to be worthwhile, along with 65% of those who attend monthly or more. These figures include those who identify with all streams of Christianity, non-Christian religious traditions, as well as religious nones.

I have written elsewhere of my twofold suspicion surrounding this argument (see Thiessen and Dawson 2008). First, the 55% figure is misleading because only 15% definitively answer "yes" they desire greater involvement while 40% respond with an ambiguous "perhaps" (may or may not desire greater involvement, but we should not by default assume that they either do or do not desire greater involvement). Second, regardless of changes to religious supply, the apparent demand for the things that religious groups offer may not be as high as is customarily assumed (also see Perry et al. 1980, 398–401; Hunsberger and Altemeyer 2006, 16).

I am pleased to see that Bibby (2011) has since tempered his assessment somewhat. Still, amid our exchanges on this subject (see Thiessen and Dawson 2008; Bibby 2008; Thiessen 2012; Bibby 2012) and his referenced work in various media outlets and other publications (Bibby 2011; Bibby and Grenville 2013), I remain surprised with the continued interpretation that there is extensive demand for religion. We agree that for religious groups to have any chance of luring back marginal affiliates and religious nones, they ought to pay attention to their supply of religion, particularly in areas that individuals have identified are important for greater involvement. But is extensive demand the same as saying that "in the face of apparent rejection and defection, many Canadians who are not actively involved in religious groups have not closed the door on potential involvement" (Bibby 2012, 94)? Should we interpret higher church attendance figures at Christmas as evidence that faith "continues to be important for a sizable number of Canadians" (Bibby and Grenville 2013, 2)? I have my doubts.

Here I turn to my interview data that improve our methodological ability to answer these questions beyond quantitative data or open-ended survey questions. I had the opportunity to probe interviewees beyond their initial responses, to gain clarity and context surrounding their responses, and to delve into inconsistencies between their beliefs and behaviours. For instance, do those in my study desire greater involvement if they found it to be worthwhile, and more pointedly, what is the likelihood that they might pursue greater involvement in the future? Do those who answer "perhaps" really want more involvement? For those who desire greater involvement, what would lead to greater involvement? What prevents them from pursuing further involvement? Have they tried to get more involved given the many religious options available to them?

Of the 30 marginal affiliates and 30 religious nones that I interviewed, 17 say that they desire greater involvement (11 marginal affiliates and 6 religious nones), 8 say they perhaps desire greater involvement (3 marginal affiliates and 5 religious nones), and 35 say they definitely do not desire greater involvement in a religious group (16 marginal affiliates and 19 religious nones). I was surprised with these findings in that I expected fewer to express a desire for greater involvement and more to categorically reject the possibility of increased involvement, though mining the data further helps to give some context and clarity as to what these findings truly mean. Before I do so, it is helpful to know that those who do not desire greater involvement are content with their current level of involvement and, for those who left behind active involvement in a religious group, they have no regrets and they stand by their reasons for leaving as continued barriers to any possibility for greater involvement in the future (also see Bibby 2012). Beyer and Ramji's (2013) account of Muslim, Hindu, and Buddhist apostates reveals analogous levels of satisfaction with leaving behind one's faith, with no desire to pursue their faith heritage in the future.

What about those who say they definitely do or perhaps desire greater involvement in a religious group? What do they say would lead to increased attendance? Interviewees provide an array of variables and here I focus on the seven most referenced indicators. First, 9 marginal affiliates and 2 religious nones indicate that if they find and experience community in a religious group, then they would consider greater involvement. Interviewees have a few things in mind when they say this. For some it means that if they want to form new friendships, then churches could be a place to do so. Others say that if their friends attend more, then they are more likely to do so also, seeing their friends as a helpful catalyst to jumpstart greater attendance. The idea most often referenced is if they know more people at a church, then they would entertain attending more regularly. This was evident earlier in the chapter with Abigail Locke and Valerie Thomas, and again here with Valerie who says to me, "As soon as I have that belonging I think I would definitely be more likely to go."

Second, various family factors such as getting married, having children, finding a religious group with enjoyable programming for children, or children moving out could contribute to greater involvement. Seven marginal affiliates and 3 religious nones reference some combination of these factors. Oscar Jenoff is in his 30s and continues to identify as a Lutheran due to his religious upbringing. He says he would attend religious services more "if I were to have kids, just because I would want to share something with them … I would want them to have what I have … to see that there is something out there. To not only have values where this is right, this is wrong, but this is because we are a part of this … this goes back to the way that I was raised. I look back and I know that helped me." Kathryn Armstrong no longer identifies with a religion, but was raised in a conservative Protestant tradition. She says, "I really want to start going, I want to start going every Sunday. But I can't, I feel like I can't find one that I know. So I feel very confused about where to take my children … But I want to take my children to church because … they have questions. And I think … they would enjoy it." Believing that it is important to pass her religious background on to her children, Kathryn continues: "I don't know how to instill that in my kids … And so, I would like to go for my kids." As we continue the interview Kathryn reveals, similar to Rose Eskin earlier, what appears to be the real barrier for her to attend more regularly for her children: "Part of it is I'm afraid to get into a church where their belief system is either too strong … I struggle with it, because I've heard, you can get in, and I just don't want to get in to a church where all of a sudden I feel like I'm being brainwashed, or … that their religious beliefs aren't matching mine … I also don't want my kids going to the Sunday school, and then being taught things that I don't want them being taught … So, I think that's what holding me back. It's more that I don't want them going, and being taught something that I don't believe."

Kathryn's concluding reflections lead to the third factor that would lead to greater involvement. Much like the reasons for why people reduced their level of religious affiliation or involvement, if religious groups are less exclusive then marginal affiliates (2) and religious nones (5) would entertain more participation. Namely, if religious organizations stop judging others based on behaving or believing differently, cease seeking to influence the world (e.g., through proselytizing or involvement in politics), and allow individuals to think for themselves.

Fourth, 5 marginal affiliates and 2 religious nones single out many aspects of how church is "done" (see, e.g., Perry et al. 1980, 398–401). They discuss the need for more relevant preaching that is intellectually stimulating and applicable to everyday realities. Along with relevant preaching interviewees call for more dynamic and engaging religious leaders and communicators. Music is another topic to arise several times, in two contrasting ways. Some express their desire for modern and contemporary music while others lament the lame and cheesy pop culture music interpreted as really bad love songs to an invisible deity.

Fifth, some share their desire for religious people to live out their faith on a daily basis, specifically calling for religious groups to more actively participate in humanitarian efforts as a core part of who they are (3 marginal affiliates and 3 religious nones). Jenna Stock says, "If they had … food drives for charities … they were doing … something where I could help donate things, I definitely would. Like, clothes for in the winter for the unfortunate. Yeah, I would definitely join that, or donate." James Gordon echoes these sentiments: "Just doing simple things of helping out your neighbour … shoveling their driveway, just get a big group together, and … let's just go shovel driveways in the winter for free … Let's go mow people's lawns, or let's chop wood for them, or clean their windows, or … just a group of community service people … let's make big pots of coffee and go to construction workers and say … here's some coffee … just things like that."

Sixth, some interviewees exclaim they would attend religious services more regularly if there is a church closer to where they live (3 marginal affiliates and 1 religious none), and seventh, if people are less busy they would consider greater involvement in a religious group (4 marginal affiliates). Interestingly on this last point, interviewees readily accept, when pressed a bit further, that they make time for the things that are important and they are not sure that if they were less busy that they would respond with greater levels of religious involvement. This is not to diminish the importance and strains of work, parenting, household chores and errands, and the desire for "down time," but attendance at religious services does appear to diminish in importance relative to competing demands for people's time.

It is one thing for people to say that they are open to greater involvement in a religious group if they find it to be worthwhile and to list a series of variables that could increase the chance of this desire materializing into reality. It is quite another to probe people further to see if they have made any effort to pursue greater involvement or to project, in all seriousness, the likelihood that they will pursue greater involvement, particularly if their "wish list" is accounted for. This distinction enables a measurement of people's intensity and depth of desire, yielding a more accurate base to evaluate optimism about greater involvement in religious groups in the future.

The first observation is only 2 of the 25 who say they desire or perhaps desire greater involvement have attempted greater involvement. Suffice it to say, it is fair to question the intensity of the supposed desire for greater involvement that many church leaders, some academics, and the media believe is present among marginal affiliates and religious nones. The second observation is only a handful of participants say that it is very likely that they will pursue greater involvement in the future, even if religious groups account for the things that they mention. This point is reinforced when I present a series of realities to interviewees regarding church options available to them at present. For instance, I noted that there are many congregations that are theologically liberal relative to the exclusive claims that they so vehemently oppose, particularly on issues of gender and sexuality; they have female religious leaders, they openly welcome homosexuals into their congregations, and they do not condemn individuals who are divorced or who have had an abortion. I highlight many churches with all types of music styles, preaching dynamics, programs, and congregational sizes that are readily available depending on people's preferences. For those who reference church location as a stumbling block, I note that I passed a few churches within close proximity of people's homes where interviews took place. Knowing these things, how likely are they to seek greater participation in a religious group? Again, nearly all interviewees confess that their desire for more involvement is not that great and that they do not envision putting in the time and effort to change their religious activities. Put simply, even if religious groups adjust things that are reportedly in their control to change with the hope that marginal affiliates and religious nones will respond with more active attendance, the demand for greater religious involvement is not that strong. A small minority will respond with added involvement, but on the whole I do not anticipate any great reversal to current trends in this regard.

This said, it remains valuable to briefly highlight the research that does exist on how many people return to their faith group after a period of absence (and stay around long term) or the conditions that contribute to their return. David Roozen's 1980 study suggests that upwards of 80% of dropouts eventually resume active involvement in a religious group, largely due to getting married or having children. Wilson and Sherkat (1994) and Stolzenberg et al. (1995) reinforce findings on marriage and children as catalysts for returning, though Stolzenberg et al. (1995, 98) highlight that the longer the gap since one was actively involved in a religious group – which is increasingly the norm as people get married and have children later in life (Sandomirsky and Wilson 1990, 1214; Wuthnow 2007) – the less likely they are to return to heightened levels of involvement. Wilson and Sherkat (1994) additionally identify close relationships with parents as significant for returning to religious involvement. Bengtson et al. (2013, 143, 189) build on this finding in their study of "prodigals." Those who return to their religious roots tend to have parents who were patient and supportive during their child's religious absence. This includes warm, affirming mothers in particular who have strong bonds with their children, the freedom for children to come and go from their religion as they please (i.e., religion is not forced), and a strong religious foundation and upbringing that children can return to.

Edward Rauff (1979) explores the reasons for why 180 people who were not previously involved in a church (for at least the previous 5 years) decided to join a church. Rauff does not distinguish between those who had no religious background and those who were once actively involved, left for a period of time, and now returned. Nevertheless, his study offers valuable insights. Catalysts for joining a church include people inviting them to join; family factors such as marriage or children or a family crisis; a sense of community extended to them from a minister or parishioner in response to their loneliness or some tangible need (e.g., hospital visit); a personal crisis like the death of a loved one, a lost job, or a divorce; a search for more meaning in life; a desire to end their rebellious years away from their childhood religion; a sense of guilt or fear tied to sin in their life; and attendance at a one-off religious service for a wedding or funeral or special Christmas production.

Dillon and Wink (2007) show a shallow U-shaped curve to people's religiosity over time, identifying marriage, children, more time in life, the death of a loved one, or one's proximity to death as catalysts for increasing one's religious involvement (also see Ingersoll-Dayton et al. 2002). However, their research shows that levels of religiosity later in life are lower than one's earlier years.

The benefit of studies like these are the variables that contribute to greater levels of religious involvement. The limitation is these studies do not track individuals later into adulthood, to see if returnees stick around long term the further they get from their wedding and having children. Thankfully a few studies fill this gap. Some research shows that people who increase their levels of religiosity between marriage and child-rearing do so until their mid-50s, at which point their religiosity diminishes to pre-marriage levels (Bahr 1970; Stolzenberg et al. 1995, 85; McCullough et al. 2005). Smith and Snell (2009, 208) contend that while people's religiosity ebbs and flows over the lifespan, "The default of most people's lives is to continue being what they have been in the past." That is, levels of religiosity later in life tend to resemble a person's teen or young adult years (also see Shand 1990; McCullough et al. 2005; Voas and Crockett 2005; Crockett and Voas 2006; Dillon and Wink 2007; King-Hele 2009; Voas 2009; Wilkins-Laflamme 2014). Put simply, while there are always exceptions, even if those in my sample or elsewhere in Canada do pursue greater involvement (and some may), I do not expect a great resurgence in religious affiliation or involvement among marginal affiliates or religious nones in the short or long term.

RELIGIOUS SOCIALIZATION

Unfortunately I do not track active affiliates, marginal affiliates, and religious nones over the life course in this study, and thus I cannot speak directly to the assumptions outlined in the previous section (I plan to conduct a longitudinal panel study with my interviewees in the future). However, I did ask interviewees a series of questions about religious socialization and the results add credence to my argument that we should not expect greater levels of religious involvement among marginal affiliates and religious nones. How do marginal affiliates and religious nones approach religious socialization? If they already have children, how did they handle this subject, and if they plan to have kids in the future, what do they anticipate their approach will be? What do their responses reveal about the likelihood of greater involvement down the road?

Based on research to date little is known about how marginal affiliates tackle this subject, though from their reasons for maintaining an arm's-length connection with their religious group it is fair to expect that they will provide some religious exposure to their children. From my interviews with marginal affiliates this is evident in two ways. For some they either did or plan to provide regular and active religious socialization for their children through some combination of regular church attendance, Sunday school involvement, religious practices in the home, religious rites of passage (e.g., baptism or catechism), or religious schooling. For others they did or intend to provide nominal religious exposure by baptizing their children, explaining some religious beliefs in the home, or sending their children to Sunday school from time to time (though parents have no intention of attending church) (see Dudley 1978, 73; Perry et al. 1980, 398; Altemeyer and Hunsberger 1997). Why? Several reasons emerge from wanting to pass on the religious tradition that marginal affiliates were raised with to pleasing the grandparents to providing children with a moral base. These findings are not shocking since those who return to their religious groups tend to do so when they get married or have children. Recall, some of those in my sample claim that these life transitions will eventually bring them back to regular church involvement. Some marginal affiliates in this study and elsewhere will likely pursue greater involvement when they have children, and some may even maintain higher levels of religiosity for the long haul. But I have my doubts that this will characterize most based on the cumulative evidence put forward in this chapter. Only follow-up interviews with marginal affiliates in 10, 20, and 30 years from now will help to definitively resolve these suspicions, one way or the other.

Recently more attention has been given to religious nones and religious socialization. Studies show that for those raised in a family where one or both parents are non-religious, they are unlikely to be religious themselves (see, e.g., Voas and Crockett 2005; Wuthnow 2007, 86–7; Schwadel 2010; Zuckerman 2012, 139–45; Bengtson et al. 2013). In Zuckerman's (2012, 145–9) research on apostates he identifies three common approaches to religious socialization: expose their children to some of the same religious experiences that they had when they grew up such as Sunday school, church songs, Bible stories, and prayers; avoid any and all exposure to religion, leaving it to their children to explore religion later in life if they choose (i.e., "irreligious socialization" – see Merino 2012, 13); or somewhere in-between, casually exposing their children to some religious experiences, but teaching their children that religion or irreligion is not an important aspect to life.

In her article "Unaffiliated Parents and the Religious Training of Their Children," Christel Manning (2013) discusses five approaches to religious socialization. Non-provision means that parents do not intentionally include any religious instruction in the home nor do they place their child in any setting where they would receive religious instruction (e.g., Sunday school or a religious school). Outsourcing is similar to non-provision in that parents do not provide any religious instruction in the home, but they will expose their children to some form of religious education through a local religious group or a school. Self-provision involves some religious instruction in the home (even though parents do not identify with any religion) where children learn about God or a higher power, potentially pray or meditate, read religious stories, or discuss the religious significance of various holidays throughout the year. Alternative approaches entail that children are enrolled in programs that teach about different religions and where different religious views and images are spoken of and incorporated into home life (e.g., celebrating different religious holidays), often with the goal that the child might join a community that respects religious differences including those who are not religious. Finally, there are those who, after having children, return to regular religious involvement in the tradition that they were raised with and proceed to integrate religion into home life, and to place their children in some form of religious education outside the home.

A few religious nones that I interviewed are married to someone who is fairly religious and thus plan to actively expose their children to their spouse's religion. Some others who make a positive link between religion and morality regret not baptizing their children or even exposing their children to any religious belief or practice. Most religious nones, like Wendy Yandle in chapter 4 however take a hands-off and inclusive approach to religion (see Altemeyer and Hunsberger 1997; Hunsberger and Altemeyer 2006, 71–3). They reject forcing a particular world view on to their children (including their own non-religious views, in the case of atheists and many agnostics), preferring that their children discover a world view (or multiple world views) for themselves. They do not actively promote or discourage religion in the home, they are not bothered if their children encounter religion elsewhere, and people like Christopher Rearden in chapter 4 are open to discussing religion with their children should their children raise the subject. It is not unexpected, therefore, that today young people of all religious backgrounds stress individual agency in their religious development, reject external authorities telling them how they ought to believe or behave, and resist forcing their religious views on to others including those closest to them (Smith and Denton 2005; Beyer and Ramji 2013; Madge et al. 2014).

Moving forward I agree with three points that Stephen Merino (2012) makes regarding religious nones and religious socialization. First, saying that one has no religion is more culturally acceptable today than in previous generations. This fact is verified in Bibby's (2006) account of the Canadian shift away from cultural obligations or pressures to conform to religious identity, belief, or participation. As such, irreligious socialization is likely to steadily increase for the foreseeable future as the cultural stigma toward religious nones decreases. Second, as more teens are raised without a religion they are prone to move into adulthood as religious nones who do not desire to turn to religion (also see Hadaway and Marler 1993; Hunsberger and Altemeyer 2006, 42; Kosmin and Keysar 2006, 56–64). In turn fewer children and young adults will rub shoulders with friends who are religious mainly because of a lack of religious socialization, and individuals tend to be similar, religiously, to their peers (Perry et al. 1980, 396; Baker and Smith 2009). Third, acknowledging that marriage is a common catalyst for some people to newly or re-explore religious belief and practice, particularly if a non-religious person marries someone who is religious, more religious none adults exist today than any other point in Canadian history. In the context of marriage then, religious nones will have more non-religious partner options to marry, possibly diminishing the occurrence of religious and non-religious intermarriages where religious conversion due to marriage between religious nones and religious individuals takes place.

WHO CARES ABOUT RELIGIOUS SUPPLY?

This question is both playful and rhetorical. Rational choice theorists, Reginald Bibby, and religious leaders understandably care about religious supply (even though religious demand variables are accounted for – see, e.g., Bibby 2002, 221), yet I believe I have advanced a compelling case against this ongoing concern with religious supply. I will not belabour what I hope is an obvious point by now: the demand for religion is not as strong as once thought. Both supply and demand-side explanations help to account for interviewee's religious decision-making processes, including the reasons for diminished religious involvement and/or affiliation or potential greater involvement. Still, far more attention needs to focus on the demand side of the religious equation. Supply is undeniably a necessary but not sufficient cause to help explain religious behaviour. Religious groups are unlikely to thrive if they do not provide relevant preaching, lively music, effective programming, a caring and loving environment, and reach out beyond their walls. Nonetheless, even if these things exist success is not guaranteed or even likely in many situations, other than to maybe keep those already in attendance. The data from this study help to explain why. It is because the reasons for diminished involvement and the potential reasons for greater involvement are largely beyond what religious groups can control. This is clearest when marginal affiliates and religious nones, by their own admission, acknowledge that even if the religious supply changes, they are not likely to reciprocate with greater levels of involvement in a religious group. If I extend this discussion to religious socialization, while marginal affiliates are more open to exposing their children to some semblance of religious belief and practice, there is little reason to expect such exposure to lead to long term active religious affiliates among current marginal affiliates or their children. The hands-off approach to religious socialization among most religious nones should similarly lead one to low expectations for religious nones or their children to eventually become active affiliates. These findings, and the discoveries in the previous chapters, can be understood best in the context of Canadian cultural values toward religion, diversity, pluralism, individualism, and tolerance – themes that I expand on in the next and final chapter.

6

Canada's Seat at the Secularization Table

In recent years I have presented many of the findings from this study in various academic and practitioner settings. Amidst the feedback that I receive one of the most consistent affirmations pertains to the lack of demand argument, and more generally that religious belief and practice, if present, is best served in Canadian society when confined to one's personal world. Even religious leaders acknowledge that while they would like to believe that there is unending demand and that changes to religious supply will generate greater levels of involvement, their anecdotal experiences and the evidence from my research does not bear this out. It is clear to me that a full understanding of active affiliates, marginal affiliates, and religious nones must account for this changing narrative – a storyline that, among other findings in this research, intersects with many of the ideas advanced by secularization proponents.

With this argument at the forefront I return in this final chapter to the three central questions in this study. First, what explains higher and lower levels of religiosity? In what ways are active affiliates, marginal affiliates, and religious nones similar or dissimilar? Second, how might one assess scholarly debates about religiosity or secularity in light of the religious beliefs, practices, and involvements among active affiliates, marginal affiliates, and religious nones? Third, depending on whether people are highly, moderately, or not at all religious, what impact does or could this have on a society's social and civic fabric? On answering these questions I identify opportunities for further research based on some of the topics explored and not handled this project.

WHAT EXPLAINS HIGHER AND LOWER LEVELS OF RELIGIOSITY?

From my interviews with active affiliates, marginal affiliates, and religious nones two overarching explanations help to account for higher and lower levels of religiosity: personal experience and social influence. An individual's propensity to adopt various religious beliefs and practices is correlated to their personal experiences with the supernatural, other people, and religious organizations, and to the perspectives and habits of those around them who either encourage or discourage religious identification, belief, or practice. These two unifying variables overlap with three topics to surface during my interviews that demarcate active affiliates from marginal affiliates from religious nones along a gradual continuum from higher to lower levels of religiosity. These themes pertain to how important religion is to one's life and identity, a person's perspective on supernatural versus human activity in the world, and how individual or social one's religious life is. Consistent with the opening narratives from Larry Masters and Trent Hooper in chapter 1, most that I interviewed hold some belief that religion is primarily an individual matter that should not be pushed on to others. These beliefs are held more stridently the less religious one is, in large part because of an individual's personal experiences and social influences.

Religion as Master Status

The importance given to religious affiliation, belief, or practice influences the extent to which a person is religious (see, e.g., Campbell 1971; Pew Research Global Attitudes Project 2012; Manning 2013, 151). Active affiliates, marginal affiliates, and religious nones are very different in this regard. As with Stephen Nettle in chapter 2, most active affiliates believe that religion should have a "master status" in their life. Recalling from chapter 2, Stephen declares: "My Christian faith isn't something which is ... laid on top ... it's not *part of* my life. My religious faith is an expression of what is ultimately true in my life ... Being a committed Christian doesn't mean that you say goodbye to all the other parts of life. It is something which is part *of* life ... the Christian faith is a way of looking *at* life as a whole ... There is no conflict between the ordinary and the spiritual. There is no conflict. It is the same thing as two things." Another interviewee states, "God wants all of me." Active affiliates generally think that their religion should influence all aspects of their life, from family to work to leisure. Hence, as reminders of this world view, many faithfully observe religious practices in the home (e.g., prayer) and with public rituals such as church attendance. They acquired this strong religious orientation to life in their home, at church, with friends, in the Bible, and through religious music or books. Moreover, they believe this "master status" approach to faith works based on their personal experiences that God is dependable and responsive in their life. These conclusions are not confined only to active affiliates in Christian contexts. Peter Beyer (2013a, 84) offers comparable conclusions about devout Muslims in Canada who consider "Islam not only as important but central, as the axis around which their lives were organized and in terms of which they took their meaning." Similar observations arise among young Muslims and Sikhs in the United Kingdom (Madge et al. 2014, 75, 94).

In contrast, marginal affiliates and religious nones do not convey a strong belief that their religious identification or set of religious beliefs and practices ought to function as a "master status" in their life (religious nones are even less likely to adopt this perspective). It is not that their religious identity, attitudes, and behaviours or the lack thereof are altogether unimportant. Their approach to religion just does not resonate as all-encompassing as that of active affiliates. The explanation for this difference is largely found in their individualist orientation to faith, believing that religion is a private matter that should not enter the public arena nor should it be pushed on others. These views are nurtured and reinforced in marginal affiliate and religious none social circles and Canadian society at large. They are also based on people's observations and experiences of individual and societal destruction when religion is too pervasive a force in an individual or group's life.

The implication of this distinction is straightforward: levels of religiosity co-exist with beliefs about religious saliency in one's life. The one possible exception to this argument, from the secular end of the continuum, is "new atheists." Their identity takes on a "master status" evident in joining atheist groups, lobbying the government, and sometimes trying to "evangelize" others to also become committed atheists. Such individuals did not emerge in my study, and I suspect that these individuals, though they exist, are relatively rare in Canada compared to other places like the United States, where debates over religion and its place in the public sphere are far more polarized (see, e.g., Niose 2012; Williamson and Yancey 2013). Religious none interviewees, including atheists, seem to be content to keep their beliefs and practices to themselves for the time being.

Supernatural versus Natural Activity

Connected to views about religion as a "master status" are perspectives on how active or inactive the supernatural is in the world. Active affiliates are the most likely to maintain that God is actively involved in events on earth, followed by some marginal affiliates and then religious nones, who largely adopt the humanist belief that humans have greater or all control over their life and circumstances. In turn these views inform the nature and extent of people's religiosity.

Active affiliates believe that God is actively involved in their world and therefore with religion as a "master status" in their life, they should submit their lives to God's will. They do not view their lives as their own, but instead as belonging to God to do with what He wants. Over half of active affiliates share something along the lines of David Diamond, introduced in chapter 2, who says, "You don't get to make your own decisions. Your life isn't your own anymore. If you're serious about it, it's not your own anymore ... you're not the boss." Church attendance, among other activities such as reading the Bible or praying are some of the religious practices that they believe are helpful for knowing how and why God is working in their life. The words people hear at church help to give them a framework for interpreting their experiences and the social world. Though many see submitting one's will to God as a significant cost of faith, active affiliates strongly value the subsequent direction and purpose that God offers them in exchange.

Part of the reason that most active affiliates believe they can submit their lives to God is because they claim to have personally experienced God's active involvement in their life and in the world at large. Reflective of many other active affiliates, Elizabeth Hickory's vignette in chapter 2 reveals how she depends on God, and when she prays, she believes that God answers her prayers. Personal experience validates this belief that God is dependable. When good things happen in life active affiliates are quick to acknowledge God's hand in such events. Further, if or when bad things happen, such as when Gail

Robbins, referred to in chapter 2, lost her job, active affiliates tend to justify such events by pointing to human error or they claim that God has a bigger plan in place. Bolstering the social aspects of their faith experiences, active affiliates' personal experiences of a God who is active in the world is reinforced in the words, prayers, and songs that are lifted unto God in their religious gatherings each week, which in turn reminds individuals to constantly go to God with all of their joys and pains in life.

Some marginal affiliates agree with active affiliates that there is supernatural involvement in human affairs. Those like Larry Masters or Rose Eskin in chapter 3 have a favourable view of God's dependability and responsiveness based on personal experiences in the past. Others acknowledge God's involvement in the world but in a less dependable and responsive way, stridently asserting that God has let them down. For example, Cynthia Schellenberg in chapter 3 lost her husband at a young age and Norman Patterson in chapter 5 lost his brother to a car accident. They attribute these negative personal experiences to God who they believe either caused or at the very least did not prevent their hardship. It is not surprising that Cynthia or Norman are not as prone to pray, read religious texts, or attend religious services as regularly because each of these practices is to some degree premised on the existence of a supernatural that intervenes in positive and meaningful ways in human affairs.

Marginal affiliates tend to align more closely with religious nones and their guiding belief that humans have control over what happens on earth. Fewer marginal affiliates believe in God or a supernatural entity compared to active affiliates and religious nones are even less likely to believe in the supernatural. Most religious nones also reject any supernatural existence or involvement in human affairs. Even among those who do believe in God or the supernatural, some reject that God is dependable or responsive based on negative past experiences and thus are unwilling to submit their life to God in the ways that active affiliates do. Yet most are like Matthew Walter in chapter 3 or Wendy Yandle in chapter 4, who assert that individuals control their destiny and people need to depend on themselves or those around them, not on a supernatural being, in all of life's circumstances. Here, too, lower levels of religiosity among marginal affiliates and religious nones is not unexpected given that things like prayer or church attendance are generally predicated on making exchanges with the supernatural. Again, these narratives are developed and strengthened from personal experiences, both successes and failures that they attribute to human effort, and in people's social interactions at home, work, school, or online.

The Social and Individual Context for Religiosity

Inherent in the discussion to this point is that social influences play a notable role in a person's level of religiosity. For active affiliates one or more of the following descriptors apply: raised in religious homes where their parents were actively religious themselves; consistently attended religious services with friends or neighbours while growing up; joined a religious group because a close friend invited them; currently surrounded by close friends who, like them, are actively involved in a religious group. Nearly all marginal affiliates and many religious nones were also raised in religious homes. The difference is that many of their parents nominally practiced religion in the home or infrequently attended religious services, their parents were more likely to give interviewees the option to attend religious services when they reached their teen years (a choice that interviewees adopt today with their own children, resulting in most cases with teenagers who choose to set religious belief, practice, or identification to the side), and many of their parents stayed clear of teaching religious "absolutes" that were seen as too exclusive in a pluralist and individualist culture (an approach that marginal affiliates and religious nones either did, do, or plan to incorporate when raising their own children). As Bagg and Voas (2010, 108) note, "The religious decline seems to be a result of a failed transmission of religious identity from parents to children, which is in turn caused by a decrease in the prominence of religious activities in childhood. Parents may not have stopped attending and may still identify with the beliefs and denomination of their childhood, but they are unwilling or unable to make their children follow in their religious footsteps ... If maturing adults have less reinforcement from home, see plenty of attractive secular alternatives to religious beliefs and practices, and have few social incentives to remain regular participants, they will be less likely to become religious adults."

Social ties played an important role for some marginal affiliates and religious nones to reduce their affiliation or involvement in a religious group. Some marginal affiliates and religious nones left their religious group because their friends or family discouraged their continued involvement in a religious group, or in some cases, they diminished their level of involvement because they or their close friends moved away and they did not want to attend religious services on their own. Others like Rose Eskin, Opal Lackey, and Ronald Darling from chapter 3 left because they had negative experiences with others in their religious group, and people like Jacob Hewson, Jasmyne Court, Victor Chancel, and Nicholas Wallen in chapter 5 identified scandals and hypocrisy in their congregation or the church at large that facilitated their eventual departure from regular church involvement. It is logical that most marginal affiliates and religious nones are at present surrounded by close friends who do not identify with a religious group or do not subscribe to many religious beliefs or practices.

Moving beyond their social ties, when I ask individuals if religious beliefs and practices are primarily up to the individual to develop and foster or if this should occur in the context of other people, active affiliates are much more likely to suggest that this is a communal activity than are marginal affiliates and religious nones, who share the view that religion is mainly a private matter. These beliefs are mirrored in their religious practices as well, evidenced in each group's level of participation in a religious group, for example.

For active affiliates regularly gathering with others who are like-minded helps to remind them of what they believe, how they should act, and how they should interpret their daily existence. Reflective of the data presented in chapter 2, Jacqueline Airhart says that she attends because "you can meet people who relate with you or who you can help grow together in your faith or just have moral support with regarding your faith ... even just to have someone who ... you know is there for you and will pray for you if you're going through a tough time." This sense of community is one of the primary rewards that active affiliates attach to regular church attendance in many respects because of their good experiences with fellow congregants who they believe are dependable and responsive; religious community helps to provide active affiliates with stability and certainty in a chaotic and fragmented world. At the same time, however, many active affiliates are elevating their personal attitudes and behaviours above official church doctrine, religious leaders, or others in their congregation, especially on controversial subjects such as gender and sexuality.

As some active affiliates take an individualist approach to their religion, one of the defining features of marginal affiliates and religious nones is their belief that religion is primarily an individual phenomenon. As Larry Masters, Matthew Walter, Rose Eskin, Wendy Yandle, and Christopher Rearden's vignettes reveal, marginal affiliates and religious nones largely reject external authorities telling them what to believe or how to behave, and they value their ability to pick and choose which religious beliefs and practices they adopt. This perspective led many to abandon their religious involvements or religious identification altogether, maintaining that religious exclusivity was too great a cost to remain actively part of a religious group. Since leaving their religious group religious nones particularly value the individualist approach to religion because as they put it, they are more open-minded and free in their world view than are those formally tied to a religious organization. They do not feel constrained to adopt beliefs or practices imposed on them by a religious group. One could extend this line of reasoning regarding individualism to interpret busyness as a common justification for reduced involvement in one's religious group. Where church attendance was once viewed in society as a non-negotiable priority amidst the things that competed for people's time, today Canadians are less inclined to bow to tradition or religious authorities to compel them to attend religious services regularly (Bibby 2006).

Combined, a person's social ties that include family upbringing, friends, co-workers, and neighbours as well as continued exposure to and consumption of Canadian culture via the media and internet, education, and politics contribute both subtly and explicitly to a person's approach to and consumption of religion. Active affiliates are more likely than marginal affiliates and religious nones to maintain that religious beliefs and practices should develop in religious community, and that religious groups should have some authority over how one believes and behaves. Yet, the gap is diminishing on this front as active affiliates appear to more openly embrace individualism in ways similar to the rest of my interviewees. The reason for this could be attributed to a shifting Canadian consciousness toward individualism that encourages inclusiveness, tolerance, and freedom for individuality amidst a plural and diverse social setting. I find Madge et al.'s (2014, 207) analysis of young people and religion in Britain helpful for thinking about individualism over religion as a possible binding narrative in a Durkheimian sense in the Canadian context: "Young people in these locations espouse an ethos of liberal individualism embracing personal agency and morality. It is suggested that these common values, instilled through faith communities, families, schools and other institutions, may be part of the 'glue' that Durkheim was referring to. In other words, a common ideology of respect, tolerance, and a concern to do right unto others may be a major factor, combined with other elements, contributing to healthy cohesive communities." Simply put, individualism, respect, and tolerance – not religion – are the common social bonds that bind the majority of Canadians, and this orientation infuses how many in my study, and I suspect beyond, approach religion.

THE DIMINISHING PRESENCE AND IMPACT OF RELIGION

In chapter 1 I detailed Karel Dobbelaere's (2002) threefold approach to secularization. Societal secularization entails that religious belief, practice, and authority now have less influence, if any at all, over social institutions like politics, education, the law, or health care. Organizational secularization refers to shifts within religious groups away from strict and rigid beliefs and practices, in an effort to remain current and modern relative to society. Individual secularization encompasses declining levels of individual religious belief and practice.

My interviews with active affiliates, marginal affiliates, and religious nones intersects most with discussions of individual secularization, and to a lesser degree with societal and organizational secularization. But as Peter Berger and Steve Bruce indicate, these three levels are connected. Individual secularization is a result of societal secularization, and in some circumstances organizational secularization. On one hand, interviews with ninety individuals in a single Canadian city do not yield sufficient data to conclude if Canada as a nation is closer to the religious or secular end of the continuum. On the other hand, the detailed accounts in this study, along with nationally representative survey findings in Canada and abroad, provide some important clues about how religious or secular Canada and Canadians are.

Starting with research beyond my interview data, the clearest and most recent signs of individual secularization arise from Reginald Bibby's data in *Beyond the Gods and Back* (2011) that I outlined in chapter 1. For every indicator of adult or teen religious affiliation, belief in God, and attendance at religious services over the past 30 to 40 years, the "religious" end of each continuum decreased and the "non-religious" end increased. That is, fewer Canadians claim to identify with a religion, to believe in God, or to attend religious services regularly, while more Canadians say they have no religion, they do not believe in God, and they never attend religious services. These trends are particularly evident among Canadian teens. These findings add to the mounting evidence concerning secularizing trends at the individual level and generation over generation religious declines in Canada (Bibby et al. 2009, 162–87; King-Hele 2009; Eagle 2011; Wilkins-Laflamme 2014).

Truth be told, levels of individual secularization would likely be worse if it were not for immigration. Immigration keeps Christian identification, belief, and practice afloat, notably in Roman Catholic and conservative Protestant settings (Bowen 2004, 56–7; Bramadat and Seljak 2008; Bibby 2011, 30–1). In part this is because foreign-born individuals who are religious tend to hold more theologically conservative stances that fuel higher rates of religiosity. Religion also helps immigrants psychologically and socially to adjust to a new social setting. Nevertheless, as Steve Bruce (2002) notes, cultural transitions of this kind can help to slow down secularization processes in a country, but are unlikely to altogether reverse secularization.

Some understandably refer to growth in non-Christian religions in rejecting secularization assertions. What is known about religiosity levels in these settings? Beyer and Martin (2010) rightly note that religiosity measurements vary between and within religions; thus comparisons of this kind are not comparing apples with apples, so to speak. The following indicators are therefore by no means perfect, but they do offer some insights relative to the religiosity indicators used among active affiliates, marginal affiliates, and religious nones.

In terms of religious affiliation there are signs of religious growth, mainly due to changing immigration patterns. As of 2011, 7.8% of Canadians identified with a non-Christian religious group, up from around 6% in 2001 and approximately 4% in 1991 (Statistics Canada 2001, 2013). Between 1984 and 2008 religious affiliation increased among young people across Muslim, Buddhist, Jewish, Hindu, and Sikh settings, from 3% to 16% overall (Bibby 2011, 32). Projections suggest that these groups could make up about 10% of the Canadian adult population by 2017 (Beyer and Martin 2010, 15; Valpy and Friesen 2010), and upwards of 8% of the Canadian population could identify as Muslim by 2031 (Friesen and Martin 2010; Statistics Canada 2010). Muslims are singled out for having higher birthrates, stronger retention rates, high religious demands, and a bright future connected to Islam's global spread (Bibby 2011, 199–201).

With respect to attendance at religious services, in 1957, 35% of members from "other faith" groups attended religious services weekly, gradually diminishing to 17% in 1975, 12% in 1990, and 7% in 2000 before rebounding to 22% in 2005 (Bibby 2011, 29, 37). When comparisons are drawn between different religious traditions, members of non-Christian religions are the most likely never to attend religious services (19%) and the second least likely to attend religious services weekly (22%, followed by 20% among mainline Protestants) (Bibby 2011, 54). It is too early to know what to make of these findings, and in particular the 2005 rebound among weekly attenders. If data from the United States are any indication, weekly attendance at religious services in "other faith" settings has declined since 2000 (Putnam and Campbell 2010, 106–8). Regardless, Beyer and Martin (2010) wisely caution against reading too much into figures like these relative to Christian contexts due to different religiosity standards across religions. For example, Buddhists may not regard weekly attendance as important as Catholics or Muslims. Moreover, gender variations exist so that Muslim and Jewish males have stronger expectations to regularly attend than do women.

It is well known that religiosity levels (e.g., attendance at religious services) among first-generation immigrants from all religious backgrounds are higher than in the population as a whole (Clark 2003; Bramadat and Seljak 2005, 2008; Beyer and Martin 2010). Further, immigrant families tend to have higher birth rates, and non-Christian religious groups are disproportionately younger than the Canadian population (Beyer and Martin 2010, 28–9). The question relative to secularization theory is what happens the longer that one settles into Canadian life, and what about second- and third-generation immigrants? Beginning with birth rates, McDaniel and Tepperman (2011) show that immigrant families tend to regress to the mean within one or two generations. In other words, any signs of religious revitalization in Canada due to higher birth rates in immigrant families could be relatively short lived. Regarding religious involvement, variations exist for individuals and pockets of some religious groups, but mounting evidence points toward diminished levels of attendance at religious services across religious traditions among first- and second-generation immigrants (see, e.g., Wuthnow and Christiano 1979; Connor 2008, 2009; Collins-Mayo and Dandelion 2010; Beyer and Ramji 2013; Madge et al. 2014). Based on ten thousand surveys and 160 interviews with young people from many religious backgrounds in the United Kingdom, Madge et al. (2014, 149) conclude that there is "suggestive evidence that the longer a family has been in the UK, the more individuated young people become in terms of their religiosity. There is no direct evidence from the study on whether members of the younger generation in these families are necessarily less religious than their parents, though the qualitative data would suggest this is usually the case. Regardless of specific patterns, it can nonetheless tentatively be concluded that these findings underlie the effects of Westernisation on a tendency toward greater secularisation among minority faith groups in Britain."

Much research still needs to be conducted on religiosity in Muslim, Buddhist, Sikh, Jewish, and Hindu settings, to know more definitively about the trajectory of religious belief and practice following immigration to Canada and across subsequent generations. Until we have more clarity on these matters I think it is important to keep the larger context in mind. Canada is more religiously diverse today than one generation ago, but not to the extent that the media, the state, and even some academics would have us to believe (even if statistics follow the current trajectory). Fewer than 10% of Canadians identify with a non-Christian religious tradition (in the United States figures are around 2%–3% [Putnam and Campbell 2010, 16]). In addition, signs of growth in non-Christian religious contexts do not compensate for continuous declines in religious affiliation, belief, and involvement in Canada at large. To reiterate, religious nones are the greatest beneficiaries of declines in Christian identification, belief, and involvement. These facts do not discount the presence of religious diversity, the lived experiences among Jews, Hindus, Muslims, Buddhists, or Sikhs, or the very real and intense debates about the public place of religion in a religiously diverse environment. But conflating the presence of religious diversity with rejecting secularization interpretations for all of Canada is problematic.

Returning more closely to my interview data, how might the recent past and present levels of individual religiosity impact religious belief and practice in 10, 20, or 30 years? An important clue is found among teenagers. Earlier I demonstrated, based on surveys in different social contexts that it is unlikely that people take on faith later in life if they have little or no religious background. Further, based on my interviews along with assertions from other scholars, parents are less likely to pass on faith to their children in this generation compared with previous generations – at least among marginal affiliates and religious nones, who together comprise upwards of 75% of the Canadian population (and growing). The religious none category is also growing fastest among young people, Canadians increasingly accept and normalize religious nones in the religious landscape, and religious nones generally have lower levels of religiosity relative to marginal affiliates. Moreover, even if today's teenagers eventually (re)turn to religious groups for key life events such as marriage or having children (an unlikely event in my estimation based on the reasons noted in the previous chapter), which is less likely given that fewer have a religious point of departure, the evidence presented in chapter 5 reveals that few maintain increased levels of religiosity throughout the remainder of the life course.

Another insight from my interviews concerns future religious involvement among marginal affiliates and religious nones. Unlike Reginald Bibby and rational choice theorists I am less convinced that individuals desire greater involvement in their religious group or that there is an unending desire for the things that religious groups offer, despite what individuals indicate on a survey. One of the benefits of this qualitative study is that I could probe interviewees about their past, present, and potential future levels of religious involvement in ways not possible in survey data. In the end my findings confirm what one should intuitively assume in looking at survey data about future religious involvement: if people say they want to pursue greater involvement, they provide a list of variables that would lead to greater involvement, and such variables are readily available within the religious marketplace, then it is reasonable that if we are not witnessing changes on nationwide statistics regarding individual levels of religiosity, the demand for the things that religious groups offer is not all that great. My interviewees do not strongly desire greater involvement in a religious group, certainly not enough to exert the time and energy to seek out a place of worship that fulfills their checklist. The reasons for diminished involvement and the barriers for marginal affiliates and religious nones to pursue greater involvement in a religious group largely rest on their own shoulders, regardless of changes to religious supply. Furthermore, marginal affiliate religious belief and practice is in many respects more similar to those of religious nones than active affiliates. My sense is that if marginal affiliates change their level of involvement, it is most likely going to be for the religious none end of the continuum rather than the active affiliate side. As for religious nones, there is little evidence from my interviews to suggest that they will change their posture toward greater religious belief or practice in the future. Taken as a whole, I think the evidence is clear that continued secularization at the individual level is on the Canadian horizon.

My interview data provide some additional depth, context, richness, and nuance to how and why individual secularization is an accurate interpretation to explain religion in Canada today. Namely, my conversations with active affiliates, marginal affiliates, and religious nones help to unpack Berger and Bruce's assertions that societal secularization sets the conditions for individual secularization to eventually materialize (also see Bowen (2004) for an excellent exposition of social changes that have contributed to secularizing trends in Canada, and Hay (2014) for quantitative evidence that supports Berger's theory in a Canadian context). Few contest the onset of societal secularization in the 1960s (some would argue that the seeds for this started long before) where Christianity's influence over several other social institutions such as education, health, or the family gradually diminished, and religion lost its taken-for-granted status in Canadian public life. Still, religion figures prominently in public debates over education, security, the law, health care, the work place, and family life (see e.g. Beaman 2008; Buckingham 2014; Lefebvre and Beaman 2014). Most often these conversations pertain to how Canada should "neutrally" negotiate religious diversity in a fair, equal, and just society. But are these public debates evidence for or against secularization? I appreciate how a case could be made that public debates surrounding religion's place in various social institutions are evidence that religion is not disappearing. Yet both the debates themselves as well as the outcomes to several recent cases (e.g., Bill 44 in Alberta, Bill 94 in Quebec, prayer before municipal meetings in Saguenay, Quebec, or opposition to the Trinity Western University law school) reveal a prevailing discourse that wishes to relegate religion to the private realm. The dominant tenor in these public discussions is not to elevate religion's role in social life, nor to take seriously the role that religion plays in individuals' lives and how, in turn, social institutions ought to adapt to make greater room for such realities (David Seljak's [2005] discussion of education is an excellent example of this). Quite the contrary. In the name of neutrality, the ultimate goal is how to keep religion to the margins of social life, which according to Dobbelaere's definition of societal secularization epitomizes the shrinking relevance of religion for social life. From a purely descriptive level, state neutrality is, in fact, a secular orientation that privileges secularity over religion such that public social institutions are seen as independent from religion. Therefore, I do not see these public conversations about religion as evidence against secularization, but rather as evidence for societal secularization.

Societal secularization opened the door for religious and social pluralism to develop even further. Canadians gradually became less sure of the merits of their religious beliefs and practices in the context of many other attitudes and behaviours that were eventually celebrated and entrenched into Canadian law and policy (e.g., immigration policy, the Multiculturalism Act, and the Canadian Charter of Rights and Freedoms). The challenges to arise due to religious and social pluralism for continued religious belief and practice is a repeated theme documented among all three groups of interviewees, with many wondering about the merits of a definitive set of religious beliefs and practices in a plural and diverse country like Canada, never mind in a globalized era where one's awareness of social and religious pluralism is that much greater. As Jack McEwan, from chapter 5, claims: "The older you get, the more experience you have. The more people you meet, the more experiences you see. And it was just through that whole process that I really started to not see the point of identifying with any one religious group because ... there's so many of them ... So I started to say, 'Well ... there's so many ... they can all be right. They can all be wrong.'"

A logical extension of religious and social pluralism is the privatization of religion where people believe that religion functions best in the privacy of one's home and family, not in public settings such as the workplace, in politics, or in education. Privatized religion also entails that people do not seek to proselytize others with their faith. Those I interviewed communicate loud and clear that religion should not be forced on to other people for fear of alienating or offending others who may not view the world in a similar manner. Alongside the chapter 4 discussion of Canadian alarm bells that go off if a political leader is overtly religious or allows religion to inform public policy, Canadian preferences for privatized religion are strongly evident in public sentiment over the place of religion in Canadian schools, wearing public religious symbols (in Quebec), or in any array of public online comments to news stories about religion. I disagree with Casanova's (1994) suggestion that these public discussions and reactions to religious matters are evidence of the "deprivatization" of religion, and thus a refutation of secularization at the societal level. Rather, these debates largely centre on the majority of Canadians who long for religion to take a back seat in the public arena, giving further evidence of societal and individual secularization.

If the above assumptions and findings are true, then it makes sense, as Berger and Bruce discuss, that individuals will approach religion in a highly subjective, experiential, individual, and relativist manner. The cumulative evidence in this study strongly supports this line of reasoning, showing how interviewees modernize and liberalize their faith relative to values and behaviours traditionally associated with their religious group (i.e., organizational secularization). In chapter 2 on active affiliates, individualist approaches to faith were sometimes at odds with formal religious teaching and practice. Indicative of some active affiliates Cam Mack states, "I have my own beliefs and ... things that I hold dear and that I sort of know in my heart ... I think that that's why ... I found the church that I did. Because it ... embraced the things that I ... believed in. And they're teaching me more about what I wanted to know." In other words, some active affiliates claim authority over their religious beliefs and practices rather than deferring authority to their church tradition or religious leader. These individuals associate only with congregations that conform to what they already hold as true.

In chapter 3 on marginal affiliates organizational secularization was clear in those like Rose Eskin who maintains that she can and will continue to identify as Roman Catholic even though she vehemently disagrees with formal church teachings on sexuality. A further sign of organizational secularization is that two of the three leading reasons for church attendance among marginal affiliates, tradition and family pressures, are relatively irreligious motivations for participating in a religious activity. Some scholars prefer to emphasize the behaviour of church attendance as a sign of continued religiosity, and this should not be ignored. However the case I am making is that behaviour is only part of the equation. The motivation for behaviour is another significant clue for how to interpret people's religiosity, which I think is one of this study's scholarly contributions. If marginal affiliates do not ascribe religious motivation or meaning to a religious behaviour, it is premature to focus squarely on the behaviour as evidence that religion is alive and well as Bibby has put it.

Chapter 4 on religious nones most strongly reinforces the individualist and relativist approach to matters of faith. Most believe that religious belief and practice should exist on an individual level and that one's faith should not be forced on to others.

In total, the absence of an overarching shared religious narrative that is reinforced in many spheres of social life makes it difficult for individuals to share a "common" religion with others. As Steve Bruce (2011, 2–3) articulates, this social context facilitates declining levels of religiosity, reduced levels of religious socialization within the home, porous boundaries between one set of beliefs and practices to the next, and general indifference toward maintaining or spreading a unique set of religious beliefs and practices on to others. My research and other Canadian studies support Bruce's projections, with the following exception: active affiliates, marginal affiliates, and religious nones appear to hold a shared narrative around privatized religion and individualism that limits religious belief and practice to one's self and their family. Many of those I interviewed were socialized with this set of assumptions in their home and they similarly have or plan to pass these views on to their children. This social script toward religion is also reinforced, implicitly and explicitly, in Canadian media, education, law, and political discourse. This social context does not mean that there is a definitive and linear relationship between modernity and secularization, only that these conditions make it more difficult to establish religious belief and practice on a societal or individual level that is sustainable or that has much social significance.

It is true that there are signs of religious life among some individuals and groups across Canada and elsewhere (e.g., Pentecostals, Muslims, and Mormons). Yet when surveying the entire religious landscape these signs pale in comparison to what I argue here is a downward trajectory in individual levels of religiosity, which is a consequence of societal secularization that started half a century ago in Canada. Simply put, at least in Canada religion has, is, and will be on the decline. Religion plays less of a role in Canadian society today than when my parents or grandparents grew up, religious beliefs and practices are less salient today among individual Canadians than in the past, and these trends are likely to continue into the foreseeable future. Like several other modern Western nations, Canada is holding on to its seat at the secularization table.

RELIGION AND CIVIC ENGAGEMENT

Few sociologists across Canada give attention to religion in their academic work, believing that secularization accompanies modernization and thus there are few reasons to study religion sociologically. Countless Canadians also maintain that as a plural and diverse society that prides itself on the privatization of religion, religion does not or should not have much social significance. As a result energy or money should not be invested into studying religion. Going one step further there are some who assume that only the religious few in Canada do or should have an interest in sociological studies on religion. Even though my conclusions point toward secularization and could cause some to wonder the point to studying religion, the interview data in this study partially reveal the errors in these reflections. Religion as a "master status" makes a difference in how active affiliates live their day-to-day lives, in areas of morality for instance (this applies to some marginal affiliates and religious nones). The same conclusion applies to active members of non-Christian religious group in Canada (Bramadat and Seljak 2005; Beyer and Ramji 2013). The tragic religiously inspired attacks in Saint-Jean-sur-Richelieu, Quebec and Ottawa, Ontario in October 2014 are a stark reminder of the real power that religion holds in society.

It is important, therefore, to understand the correlations between varying levels of religiosity and individual and social well-being. Is religious belief and practice ultimately beneficial or harmful or both for society? What impact, if any, might diminished religious identification, belief, and involvement have on society? What is the relationship between levels of religiosity and a range of social and civic attitudes and behaviours? Active affiliates tend to believe that religion is good for society and religious nones are more likely to believe that religion is problematic for society. Marginal affiliates fall somewhere between, though they are closer to religious nones than to active affiliates. What do large-scale national studies reveal on this subject?

In his book *Christians in a Secular World: The Canadian Experience* (2004), Kurt Bowen documents that those with higher levels of religiosity – measured by things such as church attendance, claims that religion is personally important, prayer, and reading religious texts – are more satisfied with life, have more close relationships, place more importance on relationships with family and neighbours, and demonstrate higher levels of honesty, ethical behaviour, and general concern for the welfare of others. Zuzanek et al. (2008) examine teenagers in Canada and also show positive correlations between teens' religiosity and their overall well-being measured, for example, by higher levels of personal happiness, stronger ties with family members, greater concern with doing well at school, and lower levels of anxiety or feelings of boredom and loneliness. Reginald Bibby (2007, 2009, 2011) uncovers similar findings among Canadians teenagers and adults. Bibby explores a series of attitudes and behaviours pertaining to honesty, concern for others, politeness, forgiveness, generosity, patience, working hard, trouble with the law, and helping others in need (e.g., those without medical coverage, victims of human rights violations, those with aids, or those who are poor). Bibby shows that pro-social attitudes and behaviours characterize most Canadians in many of these areas, yet across the board, the more religious that one is (particularly among Christians, Muslims, and Hindus), the more likely they are to believe and behave in pro-social ways.

At the same time Bibby's (2011, 104–7) recent research on the relationship between religiosity and happiness reveals that regardless of one's level of religiosity, Canadian adults show strong signs of overall happiness, marital satisfaction, and quality of life. Canadian teens also tend to respond similarly to questions about self-image or personal concerns irrespective of their level of religiosity. These latter findings lead Bibby to conclude that religion is not necessary for people to be happy, though religion is one of the variables that contributes to some people's happiness. The results among my interviewees add support to Bibby's work. Most that I interviewed believe that they have meaning and purpose in life, a significant indicator of happiness, regardless of their level of religiosity. For some religion is an important source of their meaning and purpose while for others it is their friends, family, job, and leisure opportunities.

In addition to these discoveries Kurt Bowen (2004) suggests that higher levels of religiosity are positively correlated to social capital, volunteering and charitable giving, and political engagement. Bowen's findings are supported in many other studies. When it comes to donating money to charitable organizations Hall et al. (2009, 20) show that 49% of weekly attenders are in the "top donor" category (the 25% of Canadians who account for 82% of all donated dollars) compared with only 15% of those who do not attend weekly (also see Reed and Selbee 2001). Of weekly attenders 94% made donations in 2007, compared to 82% of non-weekly attenders, and weekly attenders donated an average of $1,038 annually versus $295 for those who do not attend weekly (23). Among Canadians who volunteer their time, 66% of weekly attenders volunteered somewhere in 2007, compared with 43% of non-weekly attenders, and weekly attenders volunteered nearly twice as many hours than non-weekly attenders (43). With 25% of volunteers contributing almost 80% of the total volunteer hours (36), 23% of weekly attenders are in the "top volunteer" category compared with 9% of non-weekly attenders (41). These findings are all supported in other studies by Piché (1999), Putnam (2000, 117), Cnaan (2002), Campbell and Yonish (2003), Nemeth and Luidens (2003), Smidt et al. (2003), Wuthnow (2004, 2007), Berger (2006), Putnam and Campbell (2010), and Johnston (2013). Hall et al. (2009, 22, 41) additionally demonstrate that if children learn at a young age to volunteer and give money to charitable organizations, then they are more likely to do so as adults (also see Wilson and Janoski 1995; Hodgkinson and Weitzman 1996; Dillon and Wink 2007). Further, children who are active in a religious organization when growing up tend to give more often and in greater amounts when they are adults, compared to any other social setting where children are taught to volunteer and donate money (Hall et al. 2009, 22). The same is true in the volunteering realm (41).

It is true that many regular church attenders give significant time and money to their religious organization (see Campbell and Yonish 2003; Nemeth and Luidens 2003; Hall et al. 2009, 24; Johnston 2013), which begs the question: does their charitable work benefit the broader society? The answer is categorically yes. Regular attenders actively contribute money and time to secular initiatives. Hall et al. (2009) document that weekly attenders in Canada account for 20% of donations to secular agencies and 23% of volunteer hours to non-religious organizations. Putnam and Campbell (2010, 448) reveal that in the United States, "regular churchgoers are more likely to give to secular causes than non-churchgoers, and highly religious people give a larger fraction of their income to secular causes than do most secular people." Bowen's (2004, 157) research in Canada shows that 35% of those who attend weekly volunteered in a secular agency in 1997 versus 25% of the least religious. Putnam and Campbell (2010, 446) demonstrate that 45% of weekly attenders volunteer in secular organization (e.g., helping the poor or elderly, serving in school or youth programs, assisting in health care) versus 26% of non-attenders. As several scholars note, those who regularly attend religious services share a theological conviction (and are reminded each week at church) to make a positive impact on society, and they are given opportunities through their church to do so beyond the walls of their church (see Cnaan et al. 2003; Harris 2003; Smidt 2003; Bowen 2004; Wuthnow 2004; Berger 2006; Putnam and Campbell 2010; Johnston 2013).

Religious organizations also offer services that benefit Canadian society, thus giving time and money to one's church helps those outside of congregations. For example, religious organizations provide social services to fill the gap where state financial or human resources do not (Cnaan 2002; Cnaan et al. 2003; Smidt 2003; Wuthnow 2004; Ammerman 2005; Putnam and Campbell 2010; Janzen et al. 2012; Friesen and Clieff 2014). Bowen (2004) points out that despite religious organizations spending large sums of money on buildings and facilities, religious properties serve outsiders' needs (e.g., shelter for the homeless, Boy Scouts, Alcoholics Anonymous, and immigrant settlement groups). Expenditures on clergy also save the government money in areas of counselling. At an individual level religious group members develop practical skills such as letter writing, planning and chairing meetings, giving presentations, and teamwork that are transferrable into the workplace and overall civic participation (Brady et al. 1995; Verba et al. 1995) – skills acquired in non-religious volunteer settings too (Hall et al. 2009, 49). These skills are especially helpful for disenfranchised populations looking to establish themselves in the economic sector.

A consistent variable within the literature is that more regular church involvement yields the social capital necessary for civic engagement. Referencing Robert Wuthnow (1994), Coleman (2003, 37) states that "even intense, purely personal spirituality that is cut off from churches or some ongoing groups has almost no predictive value for civic engagement or social activism." Nemeth and Luidens claim that "the social capital produced by the relations found in churches and synagogues is evident only among the most frequent attenders. Simply being a member or being an infrequent attender, it appears, does little to increase one's financial support for nonreligious charities" (2003, 114–15). Putnam and Campbell (2010, 472) confidently conclude, "Having close friends at church, discussing religion frequently with your family and friends, and taking part in small groups at church are extremely powerful predictors of the entire range of generosity, good neighbourliness, and civic engagement ... devout people who sit alone in the pews are not much more neighbourly than people who don't go to church at all. The real impact of religiosity on niceness or good neighbourliness, it seems, comes through chatting with friends after service or joining a Bible study group, not from listening to the sermon or fervently believing in God."

Siobhan Chandler (2008) is not as convinced. She summarizes the sentiments of many who argue that just because individuals practice their religion privately or are involved in New Age forms of spirituality, this does not mean that they are by default selfish or non-contributing members to society: "Autonomy and self-expression are not synonyms for negative freedom. By the same measure, the autonomous and self-expressive nature of contemporary 'New Age' does not make it *de facto* a selfish religion, even if it is a religion of the self. Sweeping generalizations condemning a massive cohort of post-materialist seekers as narcissists is untenable. That some spiritual but religiously unaffiliated individuals are selfish is inevitable, but so are many of the religiously affiliated. Not all individuals are equally benevolent and moral, no matter what their religious beliefs" (2008, 13). For instance, in a study of New Age students, a group of people who are typically identified as more individualistic than non-New Age followers, Franz Hollinger (2004) shows that New Agers have higher levels of political activism, involvement in political party activities, and charitable donations when compared with non–New Agers (also see Heelas et al. 2005; Stanczak 2006; Dillon and Wink 2007).

However one resolves the debate over the individual versus social nature of one's faith relative to social and civic engagement, the evidence seems clear that there is a positive correlation between religiosity and individual and societal well-being. Putnam and Campbell (2010, 444) submit that "religiously observant Americans are more civic and in some respects simply 'nicer.'" Bibby cautiously concludes, "Religion is one important source of positive interpersonal life. Those who are not religious do not lack for civility and compassion. But, collectively, they tend to lag behind Canadians who are religious" (Bibby 2011, 153). In saying these things scholars do not believe that religion is necessary for social and civic health, but on the surface it appears to at least help. In many ways this conclusion mirrors how active and marginal affiliate interviewees perceive the relationship between religion and personal and social well-being.

Like the religious nones that I interviewed, not everyone agrees with this interpretation. In his book *Society without God* (2008), Phil Zuckerman examines Denmark and Sweden, two of the world's least religious nations and the happiest and most content countries in the world. Far less than 50% of Swedes or Danes believe in God, believe that religion is important to their life, believe in life after death, or attend religious services, among several other indicators of religiosity (24–5). Yet when looking at the "Human Development Index," which is based on having a long and healthy life (e.g., life expectancy), high knowledge levels (e.g., literacy and school enrolment rates), and a decent standard of living (e.g., GDP per capita), Sweden and Denmark rank in the top twenty in the world, surrounded by several other non-religious nations such as Norway, Britain, and the Netherlands (26). Other indicators of societal health such as the "Quality of Life Index" or low crime rates or suicide also position Sweden and Denmark, alongside other irreligious societies, among the world's leaders. Zuckerman concludes that "it is not the most religious nations in our world today, but rather the most secular, that have been able to create the most civil, just, safe, equitable, humane, and prosperous societies" (30). He also states that he is "not arguing that the admirably high level of societal health in Scandinavia is directly *caused* by the low levels of religiosity. Although one could certainly make just such a case ... I simply wish to soberly counter the widely touted assertion that without religion, society is doomed" (18).

In addition to Zuckerman's observations, religious individuals and groups are the source of intense conflict in the world. At the macro-level staunch atheists like Richard Dawkins (2006), Sam Harris (2006), and the late Christopher Hitchens (2007) draw attention to the Middle Ages which were riddled with religious conflict, the ongoing religious tensions in the Middle East, and the current war on terror that is steeped in religious ideologies. At the individual level religious belief and practice also has a destructive impact. Marginal affiliates and religious nones encountered tension with others in their religious group, negative experiences due to religious exclusivity, and religious scandals or hypocrisy. Kinnaman and Lyons (2007) detail perceptions of Christians as hypocritical, anti-homosexual, sheltered, overly political, judgmental, and insincere. Piché (1999) shows that highly religious Canadians, particularly conservative Christians, are the least tolerant of homosexuals acquiring equal rights and the most likely to contest that all religions are equally good and true. Robert Wuthnow highlights similar things in *America and the Challenges of Religious Diversity* (2005), and Putnam and Campbell (2010, 444) state that religious Americans are "less tolerant of dissent than secular Americans, an important civic deficiency." My interviews with marginal affiliates and religious nones reveal that these negative perceptions and realities contributed to them leaving behind their religious affiliation or involvement, and are barriers for them to realistically turn to active religious involvement in the future.

If my conclusions about secularization are accurate, what are the likely implications for social and civic engagement? For instance, should social and civic concern arise as fewer teens are raised in religious homes, adopt basic religious beliefs, or are involved in a religious organization? What about marginal affiliates who are unlikely to eventually become active affiliates, or the all-time high presence of religious nones (likely to increase in the future)? On one hand it is hard to ignore the repeated and compelling evidence that correlates higher levels of religiosity, particularly regular attendance at religious services, with various pro-social attitudes and behaviours. Yes, there is evidence abroad that nations can get on just fine without religion and there are distinct historical and cultural explanations (e.g., economic and political structure) for why this is that go beyond my purposes here, but there is reason to believe that religion does help some to be more socially and civically engaged. Could Canada's social and civic fabric survive without religion? I think it could, but there is some cause – not a lot, but some – for concern if Canadians are less religious. This unease is especially justified if people's religiosity exists apart from formal religious organizations centred on regular gatherings that we know, sociologically, are important hubs with which to encourage members toward collective pro-social and civic attitudes and behaviours.

On the other hand there is a line of research that links strong social networks as the catalyst for why religious individuals generally adopt more pro-social attitudes and behaviours. That is, if individuals form strong bonds in any social setting, religious or otherwise, they too are more likely to believe and behave in ways that are beneficial for individuals and society as a whole (see, e.g., Ammerman 1997; Putnam 2000; Putnam and Campbell 2010; Berghuijs et al. 2013; McClure 2013; Merino 2013). In this vein it is plausible to argue that a "collective conscience" continues to build in Canada around fundamental human responsibilities to help those in need and to treat people respectfully, equally, and with dignity. In contrast to treating others well because people want to earn their way to heaven or at least avoid going to hell, Canadians are encouraged via multiple outlets (e.g., education, politics, health care, workplace, law, media, community associations, social media, and some atheist groups) to simply make a positive difference in society because it is the right and humane thing to do. This narrative reveals one of many impacts that globalization has on individuals and social institutions as worldwide conversations about what it means to be human abound (Robertson and Chirico 1985). As just one example, Canada is a world leader in volunteerism (Curtis et al. 1992, 2001) despite relatively low levels of religiosity, and Canada is highly regarded as an international leader in promoting and embodying equality and fundamental human rights (areas of inequality remain in Canada on many fronts, but internationally speaking, Canada is much further ahead than many nations). Relative to religion then, a developing social ethos of social and civic engagement could very well fill the void that lower levels of religiosity may leave behind.

As for the negative impact that religious belief and practice has in society, particularly religious exclusivity where highly religious individuals and groups discriminate against those who do not view the world in the same way, diminished religiosity can be seen as a welcome change. Even religiously conservative folk like some of the active affiliates that I interviewed are tempering some of their exclusivist views in favour of pluralism, tolerance, and acceptance (see Reimer 2003) – an outcome that one could have predicted following Berger and Bruce's ideas surrounding the social conditions that give rise to secularization. However, Steve Bruce (2002) also contends that secularization processes can be stunted, but not reversed, when religious groups feel threatened and need to reassert themselves in society. I suppose it is possible that some religious conservatives as well as passionate atheists could conceivably push back in society. For example, if Canada becomes more secular, evident in perceived or real state neutrality or overt secular policies relative to religious belief and practice, a vocal conservative religious minority may assert themselves more forcefully in the public square. Furthermore, if conservatives in other religious traditions emerge on to the national scene (e.g., home-grown Muslim radicals), conservative Christian groups or new atheist groups might strive for greater public influence that both enhances their influence in society and diminishes another group's influence. In either possibility Christian evangelicals are the most likely to create a fuss, fearful that they are losing whatever little impact they have left in Canadian society. In part this potential reaction is tied to a perception that Canada was once a Christian nation that needs to return to its roots. It is also informed by the strong evangelical narrative in the United States that some Canadian evangelicals could interpret as a sign for reasserting evangelical influence in Canadian society. As much as these scenarios could play out in Canada, in the end the degree of polarization in Canada pales in comparison to the United States because of the small size and public sway that religious conservatives as well as "new atheists" have in Canada (see Bibby 2011, 62–97). I doubt either of the aforementioned circumstances will figure prominently in Canadian social life mainly because of the dominant belief in Canada that shies away from projecting exclusive attitudes and behaviours on to others – of course, except for the exclusive claim to inclusiveness that informs much of Canadian public and private life.

OUTSTANDING QUESTIONS AND ISSUES

In this study I investigated questions that sorely needed to be asked and that survey data to date have not adequately addressed. At the same time there are many issues and questions that I did not explore in detail that no doubt could add to a more comprehensive examination of religion in Canada. As it relates to non-Christian religious groups, to what extent does my guiding thesis apply among religious minority groups in Canada? What points of convergence and divergence exist between active affiliates, marginal affiliates, and religious nones relative to Buddhists, Sikhs, Jews, Muslims, and Hindus? If I conceptualize and operationalize religion differently relative to these other religious groups, how might this impact a secularization interpretation? Regarding religious transmission, how do members of other religious groups approach religious socialization in a Canadian context and how might such information help to inform a nuanced Canadian approach to thinking about how faith is (or is not) passed on from one generation to the next?

Narrowing this discussion to active affiliates, marginal affiliates, and religious nones, countless research questions arise from this study and several research opportunities exist. One logical next step is to conduct interviews with these three groups across Canada, asking similar questions to the ones posed in this study. A national initiative would help to generate a larger sample size that would permit regional, age, and denominational comparisons. This type of study would also test the reliability and validity of the findings discovered in this study. Do the conclusions and hypotheses advanced here, based on ninety interviews, hold in a larger sample across Canada?

Another opportunity is to track individual religiosity levels longitudinally as part of a panel study. For those I interviewed, what will their level of religiosity look like in ten, twenty, or thirty years from now? Will they believe and behave similarly to when I first met them, will they appear more religious, or will they become less religious, and what variables contribute to these possible realities? Following the same people over the long term is especially beneficial to conclusively resolve what happens to individuals who potentially return to religious involvement around key life events. Is their return a brief one or do they stick around? Moreover, how do people transmit religion between generations and what are the processes at work in these exchanges? This question is particularly interesting given that many marginal affiliates and some religious nones believe that religion is not necessary for people to be moral or ethical, yet they either have or plan to provide their children with some level of religious socialization for the purposes of moral instruction. What exactly is going on here and how might we explain this apparent contradiction between belief and behaviour? Many of those interviewed in this study are open to being contacted again in ten or fifteen years and thereafter for additional interviews. I hope to answer many of these questions in the years and decades to come based on an established and ongoing research base with individuals in this study and others to come on board in the future.

Individualism among active affiliates is an additional intriguing aspect worth paying attention to. Will more active affiliates adopt an individualist approach to their faith over and against their religious group, and will the extent and depth of this individualism expand? How will active affiliates, many of whom give a degree of control over to God and to others to guide their life, negotiate the stronger cultural push for individual authority in all aspects of one's life? What impact might religious individualism have on religious socialization efforts in active affiliate homes? Will active affiliates be more inclined to also give their children religious options like marginal affiliates and religious nones are prone to do? What role, if any, do religious organizations have in contributing to internal forms of secularization via growing individualism, or how might religious organizations, local congregations, and religious leaders respond to growing individualism from within?

Future research could also look into those who turn their backs on religious organizations but who claim that their faith has a "master status" in their life. Books such as *A Churchless Faith* (Jamieson 2002) or *Revolution* (Barna 2005, 13) highlight the over twenty million Americans who were once heavily involved in church organizations, often in leadership positions, who have left the church, but not their faith. They are different from marginal affiliates because religion remains highly important to them, but they are similar to marginal affiliates in their level of church involvement. Some may turn to alternative forms of religious life, such as house churches (Zdero 2007), while others may rely on Christian friends to journey through life with minus any formal commitment for regular church gatherings together. It is difficult to know if these individuals currently identify as Christian or as part of the "no religion" group, but this amorphous and growing group could yield valuable information about contemporary religious life.

A related opportunity is to research church plants where empirical research is lacking in Canada especially (see Bowen 2013), likely a function of their small size and loose affiliation with more formal religious organizations (e.g., denominations). What variables inform the rise, sustenance, or demise of church plants? Who attends church plants and why? What can we learn about their organizational and leadership structure?

Another set of questions pertains to marginal affiliates. What will happen with this group in the future? Will they become active affiliates as some believe they might, will they remain marginal affiliates, or will they gradually slide into the religious none category? Further, given the well-documented struggles of Roman Catholics and mainline Protestants in Canada, traditions where many marginal affiliates in Canada reside, will these demographic shifts inevitably diminish the marginal affiliate pool?

Concerning religious nones, this study starts a conversation that is likely to grow in the sociological study of religion in Canada in the years ahead. Quantitative and qualitative studies are needed to give us basic information about religious nones in Canada, and it will be interesting to document how religious nones develop as individuals and as a group. Will they continue to exist as religious nones on their own or will they gradually gather with like-minded individuals on a regular basis to reinforce their world view, particularly among secular and atheist religious nones? If they do begin to gather more regularly, what social processes, contexts, and meanings are at work? How might the global rise of religious nones, and atheism in particular, impact religious nones and atheists in Canada?

THE NATION'S CAPITAL

I put the finishing touches on this manuscript during a week where, in two separate incidents, Canadian soldiers were attacked on home soil. On 20 October 2014 in Saint-Jean-sur-Richelieu, Quebec Martin Couture-Rouleau, a home-grown Islamic convert and radical ran his vehicle over two soldiers, killing one, Warrant Officer Patrice Vincent and injuring another. Two days later, in Canada's capital city Ottawa, Ontario, Corporal Nathan Cirillo was standing guard at the National War Memorial when he was gunned down by Michael Zehaf-Bibeau, a Canadian-born Muslim radical. Zehaf-Bibeau then stormed the Canadian Parliament, exchanging gunfire with security officers before being killed. These events come on the heels of Canada's decade-long involvement in Afghanistan, its recent military commitment to combat Islamic insurgents in the Middle East, and a growing public awareness of home-grown religious radicals who aim to attack on Canadian soil.

Increased public, media, and academic concern with home-grown radicalization and terrorism (Bramadat and Dawson 2014) is a reflection of the world that Canadians now live in. The perfect storm between Canada's values of immigration and multiculturalism, globalization and technological connectedness, and people's quest for identity and meaning in contemporary society entails that scholars pay careful attention to the intersection between religious and social diversity and extremisms of all kinds. The question that remains to be answered is how active affiliates, marginal affiliates, and religious nones will shape and be shaped by these realities? Should we anticipate active affiliates to become more conservative in orthodoxy and orthopraxis as they stake their territory in the religious landscape against strongly conservative members of other religious groups or potentially militant atheists? Might less religious individuals turn to religion, particularly conservative streams to obtain stability and certainty in a fragmented and uncertain world? Will active and marginal affiliates progressively become less religious, or at least more privatized in their faith so as to not disturb the peace? In reality all of the above are likely to emerge in different niche markets. On the whole I expect that, as Peter Berger theorized, Canadians will individualize and privatize their faith in the face of religious diversity. Moreover, in the context of emerging fears surrounding religious radicalization, political and legal values that support religious neutrality and secularism will reign supreme in the nation's capital. As has gradually developed since the 1960s, religion no longer serves as a common base of ultimate meaning in Canadian society, for better or worse.

Similar to the themes that surfaced in my opening interviews with Larry Masters and Trent Hooper, assertions that religion is an individual phenomenon that should not be forced on others appeared through to my concluding interview with Leanne Toews, a religious none in her 50s who was raised in the Anglican church. In response to my question of how influential religious groups should be in shaping people's religious beliefs and practices, Leanne says: "I think information should be freely available. Coming to my front door on a Friday morning at eight o'clock is maybe going beyond. That I find a little intrusive, but I think, and especially in today's digital world, I mean, so much information as well. I think information should be widely available on all types of religions so that people can make the choice to go find it and make their own decision." Leanne continues to say, "I don't think I'm alone in my views, and I ... believe there are a number of people that ... are ... in similar positions that I am that consider it something personal if they have a belief or any relationship at all, and just would prefer to stay outside of the controversy."

Leanne's comments strike a chord in light of the recent terror events in Canada. From most accounts, both Martin Couture-Rouleau and Michael Zehaf-Bibeau were lone wolves who benefitted from the digital world to learn about religious and social diversity, and to mobilize their growing dissatisfaction with what in their minds were injustices in the world. No one forced religion on to them, but they were certainly involuntarily exposed to the predominant secular, individualist, pluralist, tolerant, and relativist values that dominate Canadian society. Such "extreme" Canadian values might have been enough to push these individuals, and others in the making, toward radicalized religious expressions. Today, easy access to technology, the Internet, and the media ensures that individuals can readily pursue desired religious and secular rewards on their own terms, and control the costs required in the process. It appears that in a global society where complex social structures and systems clearly alienate some individuals, there is an appeal for some to take the world into their own hands, and globalization and technology are making this easier to do with devastating precision and consequences. I wonder if interviewees still feel as strongly about faith as an individual phenomenon that should not be pushed on to others. Will an appetite emerge for greater social structural influence and monitoring relative to religion rather than a widespread acceptance of the "hands off" approach that currently dominates the Canadian religious landscape? Only time will tell.

This book is ultimately about active affiliates, marginal affiliates, and religious nones who adopt an array of religious attitudes and behaviours, but who generally share an ethos that religion is an individual matter that should not be pushed on to others who view the world differently than them. This view is not exclusive to these groups however. Peter Beyer (2013b, 15) echoes this perspective in his discussion of Muslim, Hindu, and Buddhist youth in Canada:

> Practically no one was favourable – or would admit to being favourable – to politicized religion, religion of whatever stripe that sought to impose its views on others by whatever means, including not just violence but, for a good number, any overt proselytization. Religious equality and tolerance of differences meant that it was fine and even important to share one's religion, provided that it was invited and then done in the spirit of sharing and mutual understanding and not aggressively with the intention of converting the other. In connection with this feature, religion was for most people in the first instance a personal affair.

There is little doubt in my mind that this approach to religion is an extension of a long-standing societal secularization process that is more recently manifested in organizational and individual levels of secularization. Moreover, this orientation toward religion factors greatly into why, regardless of what is done to religious supply, the demand for religion is likely to continue to diminish in light of dominant Canadian values that are generally at odds with organized religious belief and practice as once known in Canada. This is not an optimistic vision for religion, but this interpretation is realistic, and sociologists are, after all, chiefly interested in reality.

APPENDICES

APPENDIX A

Interview Schedule

PART ONE — BACKGROUND

(1) Description of Project and Demographic Information

    a. How old are you?
    b. What is your highest level of completed education?
    c. What type of occupation are you currently involved in?
    d. Are you married? If so, how long have you been married?
    e. Do you have any children? If so, how many, and how old are they?

(2) Tell me a bit about your upbringing:

    a. Where did you grow up? Did you have any siblings? What was your parents' occupation while you were growing up?
    b. Growing up, was your family affiliated with any religious group? If so, which group? *If not, skip to questions g, h, and i.*
    c. How often did your family attend religious services?
    d. Aside from religious services, what other religious activities, if any, were you involved in? What religious activities did you do at home?
    e. Would you describe your family as religious? Explain.
    f. Growing up, how much of a difference would you say religious beliefs and practices made on your family's life? Your life personally?
    g. (*Only for those not raised in a religious home*) Did your family ever talk about religion or spirituality? Was there any evidence of religious belief or practice in your home growing up?

h. (*Only for those not raised in a religious home*) Were you ever exposed to religious belief and/or practice outside of your home, growing up (e.g., neighbours, school, or extended family)?
i. (*Only for those not raised in a religious home*) Would you describe yourself as religious growing up? If so, in what way? Explain.
j. Thinking back to when you moved out of your family's place, what effect, if any, did that have on your religious journey? Did your interest in religion increase, decrease, or stay the same? Did your level of involvement in religious organizations increase, decrease, or remain the same?

PART TWO – CURRENT RELIGIOUS ATTITUDES AND BEHAVIOURS

(3) Current religious affiliation, beliefs, practices, and level of importance attributed to each:
   a. At present, are you affiliated with any religious group?
   b. How often do you attend religious services?
   c. (*Skip for Religious Nones*) Do you participate in any other activities associated with your religious group? If so, which activities, and how often are you involved?
   d. How did you decide to affiliate with this group? (If they are having trouble thinking of reasons – were there certain beliefs or practices that were appealing? Did you know others already involved with this group? Preacher? Music? Programs?)
   e. Could you indicate for me how important your religious affiliation is relative to other aspects of your life (e.g., family, job, or social activities)? Explain.
   f. Have you ever seriously considered affiliating or getting involved with any other congregation, denomination, or religious group? Why or why not?
   g. (*Religious Nones*) Tell me about any (quasi) religious/spiritual beliefs that you hold as well as any (quasi) religious/spiritual practices that you participate in. Probe the following too:
      i. Would you identify yourself as an atheist (God does not exist), agnostic (does not definitively believe or disbelieve

that God exists), or theist (God does exist)? Do you believe in a supernatural power or deity?
ii. Do you believe in the afterlife? If so, do you desire life after death? What do you think is required to obtain life after death?
iii. Do you believe that you have meaning, purpose, and direction in life? If so, what is the source of that meaning and direction?
iv. Do you associate with any particular thinker or set of readings or group that influences your approach to religion or spirituality? If so, do you agree and abide by all that they prescribe, or do you hold to some teachings and reject others?
v. If married, did you get married in a church and/or did you include any religious/spiritual elements in the service? If not married, do you plan to get married in a church and/or to include any religious/spiritual elements in the service? Do you plan to have your funeral in a church and/or to include any religious/spiritual elements in the service?
vi. If you have children someday, how will you raise them? Will you give them a religious upbringing? Will you take/send them to church? Why/why not?
vii. How much of a difference would you say your religious/spiritual beliefs and practices make to your life? If a great difference, in what way? If not much of a difference, why not? Explain.
viii. How confident are you in the religious beliefs and practices that you adopt?

h. (*Active and Marginal Affiliates*)
i. Overall, what, if any, beliefs and practices shape your life?
ii. Do you believe in the afterlife? If so, do you desire life after death? What do you think is required to obtain life after death?
iii. Thinking beyond your religious organization, what other religious activities, if any, do you do at home?
iv. To what extent do you follow the religious teachings of your religious group? Do you agree and abide by all that

they prescribe, or do you hold to some teachings and reject others? Probe for both beliefs and behaviours.
  v. How much of a difference would you say your religious beliefs and practices make to your life? If a great difference, in what way? If not much of a difference, why not? Explain.
  vi. How confident are you in the religious beliefs and practices that you adopt?

PART THREE – RATIONAL CHOICE THEORY

(4) Religious Costs and Rewards:

   a. (*Skip for Religious Nones*) Why do you attend religious services?
   b. (*Skip for Religious Nones*) Do you think you gain something specific from attending religious services?
   c. (*Skip for Religious Nones*) Do you think you gain anything in particular from your religious beliefs and practices outside of attendance at religious services? (*If nothing, skip to question e.*)
   d. (*Religious Nones*) Do you think you gain anything in particular by not being religious?
   e. Keeping in mind some of these benefits, what are some of the sacrifices that you have made along the way? In other words, what are the "costs" associated with obtaining these benefits? (*Religious Nones* – are there any "costs" for not belonging to a religious group or attending religious services regularly?)

(5) Dependable and Responsive

   a. Do you have a sense that you can depend on God and/or another spiritual entity? If so, how? Can you provide an example? If not, why?
   b. Do you believe that God and/or another spiritual entity is concerned about, and acts on behalf of humans? Explain.
   c. To what extent do you feel that you belong to or identify with a particular congregation? *If they do not feel connected to a congregation, ask*: do you remember a time when you did feel like you belonged to or identified with a particular congregation? *If the answer is still "no," skip to section 6.*

Interview Schedule

    d. With this congregation in mind, do you have a sense that you can depend on others in the group (either among leadership or laypeople), that others in the group could be relied upon in times of need? If so, how? Can you provide an example? If not, why?

    e. Do you believe that your congregation is concerned about, and acts in the interests of its members? Explain.

(6) Role of others in shaping one's religious life:

    a. Would you say that religious beliefs and practices are primarily up to the individual to develop and foster or should this occur in the context of other people? If shared with others, what sort of activities do you have in mind? How are these beliefs reflected in your religious journey?

    b. How influential do you think religious groups should be in shaping people's religious beliefs and practices? How influential is your religious group in shaping your religious beliefs and practices? *Religious Nones* – if it hasn't come up already, probe to see if there is any guiding group or influential figures that shape their views on religion.

    c. Of your closest friends, how many of them are from your local congregation? How many of them share the same religion as you?

PART FOUR – SECULARIZATION AND GREATER INVOLVEMENT

(7) Secularization and Greater Involvement:

    a. There is some research that suggests that attendance at religious services is on the decline. Presuming for a moment that this is true, what do you think explains this?

    Marginal Affiliates: How would you explain your own level of participation?

    b. (*Marginal Affiliates*) Some Canadians have suggested that they draw selective beliefs and practices from their religious tradition, even if they do not attend frequently. They indicate that they do not plan on changing religious traditions, but they will turn to religious groups for important religious

holidays and rites of passages. How well does this describe you? What draws you to religious services on such occasions? What meaning and significance do you find in these activities?
   c. (*Marginal Affiliates and Religious Nones*) Would you consider the possibility of being more involved in a religious group if you found it to be worthwhile for you or your family?
   d. If participants are interested in greater involvement, what factors do you think would make greater participation more worthwhile? If participants are not interested in greater involvement, why not (and then skip to question g)?
   e. If religious groups received the responses that you have just provided and they adjusted their supply of religion to provide some of the things that you mention, how likely would you be to increase your level of participation?
   f. For yourself (if they desire greater involvement), are there any efforts that you have made to find a suitable congregation to participate in, one that meets some of your criteria? If so, describe one of those instances.
   g. (*If this has not come up yet ...*) If you have children someday, how will you raise them? Will you give them a religious upbringing? Will you take/send them to church? Why/why not?

PART FIVE — CIVIC ENGAGEMENT

(8) Religious Involvement in the context of other Social Involvements:

   a. Overall, do you think that religion is a positive or a negative social force in society? Explain.
   b. Do you believe that people need religion in order to be moral or ethical beings?
   c. Are there other organizations, social activities, or volunteer initiatives that you dedicate your time to? If so, what does this commitment entail? If they have trouble thinking of any, suggest things like sports activities, book clubs, political activities, social protests or movements, and regular meetings with friends and family.
   d. How important are these involvements for you? Is there any correlation between these involvements and your religious

involvements? Put another way, does your religious involvement influence the type or amount of time given to other activities, or would you be more involved in church activities if you were not involved in any of the above activities?
e. Anything you want to add?

APPENDIX B

Interviewee Demographics

	Actives	Marginals	Nones	Total
GENDER				
Female	15	15	17	47
Male	15	15	13	43
AGE (YEARS)				
18–34	11	10	11	32
35–54	11	13	11	35
55+	8	7	8	23
HIGHEST COMPLETED EDUCATION				
Less than high school	0	1	1	2
High school	3	2	2	7
Diploma/certificate	3	6	8	17
Some college/university	5	6	2	13
Bachelor of arts/education	12	13	14	39
Master's	5	2	3	10
Doctorate	2	0	0	2
CURRENT MARITAL STATUS				
Single	6	11	6	23
Common law	0	0	2	2
Engaged	0	2	1	3
First marriage	16	9	18	43
Second marriage	5	3	1	9
Separated	0	0	1	1
Divorced	2	1	1	4
Widowed	1	4	0	5
CURRENT (PAST FOR NONES) DENOMINATION				
Roman Catholic	11	9	7	27
Mainline Protestant	9	9	10	28
Conservative Protestant	7	7	6	20
Non-denominational	3	5	0	8
Mormon	0	0	1	1
No religious upbringing for nones	0	0	6	6

Bibliography

Adams, Michael. 2006. *Sex in the Snow: The Surprising Revolution in Canadian Social Values*. Toronto: Penguin.
Altemeyer, Bob, and Bruce Hunsberger. 1997. *Amazing Conversions: Why Some Turn to Faith and Others Abandon Religion*. Amherst, NY: Prometheus.
Ammerman, Nancy T. 1997. *Congregation and Community*. New Brunswick, NJ: Rutgers University Press.
– 2005. *Pillars of Faith: American Congregations and Their Partners*. Berkeley: University of California Press.
Arweck, Elisabeth, and Eleanor Nesbitt. 2010. "Growing Up in a Mixed-Faith Family: Intact or Fractured Chain of Memory?" Pp. 167–74 in *Religion and Youth*, ed. Sylvia Collins-Mayo and Pink Dandelion. Aldershot, UK: Ashgate.
Asad, Talal. 1993. *Genealogies of Religion: Discipline and Reasons of Power in Christianity and Islam*. Baltimore: Johns Hopkins University Press.
Bagg, Samuel, and David Voas. 2010. "The Triumph of Indifference: Irreligion in British Society." Pp. 91–111 in *Atheism and Secularity*, vol. 2, *Global Expressions*, ed. Phil Zuckerman. Santa Barbara, CA: Praeger.
Bahr, Howard M. 1970. "Aging and Religious Disaffiliation." *Social Forces* 49 (1): 59–71.
Baker, Joseph O'Brian, and Buster Smith. 2009. "None Too Simple: Examining Issues of Religious Nonbelief and Nonbelonging in the United States." *Journal for the Scientific Study of Religion* 48 (4): 719–33.
Barna, George. 2005. *Revolution*. Carol Stream, IL: Tyndale.
Baum, Gregory. 2000. "Catholicism and Secularization in Quebec." Pp. 149–65 in *Rethinking Church, State, and Modernity: Canada*

Between Europe and America, ed. David Lyon and Marguerite Van Die. Toronto: University of Toronto Press.

Beaman, Lori. 2008. *Defining Harm: Religious Freedom and the Limits of the Law*. Vancouver: University of British Columbia Press.

Beaman, Lori, and Peter Beyer, eds. 2008. *Religion and Diversity in Canada*. Boston: Brill.

Bebbington, D.W. 1989. *Evangelicalism in Modern Britain: A History from the 1730s to the 1980s*. London: Unwin Hyman.

Becker, Gary. 1976. *The Economic Approach to Human Behavior*. Chicago: University of Chicago Press.

Bellah, Robert, Richard Madsen, William N. Sullivan, Ann Swidler, and Steven M. Tipton. 1985. *Habits of the Heart: Individualism and Commitment in American Life*. Berkeley: University of California Press.

Bengtson, Vern L., with Norella M. Putney, and Susan Harris. 2013. *Families and Faith: How Religion Is Passed Down Across Generations*. New York: Oxford University Press.

Berger, Ida. 2006. "The Influence of Philanthropy in Canada." *Voluntus* 17: 115–32.

Berger, Peter. 1967. *The Sacred Canopy: Elements of Sociological Theory of Religion*. Garden City, NY: Doubleday.

– 1979. *The Heretical Imperative: Contemporary Possibilities of Religious Affirmation*. Garden City, NY: Doubleday.

Berger, Peter, ed. 1999. *The Desecularization of the World: Resurgent Religion and World Politics*. Grand Rapids, MI: Eerdmans.

Berger, Peter, Grace Davie, and Effie Fokas. 2008. *Religious America, Secular Europe?: A Theme and Variation*. Burlington, VT: Ashgate.

Berghuijs, Joantine, Jos Pieper, and Cok Bakker. 2013. "New Spirituality and Social Engagement." *Journal for the Scientific Study of Religion* 52 (4): 775–92.

Beyer, Peter. 1999. "Secularization from the Perspective of Globalization: A Response to Dobbelaere." *Sociology of Religion* 60 (3): 289–301.

– 2005. "The Future of Non-Christian Religions in Canada: Patterns of Religious Identification among Recent Immigrants and their Second Generation, 1981–2001." *Studies in Religion* 34 (2): 165–96.

– 2013a. "From Atheism to Open Religiosity: Muslim Men." Pp. 74–111 in *Growing Up Canadian: Muslims, Hindus, Buddhists*, ed. Peter Beyer and Rubina Ramji. Montreal: McGill-Queen's University Press.

– 2013b. "Growing Up Canadian: Systemic and Lived Religion." Pp. 3–20 in *Growing Up Canadian: Muslims, Hindus, Buddhists*, ed. Peter Beyer and Rubina Ramji. Montreal: McGill-Queen's University Press.

- 2013c. "Growing Up in Canada, the United States, and Western Europe." Pp. 290–306 in *Growing Up Canadian: Muslims, Hindus, Buddhists,* ed. Peter Beyer and Rubina Ramji. Montreal: McGill-Queen's University Press.
- 2013d. "Islam, Hinduism, and Buddhism: Differential Reconstruction of Religions." Pp. 53–73 in *Growing Up Canadian: Muslims, Hindus, Buddhists,* ed. Peter Beyer and Rubina Ramji. Montreal: McGill-Queen's University Press.

Beyer, Peter, and Rubina Ramji, eds. 2013. *Growing Up Canadian: Muslims, Hindus, Buddhists.* Montreal: McGill-Queen's University Press.

Beyer, Peter, and Wendy K. Martin. 2010. *The Future of Religious Diversity in Canada: A Research Report.* Ottawa: Citizenship and Immigration Canada.

Bibby, Reginald. 1987. *Fragmented Gods: The Poverty and Potential of Religion in Canada.* Toronto: Stoddart.
- 1993. *Unknown Gods: The Ongoing Story of Religion in Canada.* Toronto: Stoddart.
- 2002. *Restless Gods: The Renaissance of Religion in Canada.* Toronto: Stoddart.
- 2004. *Restless Churches: How Canada's Churches Can Contribute to the Emerging Religious Renaissance.* Ottawa: Wood Lake Books.
- 2006. *The Boomer Factor: What Canada's Most Famous Generation Is Leaving Behind.* Toronto: Bastian Books.
- 2007. "Good without God, But Better with God?" Retrieved 16 Oct. 2007 (http://www.reginaldbibby.com/images/PC_10_BETTER_WITH_GOD_OCT0807.pdf).
- 2008. "The Perils of Pioneering and Prophecy: A Response to Thiessen and Dawson." *Studies in Religion* 37 (3–4): 417–25.
- 2011. *Beyond the Gods and Back: Religion's Demise and Rise and Why It Matters.* Lethbridge, AB: Project Canada Books.
- 2012. "Why Bother with Organized Religion?" *Canadian Review of Sociology* 49 (1): 91–101.

Bibby, Reginald, and Andrew Grenville. 2013. "The Christmas Onlys: A Wakeup Bell for Canada's Religious Groups." Retrieved 21 Jan. 2014 (http://reginaldbibby.com/images/Release_2013_Christmas_Onlys_Dec_23_2013.pdf).

Bibby, Reginald, Sarah Russell, and Ron Rolheiser. 2009. *The Emerging Millennials: How Canada's Newest Generation Is Responding to Change and Choice.* Lethbridge, AB: Project Canada Books.

Blau, Peter. 1964. *Exchange and Power in Social Life*. New York: Wiley.
Bowen, John, ed. 2013. *Green Shoots out of Dry Ground: Growing a New Future for the Church in Canada*. Eugene, OR: Wipf and Stock.
Bowen, Kurt. 2004. *Christians in a Secular World: The Canadian Experience*. Montreal: McGill-Queen's University Press.
Brady, H.E., S. Verba, and K. Schlozman. 1995. "Beyond SES: A Resource Model of Political Participation." *American Political Science Review* 89: 271–94.
Bramadat, Paul, and Lorne L. Dawson, eds. 2014. *Religious Radicalization and Securitization in Canada and Beyond*. Toronto: University of Toronto Press.
Bramadat, Paul, and David Seljak, eds. 2005. *Religion and Ethnicity in Canada*. Toronto: Pearson.
– 2008. *Christianity and Ethnicity in Canada*. Toronto: University of Toronto Press.
Bromley, David G., and Jeffrey K. Hadden, eds. 1993. *Handbook of Cults and Sects in America, Parts A and B. Religion and the Social Order*, vol. 3. Greenwich, CT: JAI Press.
Bruce, Steve. 1999. *Choice and Religion: A Critique of Rational Choice*. Oxford: Oxford University Press.
– 2002. *God Is Dead: Secularization in the West*. Malden, MA: Blackwell.
– 2011. *Secularization: In Defence of an Unfashionable Theory*. New York: Oxford University Press.
Bryant, Joseph. 2000. "Review Essay: Cost-Benefit Accounting and the Piety Business: Is *Homo Religiosus*, at bottom, a *Homo Economicus*?" *Method and Theory in the Study of Religion* 12: 520–48.
Buckingham, Janet Epp. 2014. *Fighting Over God: A Legal and Political History of Religious Freedom in Canada*. Montreal: McGill-Queen's University Press.
Bullivant, Stephen. 2008. "Introducing Irreligious Experiences." *Implicit Religion* 11 (1): 7–24.
Bullivant, Stephen, and Lois Lee. 2012. "Interdisciplinary Studies of Non-Religion and Secularity: The State of the Union." *Journal of Contemporary Religion* 27: 19–27.
Burkimsher, Marion. 2009. "Religiosity, Revival, and Secularisation: Cross-Country Comparisons." Paper presented at Universitair Centrum Sint Ignatius Antwerpen, Antwerp, Belgium, 6 Sept.
Campbell, Colin. 1971. *Toward a Sociology of Irreligion*. London: Macmillan.
Campbell, David, and Steven Yonish. 2003. "Religion and Volunteering in America." Pp. 87–106 in *Religion as Social Capital: Producing the Common Good*, ed. Corwin Smidt. Waco, TX: Baylor University Press.

Carrière, Kathryn. 2013. "Growing Up in Toronto: Muslims, Hindus, Buddhists." Pp. 262–89 in *Growing Up Canadian: Muslims, Hindus, Buddhists*, ed. Peter Beyer and Rubina Ramji. Montreal: McGill-Queen's University Press.

Casanova, Jose. 1994. *Public Religions in the Modern World*. Chicago: University of Chicago Press.

– 2007. "Rethinking Secularization: A Global Comparative Perspective." Pp. 101–20 in *Religion, Globalization, and Culture*, ed. Peter Beyer and Lori Beaman. Leiden: Brill.

– 2008. "Public Religions Revisited." Pp. 101–19 in *Religion: Beyond a Concept*, ed. Hent de Vries. New York: Fordham University Press.

Cavey, Bruxy. 2005. *The End of Religion: An Introduction to the Subversive Spirituality of Jesus*. Oakville, ON: Agora Imprints.

Chandler, Siobhan. 2008. "The Social Ethic of Religiously Unaffiliated Spirituality." *Religion Compass* 2: 1–17.

Chaves, Mark. 1994. "Secularization as Declining Religious Authority." *Social Forces* 72: 749–74.

– 1995. "On the Rational Choice Approach to Religion." *Journal for the Scientific Study of Religion* 34 (1): 98–104.

– 2011. *American Religion: Contemporary Trends*. Princeton, NJ: Princeton University Press.

Clark, Warren. 2003. "Pockets of Belief: Religious Attendance Patterns in Canada." *Canadian Social Trends* 68: 2–5.

Clarke, Brian, and Stuart Macdonald. 2007. "'Simply "Christian": Canada's Newest Major Religious Denomination." *Toronto Journal of Theology* 23 (2): 109–25.

Clydesdale, Tim. 2007. *The First Year Out: Understanding American Teens after High School*. Chicago: University of Chicago Press.

Cnaan, Ram A. 2002. *The Invisible Caring Hand: American Congregations and the Provision of Welfare*. New York: New York University Press.

Cnaan, Ram, Stephanie Boddie, and Gaynor Yancey. 2003. "Bowling Alone But Serving Together: The Congregational Norm of Community Involvement." Pp. 19–31 in *Religion as Social Capital: Producing the Common Good*, ed. Corwin Smidt. Waco, TX: Baylor University Press.

Coleman, John. 2003. "Religious Social Capital: Its Nature, Social Location, and Limits." Pp. 33–47 in *Religion as Social Capital: Producing the Common Good*, ed. Corwin Smidt. Waco, TX: Baylor University Press.

Collins-Mayo, Sylvia, and Pink Dandelion, eds. 2010. *Religion and Youth*. Aldershot, UK: Ashgate.

Condran, John, and Joseph Tamney. 1985. "'Religious Nones': 1957–1982." *Sociological Analysis* 46: 415–23.

Connor, Phillip. 2008. "Increase or Decrease? The Impact of the International Migratory Event on Immigrant Religious Participation." *Journal for the Scientific Study of Religion* 47 (2): 243–57.

– 2009. "Immigrant Religiosity in Canada: Multiple Trajectories." *Journal of International Migration and Integration* 10: 159–75.

Cox, Harvey. 1966. *The Secular City: Secularization and Urbanization in Theological Perspective*. New York: Macmillan.

Cragun, Ryan, Barry Kosmin, Ariela Keysar, Joseph Hammer, and Michael Nielsen. 2012. "On the Receiving End: Discrimination Toward the Non-Religious in the United States." *Journal of Contemporary Religion* 27 (1): 105–27.

Crockett, Alasdair, and David Voas. 2006. "Generations of Decline: Religious Change in 20th Century Britain." *Journal for the Scientific Study of Religion* 45 (4): 567–84.

Curtis, James, Douglas Baer, and Edward Grabb. 2001. "Nations of Joiners: Explaining Voluntary Association Membership in Democratic Societies." *American Sociological Review* 66: 783–805.

Curtis, James, Edward Grabb, and Douglas Baer. 1992. "Voluntary Association Membership in Fifteen Countries: A Comparative Analysis." *American Sociological Review* 57: 139–52.

Davidman, Lynn. 2007. "The New Voluntarism and the Case of the Unsynagogued Jews." Pp. 51–67 in *Everyday Religion: Observing Modern Religious Lives*, ed. Nancy Ammerman. New York: Oxford University Press.

Davie, Grace. 1994. *Religion in Britain since 1945: Believing without Belonging*. Cambridge, MA: Blackwell.

Dawkins, Richard. 2006. *The God Delusion*. New York: Bantam.

Dawson, Lorne L. 2006. *Comprehending Cults: The Sociology of New Religious Movements*. 2nd ed. Toronto: Oxford University Press.

Day, Abby. 2011. *Believing in Belonging: Belief and Social Identity in the Modern World*. Toronto: Oxford University Press.

Demerath III, N.J. 1995. "Rational Paradigms, A-rational Religion, and the Debate over Secularization." *Journal for the Scientific Study of Religion* 34 (1): 105–12.

– 2001. *Crossing the Gods: World Religions and Worldly Politics*. New Brunswick, NJ: Rutgers University Press.

Dencik, Lars. 2007. "The Paradox of Secularism in Denmark: From Emancipation to Ethnocentrism?" Pp. 125–38 in *Secularism and*

Secularity: Contemporary International Perspectives, ed. Barry Kosmin and Ariela Keysar. Hartford, CT: Institute for the Study of Secularism in Society and Culture.

Dillon, Michele, and Paul Wink. 2007. *In the Course of a Lifetime: Tracing Religious Belief, Practice, and Change.* Berkeley: University of California Press.

Dobbelaere, Karel. 1981. "Secularization: A Multi-dimensional Concept." *Current Sociology* 29 (2): 1–213.

– 2002. *Secularization: An Analysis at Three Levels.* Brussels: Peter Lang.

Dudley, Carl. 1978. "Alienation from Religion in Adolescents from Fundamentalist Religious Homes." *Journal for the Scientific Study of Religion* 17 (4): 389–98.

– 1979. *Where Have All Our People Gone?: New Choices for Old Churches.* New York: Pilgrim Press.

Dudley, Roger L. 1999. "Youth Religious Commitment over Time: A Longitudinal Study of Retention." *Review of Religious Research* 41: 109–20.

Duneier, Mitchell. 2006. "Ethnography, the Ecological Fallacy, and the 1995 Chicago Heat Wave." *American Sociological Review* 71: 679–88.

Durkheim, Emile. 1915. *The Elementary Forms of the Religious Life: A Study in Religious Sociology.* London: Allen and Unwin.

Eagle, David. 2011. "Changing Patterns of Attendance at Religious Services in Canada, 1986–2008." *Journal for the Scientific Study of Religion* 50 (1): 175–200.

Eck, Diana. 2001. *A New Religious America: How a "Christian Country" Has Become the World's Most Religiously Diverse Nation.* New York: HarperCollins.

Ellison, Christopher. 1995. "Rational Choice Explanations of Individual Religious Behavior: Notes on the Problem of Social Embeddedness." *Journal for the Scientific Study of Religion* 34 (1): 89–97.

Espeland, Wendy. 2005. "Thinking about Standards." Paper given at National Science Foundation, Sociology Program, Washington, DC.

Fine, Gary. 1993. "Ten Lies of Ethnography: Moral Dilemmas of Field Research." *Journal of Contemporary Ethnography* 22 (3): 267–94.

Finke, Roger. 1997. "The Consequences of Religious Competition: Supply-Side Explanations for Religious Change." Pp. 46–65 in *Rational Choice Theory and Religion: Summary and Assessment*, ed. Lawrence Young. New York: Routledge.

Finke, Roger, and Rodney Stark. 2005. *The Churching of America 1776–2005: Winners and Losers in Our Religious Economy.* Piscataway, NJ: Rutgers University Press.

Friesen, Joe, and Sandra Martin. 2010 (5 Oct.). "Canada's Changing Faith." *Globe and Mail*. Retrieved 16 Dec. 2010 (http://www.theglobeandmail.com/news/national/time-to-lead/multiculturalism/canadas-changing-faith/article1741422/).

Friesen, Milton, and Cheryl Clieff. 2014. "Strengthening Vital Signs through Urban Religious Communities." Retrieved 6 Oct. 2014 (https://www.cardus.ca/store/4139/).

Fuller, Robert. 2001. *Spiritual but Not Religious: Understanding Unchurched America*. New York: Oxford University Press.

Giddens, Anthony. 1990. *The Consequences of Modernity*. Cambridge: Polity.

Goodwin, Jeff, and Ruth Horowitz. 2002. "Introduction: The Methodological Strengths and Dilemmas of Qualitative Sociology." *Qualitative Sociology* 25 (1): 33–47.

Gorski, Philip. 2000. "Historicizing the Secularization Debate: Church, State, and Society in Late Medieval and Early Modern Europe, ca. 1300 to 1700." *American Sociological Review* 65: 138–67.

Grant, John Webster. 1998. *The Church in the Canadian Era: Updated and Expanded Edition*. Vancouver: Regent College Publishing.

Greeley, Andrew M. 1989. *Religious Change in America*. Cambridge, MA: Harvard University Press.

Greil, Arthur, and David Bromley, eds. 2003. *Defining Religion: Investigating the Boundaries between the Sacred and Secular*. Oxford: Elsevier Science.

Grenville, Andrew. 2000. "'For by Him All Things Were Created ... Visible and Invisible': Sketching the Contours of Public and Private Religion in North America." Pp. 211–27 in *Rethinking Church, State, and Modernity: Canada between Europe and America*, ed. David Lyon and Marguerite Van Die. Toronto: University of Toronto Press.

Grossman, Cathy Lynn. 2012. "Survey Finds 19 percent without Religious Affiliation." *USA Today*, 20 July. Retrieved 5 Aug. 2012 (http://wwrn.org/articles/37779/).

Hadaway, C. Kirk, and Penny L. Marler. 1993. "All In the Family: Religious Mobility in America." *Review of Religious Research* 35 (2): 97–116.

Hadaway, C. Kirk, and Wade Clark Roof. 1979. "Those Who Stay Religious 'Nones' and Those Who Don't: A Research Note." *Journal for the Scientific Study of Religion* 18 (2): 194–200.

Hadden, Jeffrey. 1987. "Toward Desacralizing Secularization Theory." *Social Forces* 65: 587–611.

Hadden, Jeffrey, and Anson Shupe, eds. 1989. *Secularization and Fundamentalism Reconsidered.* New York: Paragon.
Hall, Michael, David Lasby, Steven Ayer, and William David Gibbons. 2009. "Caring Canadians, Involved Canadians: Highlights from the 2007 Canada Survey of Giving, Volunteering, and Participating." Retrieved 28 June 28 2009 (http://www.givingandvolunteering.ca/files/giving/en/csgvp_highlights_2007.pdf).
Harper, Marcel. 2007. "The Stereotyping of Nonreligious People by Religious Students: Contents and Subtypes." *Journal for the Scientific Study of Religion* 46 (4): 539–52.
Harris, Fredrick. 2003. "Ties that Bind and Flourish: Religion as Social Capital in African-American Politics and Society." Pp. 121–37 in *Religion as Social Capital: Producing the Common Good,* ed. Corwin Smidt. Waco, TX: Baylor University Press.
Harris, Sam. 2006. *Letters to a Christian Nation.* New York: Knopf.
Haskell, David. 2009. *Through a Lens Darkly: How the News Media Perceive and Portray Evangelicals.* Toronto: Clements Publishing Group Inc.
Hay, D. Alastair. 2014. "An Investigation into the Swiftness and Intensity of Recent Secularization in Canada: Was Berger Right?" *Sociology of Religion* 75 (1): 136–62.
Heath, Anthony. 1976. *Rational Choice and Social Exchange: A Critique of Exchange Theory.* Cambridge: Cambridge University Press.
Heelas, Paul, Linda Woodhead, Benjamin Seel, Bronislaw Szerszynski, and Karin Tusting. 2005. *The Spiritual Revolution: Why Religion Is Giving Way to Spirituality.* Malden, MA: Blackwell.
Hervieu-Léger, Danièle. 2006. "In Search of Certainties: The Paradoxes of Religiosity in Societies of High Modernity." *Hedgehog Review* 8 (1–2): 59–68.
Hesse-Biber, Sharlene Nagy, and Patricia Leavy, eds. 2004. *Approaches to Qualitative Research: A Reader on Theory and Practice.* New York: Oxford University Press.
Hitchens, Christopher. 2007. *God Is Not Great: How Religion Poisons Everything.* New York: Hachette.
Hodgkinson, V.A., and M.S. Weitzman. 1996. *Giving and Volunteering in the United States: Findings from a National Survey.* Washington, DC: Independent Sector.
Hollinger, Franz. 2004. "Does the Counter-Cultural Character of New Age Persist? Investigating Social and Political Attitudes of New Age Followers." *Journal of Contemporary Religion* 19 (3): 289–304.

Homans, George. 1961. *Social Behavior: Its Elementary Forms*. London: Routledge and Kegan Paul.

Hood Jr, Ralph. 2003. "The Relationship between Religion and Spirituality." Pp. 241–64 in *Defining Religion: Investigating the Boundaries between the Sacred and Secular*, ed. Arthur Greil and David Bromley. Kidlington: Elsevier Science.

Hout, Michael, and Claude S. Fischer. 2002. "Why More Americans Have No Religious Preference: Politics and Generations." *American Sociological Review* 67: 165–90.

Houtman, Dick, and Stef Aupers. 2007. "The Spiritual Turn and the Decline of Tradition: The Spread of Post-Christian Spirituality in 14 Western Countries, 1981–2000." *Journal for the Scientific Study of Religion* 46 (3): 305–20.

Hunsberger, Bruce, and Bob Altemeyer. 2006. *Atheists: A Groundbreaking Study of America's Nonbelievers*. Amherst, NY: Prometheus.

Iannaccone, Laurence. 1988. "A Formal Model of Church and Sect." *American Journal of Sociology* 94: S241–68.

– 1990. "Religious Practice: A Human Capital Approach." *Journal for the Scientific Study of Religion* 29 (3): 297–314.

– 1992. "Sacrifice and Stigma: Reducing Free-riding in Cults, Communes, and Other Collectives." *Journal of Political Economy* 100 (2): 271–91.

– 1994. "Why Strict Churches Are Strong." *American Journal of Sociology* 99 (5): 1180–1211.

– 1995a. "Voodoo Economics? Reviewing the Rational Choice Approach to Religion." *Journal for the Scientific Study of Religion* 34 (1): 76–89.

– 1995b. "Second Thoughts: A Response to Chaves, Demerath, and Ellison." *Journal for the Scientific Study of Religion* 34 (1): 113–20.

– 1997a. "Skewness Explained: A Rational Choice Model of Religious Giving." *Journal for the Scientific Study of Religion* 36 (2): 141–57.

– 1997b. "Introduction to the Economics of Religion." *Journal of Economic Literature* 36: 1465–96.

Iannaccone, Laurence, Daniel Olson, and Rodney Stark. 1995. "Religious Resources and Church Growth." *Social Forces* 74 (2): 705–31.

Iannaccone, Laurence, and Sean Everton. 2004. "Never on Sunny Days: Lessons from Weekly Attendance Counts." *Journal for the Scientific Study of Religion* 43 (2): 191–207.

Ingersoll-Dayton, Berit, Neal Krause, and David Morgan. 2002. "Religious Trajectories and Transitions over the Life Course." *International Journal of Aging and Human Development* 55 (1): 51–70.

Inglis, Tom. 2007. "Catholic Identity in Contemporary Ireland: Belief and Belonging to Tradition." *Journal of Contemporary Religion* 22 (2): 205–20.

Jamieson, Alan. 2002. *A Churchless Faith: Faith Journeys beyond the Churches*. London: Society for Promoting Christian Knowledge.

Janzen, Rich, Mark Chapman, and James Watson. 2012. "Integrating Immigrants into the Life of Canadian Urban Christian Congregations: Findings from a National Survey." *Review of Religious Research* 53 (4): 441–70.

Johnson, John. 2002. "In-Depth Interviewing." Pp. 103–20 in *Handbook of Interview Research: Context and Method*, ed. J.F. Gubrium and J.A. Holstein. Thousand Oaks, CA: Sage.

Johnston, Joseph B. 2013. "Religion and Volunteering over the Adult Life Course." *Journal for the Scientific Study of Religion* 52 (4): 733–52.

Kelley, Dean. 1972. *Why Conservative Churches Are Growing*. New York: Harper and Row.

King-Hele, Sarah. 2009. "Generational Changes in Canadian Religiosity." Conference Presentation at the Society for the Scientific Study of Religion, Denver, CO.

Kinnaman, David. 2011. *You Lost Me: Why Young Christians are Leaving Church – and Rethinking Faith*. Grand Rapids, MI: Baker.

Kinnaman, David, and Gabe Lyons. 2007. *UnChristian: What a New Generation Really Thinks about Christianity ... And Why It Matters*. Grand Rapids, MI: Baker.

Kosmin, Barry. 2007. "Introduction: Contemporary Secularity and Secularism." Pp. 1–13 in *Secularism and Secularity: Contemporary International Perspectives*, ed. Barry Kosmin and Ariela Keysar. Hartford, CT: Institute for the Study of Secularism in Society and Culture.

Kosmin, Barry, and Ariela Keysar. 2006. *Religion in a Free Market: Religious and Non-Religious Americans*. Ithaca, NY: Paramount Market.

– 2008. "American Nones: The Profile of the No Religion Population." Retrieved 17 Feb. 2010 (http://commons.trincoll.edu/aris/files/2011/08/NONES_08.pdf).

Kosmin, Barry, and Ariela Keysar, eds. 2007. *Secularism and Secularity: Contemporary International Perspectives*. Hartford, CT: Institute for the Study of Secularism in Society and Culture.

Lamont, Michele. 2005. "Criteria for Evaluation of Qualitative Research." Paper given at National Science Foundation, Sociology Program, Washington, DC.

Lamoureux Scholes, Laurie. 2003. *The Social Authority of Religion in Canada: A Study of Contemporary Death Rituals*. MA thesis, McGill University.

Lechner, Frank. 1991. "The Case against Secularization: A Rebuttal." *Social Forces* 69: 1103–19.

LeDrew, Stephen. 2013. "Discovering Atheism: Heterogeneity in Trajectories to Atheist Identity and Activism." *Sociology of Religion* 74 (4): 431–53.

Lefebvre, Solange, and Lori Beaman, eds. 2014. *Religion in the Public Sphere: Canadian Case Studies.* Toronto: University of Toronto Press.

Levan, Christopher. 1995. *God Hates Religion.* Etobicoke, ON: United Church Publishing House.

Lewis, James R. 2004. *The Oxford Handbook of New Religious Movements.* New York: Oxford University Press.

Lim, Chaeyoon, Carol Ann MacGregor, and Robert Putnam. 2010. "Secular and Liminal: Discovering Heterogeneity among Religious Nones." *Journal for the Scientific Study of Religion* 49 (4): 596–618.

Linneman, Thomas, and Margaret Clendenen. 2010. "Sexuality and the Sacred." Pp. 89–111 in *Atheism and Secularity,* vol. 1, ed. Phil Zuckerman. Santa Barbara, CA: Praeger.

Luckmann, Thomas. 1967. *The Invisible Religion: The Problem of Religion in Modern Society.* New York: Macmillan.

– 1990. "Shrinking Transcendence, Expanding Religion?" *Sociological Analysis* 51 (2): 127–38.

Lynch, Gordon. 2007. *The New Spirituality: An Introduction to Progressive Belief in the Twenty-First Century.* London: I.B. Tauris.

Lyon, David. 1985. *The Sleepless Shadow: On the Myths and Realities of Secularization.* Grand Rapids, MI: William B. Eerdmans.

Madge, Nicola, Peter J. Hemming, and Kevin Stenson. 2014. *Youth on Religion: The Development, Negotiation and Impact of Faith and Non-Faith Identity.* New York: Routledge.

Manning, Christel. 2010. "Atheism, Secularity, the Family, and Children." Pp. 19–42 in *Atheism and Secularity,* vol. 1, ed. Phil Zuckerman. Santa Barbara, CA: Praeger.

– 2013. "Unaffiliated Parents and the Religious Training of Their Children." *Sociology of Religion* 74 (2): 149–75.

Marler, Penny L., and C. Kirk Hadaway. 2002. "Being Religious or Being Spiritual in America: A Zero-Sum Proposition?" *Journal for the Scientific Study of Religion* 41 (2): 289–300.

Marti, Gerardo, and Gladys Ganiel. 2014. *The Deconstructed Church: Understanding Emerging Christianity.* New York: Oxford University Press.

Martin, David. 1969. *The Religious and the Secular: Studies in Secularization.* London: Routledge and Kegan Paul.

– 1978. *A General Theory of Secularization.* New York: Harper and Row.

- 1991. "The Secularization Issue: Prospect and Retrospect." *British Journal of Sociology* 42 (3): 465–74.
- 2005. *On Secularization: Towards a Revised General Theory.* Burlington, VT: Ashgate.

Martin, John Levi. 2011. *The Explanation of Social Action.* New York: Oxford University Press.

Marx, Karl. 1970. *Contribution to the Critique of Hegel's 'Philosophy of Right.'* Edited with an introduction by Joseph O'Malley. New York: Cambridge University Press.

Mata, Fernando. 2010. "Religion-Mix Growth in Canadian Cities: A Look at 2006–2031 Projections Data. Retrieved 6 Oct. 2014 (http://ir.lib.uwo.ca/cgi/viewcontent.cgi?article=1018andcontext=wmc).

Mauss, Armand. 1969. "Dimensions of Religious Defection." *Review of Religious Research* 10 (3): 128–35.

McClure, Jennifer M. 2013. "Sources of Social Support: Examining Congregational Involvement, Private Devotional Activities, and Congregational Context." *Journal for the Scientific Study of Religion* 52 (4): 698–712.

McCullough, Michael E., Sharon L. Brion, Craig K. Enders, and Andrea R. Jain. 2005. "The Varieties of Religious Development in Adulthood: A Longitudinal Investigation of Religion and Rational Choice." *Journal of Personality and Social Psychology* 89 (1): 78–89.

McDaniel, Susan, and Lorne Tepperman. 2011. *Close Relations: An Introduction to the Sociology of Families.* 4th ed. Toronto: Pearson.

McDonald, Marci. 2010. *The Armageddon Factor: The Rise of Christian Nationalism in Canada.* Toronto: Random House.

McGuire, Meredith. 2008. *Lived Religion: Faith and Practice in Everyday Life.* New York: Oxford University Press.

Merino, Stephen M. 2012. "Irreligious Socialization? The Adult Religious Preferences of Individuals Raised with No Religion." *Secularism and Nonreligion* 1: 1–16.

- 2013. "Religious Social Networks and Volunteering: Examining Recruitment via Close Ties." *Review of Religious Research* 55 (3): 509–27.

Miller, Donald. 1997. *Reinventing American Protestantism: Christianity in the New Millennium.* Berkeley: University of California Press.

Mills, Charles Wright. 1940. "Situated Actions and Vocabularies of Motive." *American Sociological Review* 5 (6): 904–13.

Myers, Scott M. 1996. "An Interactive Model of Religiosity Inheritance: The Importance of Family Context." *American Sociological Review* 61 (5): 858–66.

Nason-Clark, Nancy, and Cathy Holtman. 2013. "Perpetuating Religion and Culture: Hindu Women." Pp. 145–66 in *Growing Up Canadian: Muslims, Hindus, Buddhists*, ed. Peter Beyer and Rubina Ramji. Montreal: McGill-Queen's University Press.

Neitz, Mary Jo, and Peter R. Mueser. 1997. "Economic Man and the Sociology of Religion: A Critique of the Rational Choice Approach." Pp. 105–18 in *Rational Choice Theory and Religion: Summary and Assessment*, ed. Lawrence Young. New York: Routledge.

Nemeth, Roger J., and Donald Al Luidens. 2003. "The Religious Basis of Charitable Giving in America: A Social Capital Perspective." Pp. 107–20 in *Religion as Social Capital: Producing the Common Good*, ed. Corwin Smidt. Waco, TX: Baylor University Press.

Neuhaus, John. 2009. "Secularizations." *First Things*, Feb. (190): 23–8.

Niose, David. 2012. *Nonbeliever Nation: The Rise of Secular Americans*. New York: Palgrave Macmillan.

Noll, Mark. 1992. *A History of Christianity in the United States and Canada*. Grand Rapids, MI: William B. Eerdmans.

– 2006. "What Happened to Christian Canada?" *Church History* 75 (2): 245–73.

Norris, Pippa, and Ronald Inglehart. 2011. *Sacred and Secular: Religion and Politics Worldwide*. 2nd ed. New York: Cambridge University Press.

Olson, Daniel. 1989. "Church Friendships: Boon or Barrier to Church Growth?" *Journal for the Scientific Study of Religion* 28: 432–7.

– 1993. "Fellowship Ties and the Transmission of Religious Identity." Pp. 32–53 in *Beyond Establishment: Protestant Identity in a Post-Protestant Age*, ed. Jackson Carroll and Wade Clark Roof. Louisville, KY: Westminster.

O'Toole, Roger. 1996. "Religion in Canada: Its Development and Contemporary Situation." *Social Compass* 43 (1): 119–34.

Palm, Irving, and Jan Trost. 2000. "Family and Religion in Sweden." Pp. 107–20 in *Family, Religion, and Social Change in Diverse Societies*, ed. Sharon Houseknecht and Jerry Pankurst. New York: Oxford University Press.

Pasquale, Frank. 2007. "The 'Nonreligious' in the American Northwest." Pp. 41–58 in *Secularism and Secularity: Contemporary International Perspectives*, ed. Barry Kosmin and Ariela Keysar. Hartford, CT: Institute for the Study of Secularism in Society and Culture.

Penner, James, Rachel Harder, Erika Anderson, Bruno Désorcy, and Rick Hiemstra. 2011. *Hemorrhaging Faith: Why and When Canadian Young*

Adults Are Leaving, Staying and Returning to Church. Retrieved 20 Sept. 2012 (http://tgcfcanada.org/hemorrhagingfaith/).

Perry, Everett, James Davis, Ruth Doyle, and John Dyble. 1980. "Toward a Typology of Unchurched Protestants." *Review of Religious Research* 21 (4): 388–404.

Pew Forum on Religion and Public Life. 2008. "U.S. religious Landscape Survey." Retrieved 17 Feb. 2010 (http://religions.pewforum.org/pdf/report–religious–landscape–study–full.pdf).

– 2010. "Religion among the Millennials: Less Religiously Active than Older Americans, but Fairly Traditional in Other Ways." Retrieved 17 Feb. 2010 (http://pewforum.org/newassets/images/reports/millennials/millennials–report.pdf).

Pew Research Global Attitudes Project. 2012. "Among Wealthy Nations: U.S. Stands Alone In Its Embrace of Religion." Retrieved 16 June 2012 (http://www.pewglobal.org/files/pdf/167.pdf).

Piché, Eric. 1999. "Religion and Social Capital in Canada." MA thesis, Department of Sociology, Queen's University, Kingston, ON.

Presser, Stanley, and Mark Chaves. 2007. "Is Religious Service Attendance Declining?" *Journal for the Scientific Study of Religion* 46 (3): 417–23.

Putnam, Robert. 2000. *Bowling Alone: The Collapse and Revival of American Community*. New York: Simon and Schuster.

Putnam, Robert, and David Campbell. 2010. *American Grace: How Religion Divides and Unites Us*. New York: Simon and Schuster.

Ragin, Charles. 1987. *The Comparative Method: Moving beyond Qualitative and Quantitative Strategies*. Los Angeles: University of California Press.

Ramji, Rubina. 2013. "A Variable but Convergent Islam: Muslim Women." Pp. 112–44 in *Growing Up Canadian: Muslims, Hindus, Buddhists*, ed. Peter Beyer and Rubina Ramji. Montreal: McGill-Queen's University Press.

Rauff, Edward A. 1979. *Why People Join the Church*. New York: Pilgrim.

Reed, Paul, and Kevin Selbee. 2001. "The Civic Core in Canada: Disproportionality in Charitable Giving, Volunteering, and Civic Participation." *Nonprofit and Voluntary Sector Quarterly* 30 (4): 761–80.

Reimer, Sam. 2003. *Evangelicals and the Continental Divide: The Conservative Protestant Subculture in Canada and the United States*. Montreal: McGill-Queen's University Press.

– 2008. "State of Research in Sociology of Religion in Canada." Paper presented at Religion in Canada Workshop, sponsored by Trinity Western University's Religion in Canada Institute, 9 Feb.

Robertson, Roland, and JoAnn Chirico. 1985. "Humanity, Globalization, and Worldwide Religious Resurgence: A Theoretical Exploration." *Sociological Analysis* 46: 219–42.

Roof, Wade Clark. 1999. *Spiritual Marketplace: Baby Boomers and the Remaking of American Religion*. Princeton, NJ: Princeton University Press.

Roof, Wade Clark, and William McKinney. 1987. *American Mainline Religion: Its Changing Shape and Future*. New Brunswick, NJ: Rutgers University Press.

Roozen, David A. 1980. "Church Dropouts: Changing Patterns of Disengagement and Re-Entry." *Review of Religious Research* 21 (4): 427–50.

Saha, Shandip, and Peter Beyer. 2013. " Dominance of Marginal Relations: Hindu Men." Pp. 167–91 in *Growing Up Canadian: Muslims, Hindus, Buddhists*, ed. Peter Beyer and Rubina Ramji. Montreal: McGill-Queen's University Press.

Sandomirsky, Sharon, and John Wilson. 1990. "Process of Disaffiliation: Religious Mobility among Men and Women." *Social Forces* 68 (4): 1211–29.

Schwadel, Philip. 2010. "Period and Cohort Effects on Religious Nonaffiliation and Religious Disaffiliation: A Research Note." *Journal for the Scientific Study of Religion* 49 (2): 311–19.

Seljak, David. 2005. "Education, Multiculturalism, and Religion." Pp. 178–200 in *Religion and Ethnicity in Canada*, ed. Paul Bramadat and David Seljak. Toronto: Pearson.

Shand, Jack D. 1990. "A Forty-Year Follow-Up of the Religious Beliefs and Attitudes of a Sample of Amherst College Grads." Pp. 117–36 in *Research in the Social Scientific Study of Religion*, vol. 2, ed. Misty L. Lynn and David O. Moberg. Greenwich, CT: JAI Press.

Sherkat, Darren E. 1997. "Embedding Religious Choices: Preferences and Social Constraints into Rational Choice Theories of Religious Behavior." Pp. 66–86 in *Rational Choice Theory and Religion: Summary and Assessment*, ed. Lawrence Young. New York: Routledge.

– 2003. "Religious Socialization: Sources of Influence and Influences of Agency." Pp. 151–63 in *Handbook of the Sociology of Religion*, ed. Michelle Dillon. New York: Cambridge University Press.

– 2014. *Changing Faith: The Dynamics and Consequences of Americans' Shifting Identities*. New York: New York University Press.

Sherkat, Darren E., and J. Wilson. 1995. "Preferences, Constraints, and Choices in Religious Markets: An Examination of Religious Switching and Apostasy." *Social Forces* 73 (3): 993–1026.

Singleton, Andrew. 2007. "'People Were Not Made to Be in God's Image': A Contemporary Overview of Secular Australians." Pp. 83–94 in *Secularism and Secularity: Contemporary International Perspectives*, ed. Barry Kosmin and Ariela Keysar. Hartford, CT: Institute for the Study of Secularism in Society and Culture.

Smidt, Corwin, ed. 2003. *Religion as Social Capital: Producing the Common Good*. Waco, TX: Baylor University Press.

Smidt, Corwin, John Green, James Guth, and Lyman Kellstedt. 2003. "Religious Involvement, Social Capital, and Political Engagement: A Comparison of the United States and Canada." Pp. 153–69 in *Religion as Social Capital: Producing the Common Good*, ed. Corwin Smidt. Waco, TX: Baylor University Press.

Smith, Christian. 2003. *Moral, Believing Animals: Human Personhood and Culture*. New York: Oxford University Press.

Smith, Christian, and Melinda Lundquist Denton. 2005. *Soul Searching: The Religious and Spiritual Lives of American Teenagers*. New York: Oxford University Press.

Smith, Christian, with Patricia Snell. 2009. *Souls in Transition: The Religious and Spiritual Lives of Emerging Adults*. New York: Oxford University Press.

Stanczak, Gregory. 2006. *Engaged Spirituality: Social Change and American Religion*. New Brunswick, NJ: Rutgers University Press.

Stark, Rodney. 1997. "Bringing Theory Back In." Pp. 3–25 in *Rational Choice Theory and Religion: Summary and Assessment*, ed. Lawrence Young. New York: Routledge.

— 1999a. "Atheism, Faith, and the Social Scientific Study of Religion." *Journal of Contemporary Religion* 14 (1): 41–62.

— 1999b. "Secularization, R.I.P." *Sociology of Religion* 60: 249–73.

Stark, Rodney, and William Sims Bainbridge. 1985. *The Future of Religion: Secularization, Revival, and Cult Formation*. Berkeley: University of California Press.

— 1996 [1987]. *A Theory of Religion*. New Brunswick, NJ: Rutgers University Press.

Stark, Rodney, and Roger Finke. 2000. *Acts of Faith: Explaining the Human Side of Religion*. Berkeley: University of California Press.

Stark, Rodney, Eva Hamburg, and Alan Miller. 2004. "Exploring Spirituality and Unchurched Religion in America, Sweden, and Japan." *Journal of Contemporary Religion* 20 (1): 3–23.

Stark, Rodney, and Laurence Iannaccone. 1994. "A Supply-Side Reinterpretation of the 'Secularization' of Europe." *Journal for the Scientific Study of Religion* 33 (3): 230–52.

Statistics Canada. 2001. "2001 Census: Analysis Series. Religions in Canada." Retrieved 3 Mar. 2010 (http://www12.statcan.ca/english/censuso1/products/analytic/companion/rel/pdf/96F0030XIE2001015.pdf).
– 2010. "Projections of the Diversity of the Canadian Population: 2006–2031." Retrieved 29 Nov. 2011 (http://www.statcan.gc.ca/pub/91-551-x/91-551-x2010001-eng.pdf).
– 2013. "Immigration and Ethnocultural Diversity in Canada." Retrieved 20 May 2013 (http://www12.statcan.gc.ca/nhs-enm/2011/as-sa/99-010-x/99-010-x2011001-eng.pdf).
Stirk, Frank. 2010. "United Church Losses Projected to Continue." *Christian Week*. Retrieved 8 May 2010 (http://www.christianweek.org/united-church-losses-projected-to-continue/).
Stolzenberg, R.M., M. Blair-Loy, and L.J. Waite. 1995. "Religious Participation in Early Adulthood: Age and Family Life Cycle Effects on Church Membership." *American Sociological Review* 60 (1): 84–103.
Strauss, Anselm, and Juliet Corbin. 1998. *Basics of Qualitative Research: Techniques and Procedures for Developing Grounded Theory*. 2nd ed. Newbury Park, CA: Sage.
Swatos Jr, William, and Kevin Christiano. 1999. "Secularization Theory: The Course of a Concept." *Sociology of Religion* 60 (3): 209–28.
Thiessen, Joel. 2011. Book review of Reginald Bibby's *Beyond the Gods and Back: Religion's Demise and Rise and Why It Matters*. *Church and Faith Trends* 4 (1): 1–4.
– 2012. "Marginal Religious Affiliates in Canada: Little Reason to Expect Increased Church Involvement." *Canadian Review of Sociology* 49 (1): 69–90.
Thiessen, Joel, and Lorne L. Dawson. 2008. "Is There a 'Renaissance' of Religion in Canada? A Critical Look at Bibby and Beyond." *Studies in Religion* 37 (3–4): 389–415.
Thiessen, Joel, and Bill McAlpine. 2013. "The Function of Sacred Space: A Sociological and Theological Examination." *International Journal for the Study of the Christian Church* 13 (2): 133–46.
Tschannen, Oliver. 1991. "The Secularization Paradigm: A Systematization." *Journal for the Scientific Study of Religion* 30: 395–415.
Valpy, Michael. 2010 (15 Dec.). "Young Increasingly Shun Religious Institutions." *Globe and Mail*. Retrieved 16 Dec. 2010 (http://www.theglobeandmail.com/news/national/young-increasingly-shun-religious-institutions/article1837678/).

Valpy, Michael, and Joe Friesen. 2010 (11 Dec.). "Canada Marching from Religion to Secularization." *Globe and Mail*. Retrieved 16 Dec. 2010 (http://www.theglobeandmail.com/news/national/canada-marching-from-religion-to-secularization/article1833451/page1/).

Verba, S., K. Schlozman, and H.E. Brady. 1995. *Participation in America: Political Democracy and Social Equality*. New York: Harper and Row.

Vernon, Glenn M. 1968. "The Religious 'Nones': A Neglected Category." Presented at the Society for the Scientific Study of Religion, Montreal.

Voas, David. 2009. "The Rise and Fall of Fuzzy Fidelity in Europe." *European Sociological Review* 25 (2): 155–68.

– 2010. "Explaining Change over Time in Religious Involvement." Pp. 25–32 in *Religion and Youth*, ed. Sylvia Collins-Mayo and Pink Dandelion. Aldershot, UK: Ashgate.

Voas, David, and Alasdair Crockett. 2005. "Religion in Britain: Neither Believing Nor Belonging." *Sociology* 39 (1): 11–28.

Voas, David, and Abby Day. 2010. "Recognizing Secular Christians: Toward an Unexcluded Middle in the Study of Religion." *The Association of Religion Data Archives*. Retrieved 23 Mar. 2011 (http://www.thearda.com/rrh/papers/guidingpapers/Voas.pdf).

Voas, David, and Siobhan McAndrew. 2012. "Three Puzzles of Non-Religion in Britain." *Journal of Contemporary Religion* 27 (1): 29–48.

Walliss, John. 2002. "Loved the Wedding, Invite Me to the Marriage: The Secularization of Weddings in Contemporary Britain." *Sociological Research Online* 7 (4): http://www.socresonline.org.uk/7/4/walliss.html.

Warner, Stephen R., and Rhys W. Williams. 2010. "The Role of Families and Religious Institutions in Transmitting Faith among Christians, Muslims, and Hindus in the USA." Pp. 159–165 in *Religion and Youth*, ed. Sylvia Collins-Mayo and Pink Dandelion. Aldershot, UK: Ashgate.

Weber, Max. 1963 [1922]. *Sociology of Religion*. Boston: Beacon Press.

Wilkins-Laflamme, Sarah. 2014. "Toward Religious Polarization? Time Effects on Religious Commitment in US, UK, and Canadian Regions." *Sociology of Religion* 75 (2): 284–308.

Williamson, David A., and George Yancey. 2013. *There Is No God: Atheists in America*. Lanham, MD: Rowman and Littlefield.

Wilson, Bryan. 1982. *Religion in Sociological Perspective*. New York: Oxford University Press.

– 1985. "Secularization: The Inherited Model." Pp. 9–20 in *The Sacred in a Secular Age*, ed. Phillip Hammond. Berkeley: University of California Press.

– 2001. "Salvation, Secularization, and De-moralization." Pp. 39–51 in *The Blackwell Companion to Sociology of Religion*, ed. Richard Fenn. Malden, MA: Blackwell.

Wilson, John, and T. Janoski. 1995. "The Contribution of Religion to Volunteer Work." *Sociology of Religion* 56 (2): 137–52.

Wilson, John, and Darren E. Sherkat. 1994. "Returning to the Fold." *Journal for the Scientific Study of Religion* 33 (2): 148–61.

Wright, Bradley R.E., Dina Giovanelli, Emily G. Dolan, and Mark Evan Edwards. 2011. "Explaining Deconversion from Christianity." *Journal of Religion and Society* 13: 1–17.

Wuthnow, Robert. 1994. *Sharing the Journey: Support Groups and America's New Quest for Community*. New York: Free Press.

– 1998. *After Heaven: Spirituality in America Since the 1950s*. Los Angeles: University of California Press.

– 2001. "Spirituality and Spiritual Practice." Pp. 306–20 in *The Blackwell Companion to Sociology of Religion*, ed. Richard Fenn. Malden, MA: Blackwell.

– 2004. *Saving America? Faith-Based Services and the Future of Civil Society*. Princeton, NJ: Princeton University Press.

– 2005. *America and the Challenges of Religious Diversity*. Princeton, NJ: Princeton University Press.

– 2007. *After the Baby Boomers: How Twenty- and Thirty-Somethings Are Shaping the Future of American Religion*. Princeton, NJ: Princeton University Press.

– 2011. "Taking Talk Seriously: Religious Discourse as Social Practice." *Journal for the Scientific Study of Religion* 50 (1): 1–21.

Wuthnow, Robert, and Kevin Christiano. 1979. "The Effects of Residential Migration on Church Attendance in the United States." Pp. 257–76 in *The Religious Dimension: New Directions in Quantitative Research*, ed. Robert Wuthnow. New York: Academic.

Yamane, David. 1997. "Secularization on Trial: In Defense of a Neosecularization Paradigm." *Journal for the Scientific Study of Religion* 36: 109–22.

Zdero, Rad, ed. 2007. *Nexus: The World House Church Movement Reader*. Pasadena, CA: William Carey Library.

Zinnbauer, Brian, Kenneth Pargament, and Allie Scott. 1999. "The Emerging Meanings of Religiousness and Spirituality: Problems and Prospects." *Journal of Personality* 67 (6): 879–919.

Zuckerman, Phil. 2008. *Society without God: What the Least Religious Nations Can Tell Us about Contentment*. New York: New York University Press.

- 2012. *Faith No More: Why People Reject Religion.* New York: Oxford University Press.

Zuzanek, Jiri, Roger Mannell, and Margo Hilbrecht. 2008. "Leisure, Spirituality and Emotional Well-Being in the Lives of Teenagers." Conference Presentation at the Canadian Congress on Leisure Research, Montreal.

Index

active religious affiliates, 33–64; definition, 4; demographic information, 200; God's will, 46, 48, 52, 63, 163; need for study, 8
affiliation, identification, 10–11, 168, 171; importance of, 161–3; and non-Christian religions, 169
afterlife, life after death, 10; active affiliates, 38, 42–3, 54–6; marginal affiliates, 71, 86–8; religious nones, 102, 105–6, 109, 117–20
agnostic, 82, 85–6, 95–8, 114
Anglican, Church of England: currently identifies, 3, 34–5, 67–8; formerly identified, 110, 114, 141, 189
apostasy, apostates, 111–12, 127–46, 150
atheist, 85–6, 95–8, 114–15, 122, 162, 182; identification, 10, 82; stigma toward, 97–8
attendance, 10–11, 170

baptism, 42, 66
Baptist, 86, 100–1

belief in God, supernatural, 10–12; marginal affiliates, 82; religious nones, 101, 113–16. *See also* dependable god; responsive god
Berger, Peter: anomie and alienation, 52–3; secularization, 15–20
Beyer, Peter: apostates and greater involvement, 150; Canadian approach to religion, 5, 190; measuring religion, 169–70; religious minority youth, 57, 162
Bibby, Reginald: *Beyond the Gods and Back*, 10–11, 168–9; civic engagement, 178; cultural changes, 61, 158; *Fragmented Gods*, 9; free riders, 92; greater involvement, 148–9; rational choice theory, 23–4; *Restless Churches*, 10; *Restless Gods*, 10; *Unknown Gods*, 9–10
Bible, scripture: active affiliates, 33, 38, 43, 45, 162; authority of, 55, 59–60, 163; guide for behaviour, 48; learn about from religious leader, 46; marginal

affiliates, 69–70; religious nones, 100–1, 140
Bowen, Kurt: civic engagement, 177; secularization, 173
Bruce, Steve: critique of rational choice theory, 24–5, 50; individualism, 61; privatization of religion, 7, 176; secularization theory, 15–17, 20–1, 184
Buddhism, Buddhist, 78, 130; apostates, 150; young, 5, 10, 57, 190
busy, 45, 71, 78–9; diminished involvement, 137–8, 167; greater involvement, 148, 152

children. *See* socialization
choice: cultural value 5, 63; over religion, 20, 109, 189; teenagers and religion, 134–7. *See also* rational choice theory
Christmas, church attendance, 26, 44, 68, 71–2, 78–80
civic engagement, 176–80; Canadian ethos, 183–4; religion as a barrier to, 181–3
confidence, religious explanations, 27, 29–30; active affiliates, 62; marginal affiliates, 91–2; religious nones, 110, 123–4
conservative Protestant: active affiliates, 35, 45, 47; afterlife, 55; Bible, 60; demographics, 31, 200; evangelism, 61–2; immigration, 169; marginal affiliates, 18, 88–9, 132, 139, 144; religious nones, 142, 151. *See also* Baptist; evangelical; Pentecostal; Salvation Army
costs, trade-offs, 25–6; active affiliates, 38, 47–50; marginal affiliates, 80–2; religious nones, 106, 111–13. *See also* rewards

demand, 120, 146–54, 158–9, 172; active affiliates, 56; Reginald Bibby, 24; marginal affiliates, 88; rational choice theory, 27–8; religious nones, 117. *See also* supply
dependable congregation: active affiliates, 27, 53–4, 166; diminished involvement, 143–5; marginal affiliates, 83–5. *See also* dependable god; responsive congregation; responsive god
dependable god: active affiliates, 43, 50–3, 162–4; marginal affiliates, 82–3, 162, 164; religious nones, 115–16; theory of, 25–6. *See also* dependable congregation; responsive congregation; responsive god
deprivatization, 22–3, 174–5
disaffiliation, diminished involvement. *See* apostasy, apostates
Dobbelaere, Karel, 14–16, 168

evangelical, 34, 184–5; currently identifies, 84; negative perception toward, 43, 85, 97, 139; strict, 130; United States, 99, 184–5. *See also* conservative Protestant
exclusive beliefs or practices, 38–9, 185; critique of, 43–4, 88, 97, 103, 125, 136, 165; diminished involvement, 4, 129–31, 167; evangelicals, 85, 184; greater involvement, 151–3; Mormon, 104; negative societal impact, 182, 184; Roman Catholic Church, 75–6; supply and

Index

demand, 146–7. *See also* strictness
exclusive and extended exchanges: with congregations, 27, 53–4, 83–5, 87; with God, 25–6, 50–3, 82–3, 87
experts, trained specialists, 46, 71, 131

family, 66, 79; tension with, 105. *See also* socialization
Finke, Roger. *See* rational choice theory
free riders, 27, 44, 92–3
fundamentalism, 99, 102–3, 139. *See also* evangelical
funeral, 66, 74, 78, 80, 106, 155

globalization, 141, 184, 188–9
great scope, God of. *See* exclusive and extended exchanges
greater involvement, 12, 148–56, 172–3; Reginald Bibby, 10; marginal affiliates, 68, 71, 80; religious nones, 103, 110. *See also* demand; supply

Hadden, Jeffrey, 21–2

Iannaccone, Laurence. *See* rational choice theory
immigration, 7, 17, 23, 169–71, 188
individual religion, 3, 90–1, 166–7, 176; privatistic churchgoers, 61, 63. *See also* push religion; religious authority
individualism, 14, 61, 136, 186; Canadian value, 63, 73, 122–3, 167–8

intellectual disagreement, 141–3
interpersonal tension, 143–5

Jehovah's Witness: negative perception toward, 73, 107; strict, 130

Kinnaman, David, 85

life transition, 132–4
Lutheran, 17, 66, 80, 137–8

mainline Protestant: attendance, 10, 170; demographics, 30–1, 200. *See also* Anglican; Lutheran; United Church of Canada
marginal religious affiliates, 10, 12, 24, 26, 65–93; definition, 4; demographic information, 200; need for study, 8
master status, 48, 161–3
meaning and purpose, direction, 10, 178; active affiliates, 35, 41, 45–6, 63, 163; marginal affiliates, 102; religious nones, 116–20
morals, ethics, 177; active affiliates, 33, 35, 39, 46, 55–7; marginal affiliates, 67–8, 71, 77, 87–9, 92; religious nones, 96, 113, 119–21; Ten Commandments, 69, 87
Mormon, 31, 103–8, 200; growth, 176; negative perception toward, 73, 131; strict, 130
multiculturalism, 6, 17, 129, 174, 188. *See also* immigration; pluralism
Muslim, Islam: affiliation, 7, 10, 169; apostasy, 129, 137, 150;

civic engagement, 178; homegrown radicalization, 184, 188–9; negative perception toward, 43, 57, 69, 73, 89, 131; public debates, 22; resisting stigma, 97; strict, 130; young, 5, 57, 162

New Age, 16, 20–1, 181
new religious movements, 14, 21–2

Pentecostal, 16, 36–40, 176
pluralism, diversity, 5–8, 16–19, 28–9, 61, 63, 97, 142, 174, 184; Canadian value, 90, 111, 122–3, 147, 159; relativism, 7, 20–1. *See also* tolerance
polarization, religious, 9–11, 39, 163, 184–5
prayer: active affiliates, 33, 38, 41–3, 45–6, 51, 163, 166; marginal affiliates, 68–9, 74, 77, 81–2, 164; religious nones, 100–3, 106, 114, 116 143
privatization of religion, 7, 16–19, 123, 174. *See also* secularization
push religion: aversion to, 3, 7, 18, 73, 76, 88, 90, 121–2, 161–2; apostasy, 4; culturally unacceptable, 5, 107, 125, 190. *See also* exclusive beliefs or practices; individual religion; religious authority
Putnam, Robert, 179–82

rational choice theory, 23–30, 85–6, 92, 117. *See also* Reginald Bibby; demand; supply
religious authority, 59; Bible, 60; decline of, 9; religious group, 60, 167; religious leader, 46; self, 20, 61, 91, 136, 175. *See also* individual religion
religious minorities, 7, 10, 17, 57, 78, 171. *See also* Buddhism; Jehovah's Witness; Mormon; Muslim; New Age; new religious movements
religious nones, 7–8, 12, 94–125; definition, 4; demographic information, 200; need for study, 8–9; open minded, 103, 109–13; social stigma, 96–8
renaissance, religious, 9–11, 24, 80, 148–9, 170. *See also* greater involvement
responsive congregation: active affiliates, 27, 53–4, 166; marginal affiliates, 83–5. *See also* dependable congregation; dependable god; responsive god
responsive god: active affiliates, 50–3; marginal affiliates, 82–3, 162, 164; religious nones, 115–16; theory of, 25–6. *See also* dependable congregation; dependable god; responsive congregation
returnees, 154–5
rewards, 25–9; active affiliates, 35, 45–7, 50, 54, 145, 166; marginal affiliates, 78–80, 87, 145; religious nones, 111. *See also* costs
Roman Catholic, 18, 26, 34–6, 40–4, 73–8; afterlife, 54–5; attendance, 10; demographics, 30–1, 200; individual versus group authority, 58, 60, 63, 175; negative perception toward, 68,

100, 131, 141; religion positive for society, 57; school, 37; strict, 130–1

sacred space, 79–80
salience, religious. *See* master status
Salvation Army, 34–5, 69
scandals and hypocrisy, 138–41
science, 71, 76, 114, 141–2
secularization, 9–11, 123, 176; individual, 15, 23, 168–9, 171–3; opposition to, 14, 21–3; organizational, 15–16, 21, 23, 168, 175; societal, 14–15, 23, 168, 173–4, 190; theory of, 13–21
sexuality, gender, 144, 146–7; critique church doctrine, 60–1, 75–6, 166; repressive, 88, 98, 130–1, 182
Smith, Christian, 7, 155
social ties, social capital, 29, 165–7; apostasy, 145–6; community, 45; religiosity of friends, 61–2, 91, 122
socialization, religious, 20, 155–9, 165, 176; active affiliates, 52; apostasy, 128, 134–7; religious nones, 106, 108, 116. *See also* family
Stark, Rodney. *See* rational choice theory
strictness, 49, 62, 85–6, 111, 129–31; parenting, 136; theory of, 22, 27. *See also* exclusive beliefs or practices
supernatural activity in the world, 163–5; human activity, 164–5. *See also* dependable god; responsive god

supply, 146–54, 158–9, 172; rational choice theory, 24, 27–9. *See also* demand

teenagers, 171–2; affiliation, 8, 10–11, 94, 96, 168–9; attendance, 10–11, 168–9; belief in God, 11, 168–9; choice over religion, 134–7, 165; civic engagement, 177–8; doubts about religion, 142–3; friends, 47; greater involvement, 149; socialization, 155–8
tolerance, 86, 129, 136, 167–8, 190. *See also* pluralism, diversity
tradition, custom, 40, 65–6, 71–3, 78, 101

United Church of Canada, 146–7; active affiliates, 18, 46, 49, 53, 55, 62; marginal affiliates, 70–3, 133

Voas, David, 136, 165

wedding, marriage ceremony, 65, 68, 72–5, 78–9
Wuthnow, Robert, 12–13, 180, 182

young adults, emerging adults, 7, 137, 142–3; university, 40–1, 101, 130, 132–3, 138

Zuckerman, Phil, 66, 120–1, 127–8, 130–1, 142, 156–7, 181–2